Realm

Building Modern Swift Apps
with Realm Database

By Marin Todorov

Realm: Building Modern Swift Apps with Realm Database

By Marin Todorov

Copyright ©2018 Razeware LLC.

ISBN: 978-1-942878-52-0

Dedications

"To my father. To my mom. To Mirjam and our beautiful baby."

— *Marin Todorov*

"For my wife Elia — my love, inspiration, and rock ❤. To my family and friends for their support."

— *Shai Mishali*

About the author

Marin Todorov is the author of this book. Marin is one of the founding members of the raywenderlich.com team and has worked on seven of the team's books. Besides crafting code, Marin also enjoys blogging, teaching, and speaking at conferences. He happily open-sources code. You can find out more about Marin at www.underplot.com.

About the editors

Shai Mishali is the technical editor of this book. He's the iOS Lead for the Tim Hortons mobile app, and is involved in several open source projects on his spare time - mainly the RxSwiftCommunity and RxSwift projects. As an avid enthusiast of hackathons, Shai took 1st place at BattleHack Tel-Aviv 2014, BattleHack World Finals San Jose 2014, and Ford's Developer Challenge Tel-Aviv 2015. You can find him on GitHub and Twitter @freak4pc.

Chris Belanger is the editor of this book. Chris is the Editor in Chief at raywenderlich.com. He was a developer for nearly 20 years in various fields from e-health to aerial surveillance to industrial controls. If there are words to wrangle or a paragraph to ponder, he's on the case. When he kicks back, you can usually find Chris with guitar in hand, looking for the nearest beach. Twitter: @crispytwit.

Table of Contents

Introduction

Realm is a database not exactly like any other.

Its rich feature list aside, the fact is Realm wasn't created to be an embodiment of the idea of a database — it was created as an API which answers the specific needs of app developers.

Realm sports a custom-made engine, which gets you started with a database in a single line of code and reads and writes objects as if you just kept them around in memory. With the RealmSwift API, you use native objects and can push the language to its limits as you please. You never worry about multi-threading.

The plain truth is that Realm on iOS makes persisting data actually... *fun*!

I wrote this book with two seemingly opposite goals:

- Create the *most detailed* and *exhaustive* resource about building iOS apps on top of Realm.
- Provide an *approachable* and *understandable* learning path to both Realm newcomers and experienced developers.

Luckily, Realm provides a set of very developer-friendly APIs. In this book, you'll go over each topic in detail and work through some practical examples that will give you enough experience to tackle real-life app development problems.

The only requirements for reading this book are an intermediate understanding of Swift and iOS development.

If you've worked through our classic beginner books — the Swift Apprentice https://store.raywenderlich.com/products/swift-apprentice and the iOS Apprentice https://store.raywenderlich.com/products/ios-apprentice — or have similar development experience, you're ready to read this book.

As you work through this book, you'll progress from beginning topics to more advanced concepts.

Book License

By purchasing *Realm: Building Modern Swift Apps with Realm Database*, you have the following license:

- You are allowed to use and/or modify the source code in *Realm: Building Modern Swift Apps with Realm Database* in as many apps as you want, with no attribution required.

- You are allowed to use and/or modify all art, images and designs that are included in *Realm: Building Modern Swift Apps with Realm Database* in as many apps as you want, but must include this attribution line somewhere inside your app: "Artwork/images/ designs: from *Realm: Building Modern Swift Apps with Realm Database*, available at www.raywenderlich.com".

- The source code included in *Realm: Building Modern Swift Apps with Realm Database* is for your personal use only. You are NOT allowed to distribute or sell the source code in *Realm: Building Modern Swift Apps with Realm Database* without prior authorization.

- This book is for your personal use only. You are NOT allowed to sell this book without prior authorization, or distribute it to friends, coworkers or students; they would need to purchase their own copies.

Book Source Code and Forums

You can get the source code for the book here:

https://store.raywenderlich.com/products/realm-building-modern-swift-apps-with-realm-database-source-code

There, you'll find all the code from the chapters for your use.

We've also set up an official forum for the book at forums.raywenderlich.com. This is a great place to ask questions about the book or to submit any errors you may find.

Digital book editions

We also have a digital edition of this book available in both ePUB and PDF, which can be handy if you want a soft copy to take with you, or you want to quickly search for a specific term within the book.

Buying the digital edition version of the book also has a few extra benefits: free updates each time we update the book, access to older versions of the book, and you can download the digital editions from anywhere, at anytime.

Visit our Realm: Building Modern Swift Apps with Realm Database store page here:

- https://store.raywenderlich.com/products/realm-building-modern-swift-apps-with-realm-database.

And since you purchased the print version of this book, you're eligible to upgrade to the digital editions at a significant discount! Simply email support@razeware.com with your receipt for the physical copy and we'll get you set up with the discounted digital edition version of the book.

About the Cover

The sailfish is considered one of the fastest, sleekest fish in the ocean, with modern estimates of its top speed to be well over 30mph. Sailfish raise the broad sails on their backs when they hunt; this helps them steady their head as they plow towards schools of fish to slash and stun their prey with their long bills.

The sailfish is a great choice to represent the Realm products; they're sleek, efficient and fast. We know that once you give Realm a try in your projects, you'll find that your development *sails* right along, and that Realm really does fit the *bill*!

Section I: Getting Started with Realm

This section introduces you to the basics of Realm, gives you a bit of context of the issues Realm solves for app developers, and finally guides you through quickly building a simple but complete iOS app with Realm.

Chapter 1: Hello, Realm

You will learn about Realm Database and Realm Platform, what tools to install to make the most of this book, and how to work with the included playgrounds and iOS projects.

Chapter 2: Your First Realm App

This chapter is a classic-style tutorial that leads you through creating a Realm-powered to-do application for iOS. You will work through the chapter without delving into great details about all the APIs you are going to make use of; the idea is to get a *feeling* of how it is to work with Realm.

Chapter 1: Hello Realm!

This book aims to introduce you, the reader, to the Realm database and how to create powerful, reactive iOS apps with Swift and RealmSwift.

Realm finds the sweet spot between the simplicity of storing data as JSON on disk and using heavy, slow ORMs like Core Data or similar that are built on top of SQLite. The Realm Database aims to be fast, performant and provide the commodities that mobile developers need such as working with objects, type-safety, and native notifications.

In this book you are going to learn *plenty* about Realm, how to build iOS apps with Realm, and you'll pick up some tips and tricks along the way about getting the most out of the platform.

Before getting to the code though, it's important to know what Realm *is*, and what you can expect from it — and what not to expect.

Currently, Realm offers two products:

- **Realm Database**: A free and open-source object database.

- **Realm Platform**: A syncing server solution which can be either self-hosted on your servers or used as a cloud service via **Realm Cloud**.

The primary focus of this book is the free database product (the **Realm Database**), which has been under active development for several years. It powers apps by some of the biggest names in the App Store, including Adidas, Amazon, Nike, Starbucks, BBC, GoPro, Virgin, Cisco, Groupon, and many more who have chosen to develop their mobile apps with Realm.

The database has been widely adopted due to its ease of use and the fact that it can be used on both iOS and Android, unlike other database solutions:

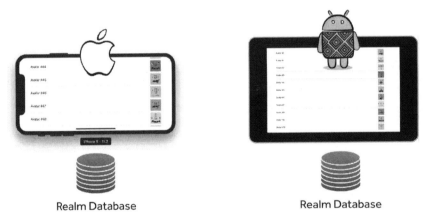

Realm Database   Realm Database

Realm Platform, on the other hand, is a relatively new commercial product which allows developers to automatically synchronize data not only across Apple devices but also between any combination of Android, iPhone, Windows, or macOS apps.

Platform allows you to run the server software on your own infrastructure and keep your data in-house, which most often suits large enterprises. Alternatively, you can use Realm Cloud, which runs a Platform for you. You start syncing data very quickly and only pay for what you use.

The good news is that once you know how to use the Realm Database to build iOS apps, which is covered in this book, enabling data sync via a cloud service is a process that takes just a few additional steps on top of what you're already doing:

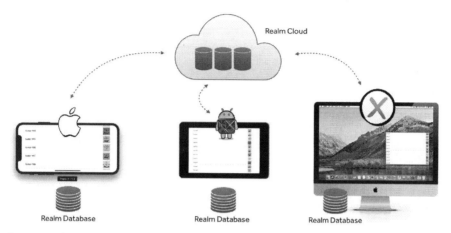

That being said, you can develop both personal and commercial projects without any restrictions using the Realm Database.

If you decide you'd like to have the app data synchronized automatically to your cloud or across platforms to Android, watchOS, macOS, Windows, or others, you can add that feature later on.

For the time being, you're going to master the Realm Database and then, in the last chapter of this book, you're going to look into using the database with Realm Cloud.

Realm Database

Realm Database fills the gap in the field of client-side data persistence. Indeed, there have been a multitude of server products released in recent years, but not much has happened for client-side needs.

Up until a few years ago, the defacto standard for building mobile apps on both iOS and Android was SQLite: a fast, but generic, all-purpose SQL database format. SQLite has a number of virtues, such as being written in C, which makes it fast, portable to almost any platform, and is highly conformant to the SQL standard.

Realm, on the other hand, is a modern database solution which focuses on the needs of modern apps. In that sense, it is not an all-purpose database. It is really good at reading and writing data extremely fast, but it requires you to master the Realm API so you can't simply use your existing SQL database skills.

So, it's precisely *because* Realm is a new type of mobile database that you should not expect to use it the same way as you would an old, generic SQL database.

That being said, ... **good news everyone**!

The Realm APIs, built with modern, best-practices code, are arguably *much* easier to use than working with the C API of SQLite from Swift.

In fact, even if you've never used Realm before, you can get started with the basics in mere minutes. After all, the code speaks for itself:

```swift
class Person: Object {
  dynamic var firstName: String?
  dynamic var lastName: String?
}

let me = Person()
me.firstName = "Marin"
me.lastName = "Todorov"

try realm.write {
  realm.add(me)
}
```

This Swift code defines a new `Person` class, creates an instance and sets its object properties, and finally tries to add the new object to a realm within a write transaction.

And let's have a look at how you get objects back from the database:

```swift
realm.objects(Person.self)
  .filter("age > 21")
  .sorted("age")
```

This Swift code asks Realm for all persisted objects of type `Person`, filters those to ones of age 21 or more, and finally sorts the results.

Sometimes Realm code almost looks *too easy* to be used in a solid, robust database API.

You might be thinking: "*I already figured out how to write data ... why do I need to work through the whole book then?*" and that's a fair question to ask!

The Realm basics are really easy to pick up; you can start using Realm in your apps after following a single tutorial. But, just like following a single tutorial on *any* topic, that gives you a very limited view into Realm's API and the specifics of building apps with Realm.

This book aims to give you some detailed knowledge of designing and building object schemas through several projects, and give you enough experience to make informed decisions when creating your next app with Realm.

Live Objects

One of the cornerstones of the Realm Database philosophy is that modern apps work with **objects**. Most persistent solutions will fetch data in the form of generic dictionaries that aren't type safe and pollute the application code with excessive logic to cast and convert fetched data to a format usable in the app.

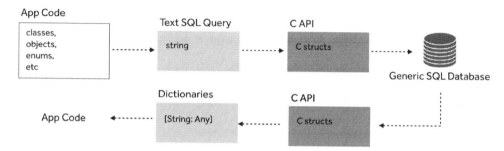

Realm, on the other hand, uses classes to define its data schema (e.g., what types of data can be persisted in the database) and the developer always works with objects, both when persisting data to a Realm and when querying the database for results.

That helps to simplify the application code when compared to persisting data other ways. You simply skip over boilerplate data-conversion code and always use native Swift objects.

The fact your data is always contained by objects allows for a number of other Realm features; it introspects your classes and automatically detects any changes you make to the database schema; it updates fetched data to the latest snapshot from the disk; and much more.

Working with data objects directly and exclusively allows for the speed, robustness, and type safety that Realm is known for across platforms. In fact, the Realm Database Core (open sourced on GitHub by Realm) is written in cross-platform C++ so it works exactly the same way on Android, iOS, macOS, or any other platform.

But don't worry: you don't ever need to use C++ in your own apps, unless you really want to. Realm provides SDKs in different languages which perform some lean wrapping of the database core engine to give developers APIs that best fit their application code.

And the best part of all is that since the C++ core is the same across platforms, the native APIs also behave similarly. That *really* helps the iOS and Android developers on a multi-disciplinary team stay in sync and work together.

The code isn't exactly the same across platforms: it's similar, but each language offers different features that Realm uses to make its APIs feel as native as possible. For example, this is how you would declare the interface of a realm object class in Objective-C:

```
@interface Person : RLMObject
@property NSString *firstName;
@property NSString *lastName;
@end
```

Defining the same class would look like this in Swift:

```
class Person: Object {
    dynamic var firstName: String?
    dynamic var lastName: String?
}
```

And just for kicks, here's the code in Kotlin:

```
open class Person: RealmObject() {
    var firstName: String? = nil
    var lastName: String? = nil
}
```

You get to work with native, custom classes in any of the supported languages you might be using to build your app, and Realm automatically read and writes the stored data to disk.

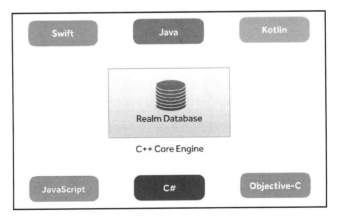

Not only does Realm allow you to use your own custom classes to persist data, but you can customize your own API in any way you'd like.

For example, if you are a big `struct` fan, you can simply add `toStruct()` and `fromStruct(_)` methods on your Swift data object class to be able to quickly read data as Swift structs from your database:

You'd be wrapping Swift objects into structs in a similar way to how Realm wraps C++ objects into Swift objects.

And since Realm data objects are fully-fledged classes, you don't need to limit yourself to only using them for storage. They can include all kinds of additional logic that makes sense in the context of data persistence. Your classes might sport methods to create new instances, fetch instances from a given realm, and to convert data between custom formats that you need to store on disk.

In any case, the Realm SDKs for each language try to give you the tools you need and provide you with native-feeling APIs to make your life as easy as possible.

Realm Studio

Another of Realm's benefits over other data persistence libraries is that it offers high-fidelity data browser and editor app.

Realm Studio (https://realm.io/products/realm-studio) lets you inspect the contents of your app's realm files and change any of the data manually, if necessary.

You will use Realm Studio throughout this book to inspect the changes your code commits to your Realm Database files. The app allows you to browse and modify all the objects stored in a file, and additionally to browse, query, and modify the stored data in a spreadsheet-like manner.

In the final chapter of this book, you will use Realm Studio to connect to Realm Cloud. Realm Studio is a streamlined way to get started with the Realm Platform, including starter code for different platforms. At launch, Realm Studio will prompt you to browse your cloud instances or explore demo apps:

Once you're connected to a server in the cloud, you can browse and modify the data manually as you would with any local file:

You will be using Realm Studio fairly often, so download and install the app for free from https://realm.io/products/realm-studio.

SimPholders

Speaking of amazing tools, you might want to consider purchasing a tool called SimPholders. It integrates very well both with your iPhone Simulator and with Realm Studio, and it allows you to inspect your app's database with a single click.

When you're working on apps in Xcode and testing them in your iPhone Simulator, SimPholders detects the activity and always gives you quick access to recently-active apps across all your simulator instances:

When you select an app from the list above, you can quickly open some folders of interest or launch Realm Studio directly:

SimPholders is a useful tool and will make your life developing apps with Realm considerably easier. You can get a 10-day trial or a (very affordable) license from the app's website:

• https://simpholders.com.

Installation

Once you are convinced that you need Realm in your app (and I hope you already are!), you need to add Realm as a dependency of your code. RealmSwift is available for free from https://github.com/realm/realm-cocoa and detailed documentation can be found here: https://realm.io/docs/swift/latest.

Realm Objective-C and Realm Swift are published under the Apache 2.0 license. Realm Core is separately available and is also published under the Apache 2.0 license.

The easiest way to include Realm and RealmSwift in your projects is via CocoaPods or Carthage.

The projects in this book use **CocoaPods**. Even if you usually use a different dependency manager, please make sure to use CocoaPods while you work through the projects in this book.

Installing via CocoaPods

You install the Realm database in your application much like any other pod:

```
use_frameworks!

target "AppTarget" do
  pod "RealmSwift"
end
```

This will pull the Realm Core engine and the Swift language SDK and make them available to your application's code.

Installing RealmSwift in the book projects

As for the projects in this book, they all come with a prepared Podfile, but without the dependency files included. We looked into this option, but it didn't make sense to include all the files for RealmSwift in every single project for each chapter in the book download.

Before you start working on the book, make sure you have the latest version of CocoaPods installed. You need to do that just once before starting to work on the book's projects. Usually executing this in Terminal will suffice:

```
sudo gem install cocoapods
```

If you want to know more, visit the CocoaPods website:

- https://guides.cocoapods.org/using/getting-started.html.

In this book, you will work on two types of projects depending on the complexity of the APIs they cover.

Xcode playgrounds

For simpler code experimentation, or examples that need a lot of iterations where you observe the output and change the code accordingly, you will use **Xcode playgrounds**.

For these projects, we've prepared a script which installs Realm and pre-builds the code to save you from waiting around while in Xcode.

For these chapters, open the book's source code folder and find the relevant chapter folder. Copy the **starter** subfolder to a convenient location and use the Terminal app to navigate to the newly copied folder.

Run the script `./bootstrap.sh` to install Realm in the playground project and build the source code. This might take a little while so you will be presented with a neat text-based UI to track the progress:

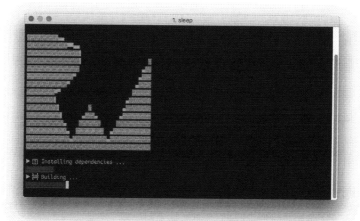

Once the script has finished, it will open the playground in your default Xcode installation and you'll be ready to start working through the chapter.

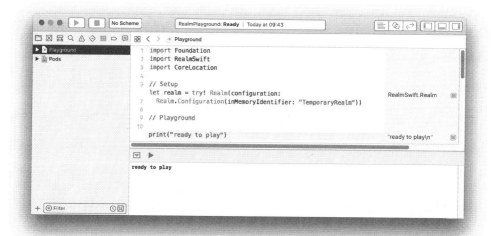

It might look a bit off at first but the generated project does not have any build targets or an active scheme. To get started, click on the playground and start adding the chapter's code as instructed.

Should you experience errors getting the playground to run that's probably Xcode acting up, try to rebuild the playground by running the bootstrap script again like so: `./ bootstrap.sh clean`. This should solve any issues related to compiling the sources and get you started working through the relevant book chapter.

Xcode projects

To give you more context, some of the chapters' projects are in the form of complete Xcode projects which you can run in the iPhone Simulator or on your device.

For these chapters, open the book's source code folder and find the relevant chapter folder. Copy the **starter** subfolder to a convenient location and use the Terminal app to navigate to the newly copied folder.

Install the project dependencies by executing:

```
pod install
```

When the process has finished, open the resulting Xcode workspace file.

> **Note**: If your CocoaPods is not up-to-date and fails to install Realm, run `pod update` once to fetch the meta-information about the latest pods published.

Installing via Carthage

The Carthage installation instructions as described in the Realm documentation are as follows:

- Add realm to your `Carthage` file: `github "realm/realm-cocoa"`
- Run `carthage update` to fetch and build Realm
- Drag **RealmSwift.framework** and **Realm.framework** from the `Carthage/Build/` sub-folder into the **Linked Frameworks and Libraries** section of your project's General section.

This will make RealmSwift available in your app. There is, however, an extra step you need to take before submitting to the App Store, which works around a bug in app submission. You can read more online in Realm's own docs:

https://realm.io/docs/swift/latest#installation.

Installing like a dynamic framework

For those that don't use dependency managers, Realm provides pre-built frameworks. Instructions on how to integrate those in your project can be found at:

- https://realm.io/docs/swift/latest/#installation

Curious to know more?

Realm is known to be very active in the developer community. They've launched a number of important iOS open source projects such as:

- **Realm Database**: A forever-free and open-source database for both personal and commercial projects.
- **SwiftLint**: A tool that enforces strict style guidelines in your Swift code.
- **Jazzy**: A modern tool for generating Swift documentation, which is the defacto standard for building API docs from Swift source code.

Besides these popular projects, Realm's GitHub account https://github.com/realm is packed with demo apps showcasing how to use Realm, additional Realm-based libraries, and more.

Additionally, the Realm Academy offers an almost endless amount of recorded conference talks, slides, articles and more:

- https://academy.realm.io.

There you will find the specialized Realm academy path. You can also explore other interesting Realm-related talks, video series, and blog posts here:

- https://academy.realm.io/section/realm

Where to go from here?

Even though there is plenty of information out there about learning Realm, the most detailed and in-depth resources on learning how to use the Realm Database in your apps could only be found in a book. Namely, this book! I hope you will enjoy learning from this light-hearted but thorough "missing" Realm manual.

Head on in to Chapter 2, where you'll learn how to quickly build a complete iOS app powered by the Realm database.

Chapter 2: Your First Realm App

In the previous chapter, you learned about the Realm Database, how it works and what problems it can solve for you as a developer.

Now you'll take a leap of faith and dive right into creating an iOS app that uses Realm to persist data on disk while following this tutorial-style chapter.

The idea of this chapter is to get you started with Realm without delving too much into the details of the APIs you're going to use. This will hopefully inspire you to try and find the right APIs, figure out what they do, and perhaps even browse through RealmSwift's source code.

Have no fear though, as the rest of this book will teach you just about everything there is to learn about Realm in detail. You're going to learn the mechanics behind everything you're about to do in this chapter and much, much more.

I invite you to work through this chapter's exercises with an open mind. This chapter is simply about getting a feeling for using Realm in your Swift code.

Getting started

The theme of to-do apps as an educational tool might be getting old by now, but the simple truth is that a to-do app does a great job of demonstrating how to build an app based on data persistence. A to-do app includes features like fetching a list of to-do items from disk, adding, modifying and deleting items, and using the data with some of the common UIKit components such as a table view, an alert view, buttons, and more.

In this chapter, you're going to work on a to-do app that's built on the Realm Database. This will be very useful as you learn the basics of CRUD operations with Realm.

> **Note:** **C**reate, **R**ead, **U**pdate and **D**elete are the basic persistence operations you can perform on mostly any data entity. Often times, this set of operations will be referred by the acronym CRUD. Just don't mix up a CRUD app with a *crude* app!

To get started, open the macOS Terminal app (or another similar app of your choice), navigate to the current chapter's starter project folder, run `pod install` (as described in Chapter 1) and open the newly created Xcode workspace.

> **Note:** The starter projects in this book contain some UI boilerplate and other non-database related code. Sometimes Xcode might show code warnings since the starter code "misses" some parts which you will add while working through the tasks in the respective chapter.

Open **Main.storyboard** to get an idea of the app's basic structure:

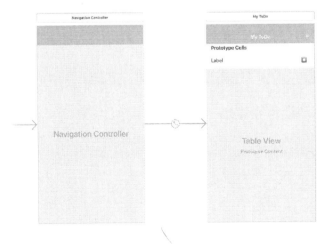

The project consist of a single table view controller with a custom to-do item cell.

The source code structure follows a general pattern for all of the projects in this book:

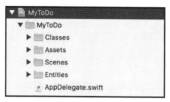

- The **Classes** folder is a catch-all location for code that doesn't fall under one of the other folders mentioned below. In this project, it includes an extension on `UIViewController` to add a simple API to present alerts on screen, as well as a handy extension on `UITableView`.

- **Assets** is where you'll find the app's launch screen, meta information plist file, and the asset catalog.

- **Scenes** contains all of the app's scenes; including their view controller, view and view model code, when available. In this project, you have a single view controller and a custom table cell class.

- **Entities** contains the Realm object classes you'll be persisting to disk. This is practically your data models, but backed by Realm. You have a single class called `ToDoItem` in this project. In later chapters, you'll be working on more complex database schemas, but this simple schema will suffice for now.

The projects in this book all follow a similar code structure, but you aren't forced to use this structure in your own work. We've provided it as a guideline so you'll know where to look for files as later projects in this book become more complicated.

If you run the starter app right now, you'll see that it compiles and displays an empty to-do list on screen:

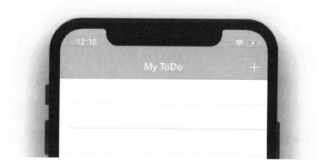

Realm objects

Realm objects are basically a standard data model, much like any other standard data model you've defined in your apps. The only difference is they're backed by Realm persistence and abilities.

You won't dive into Realm objects at this stage, as you'll be going into more detail on how to define Realm models and persist them in the next section of this book. In this chapter, you're going to waltz through these model definitions, and get straight into action.

In fact, the MyToDo starter project already includes a class that will serve as the data model for storing to-do items. Open **Entities/ToDoItem.swift** and notice the `ToDoItem` class.

There are a few interesting points to note here, but you'll be learning more about these subjects in the next chapters.

Dynamic properties

First and foremost, you should recognize that the `ToDoItem` class subclasses `Object`. `Object` is a base class all of your Realm-backed data entities must inherit from. This allows Realm to introspect them and persist them to disk.

Another interesting oddity in this class is that all of its properties are defined as `dynamic`:

```
dynamic var id = UUID().uuidString
dynamic var text = ""
dynamic var isCompleted = false
```

This allows Realm to implement some custom, behind-the-scenes logic, to automatically map these properties to the data persisted to disk.

With the help of the `dynamic` keyword, a model class serves as a loose proxy between your app's code and the data stored on disk, as seen in this simple schema:

Primary key

ToDoItem also features a convenience init(_) and overrides a static method called primaryKey() from its parent class. Realm will call primaryKey() to decide which property will be used as the object's primary key.

The primary key stores unique values that are used to identify objects in the database. For example, if you're storing Car objects in the database, their uniquely identifying primary key can be their registration plate:

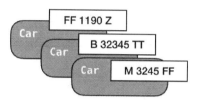

To make things easy, the id property, which is the primary key of ToDoItem, is automatically given a unique string UUID value. The UUID Foundation class lets you easily generate unique identifiers like these:

```
DB4722D0-FF33-408D-B79F-6F5194EF018E
409BC9B9-3BD2-42F0-B59D-4A5318EB3195
D9B541AF-16BF-41AC-A9CF-F5F43E5B1D9B
```

Ordinary code

You'll find that the class looks very much like a common Swift class. This is one of the greatest things about Realm! You don't have to go out of your way to adapt your code to work with the persistence layer. You always work with native classes like ToDoItem, while Realm does the heavy-lifting behind the scenes automatically.

To recap: ToDoItem is a class you can persist on disk because it inherits from Realm's base Object class. The class is pretty much ready to go, so you can start adding the code to read and write to-do items from and to disk.

Reading objects from disk

In this section, you're going to write code to retrieve any persisted ToDoItem objects and display their data in the main scene of your app.

Let's start off by adding a method to fetch all to-do items from the Realm file on disk. Open **Entities/ToDoItem.swift** and insert in the extension at the bottom:

```
static func all(in realm: Realm = try! Realm()) ->
Results<ToDoItem> {
  return realm.objects(ToDoItem.self)
    .sorted(byKeyPath: ToDoItem.Property.isCompleted.rawValue)
}
```

You just added a static `all(in:)` method which, by default, fetches all to-do items from your default Realm file. Having a `realm` parameter with a default value allows you to easily work with the default Realm, but also leaves room for using an arbitrary Realm, if needed.

You can actually have more than a single Realm file in your app, as you might want to separate out the data your app uses into different "buckets". You'll learn more about this in Chapter 7, "Multiple Realms/Shared Realms".

> **Note**: You maybe outraged by the use of `try!` and of course you will have right to be. For brevity's sake the book code will only focus on Realm's APIs but if you'd like to learn more about error handling or other Swift related topics do check the "Swift Apprentice" book on raywenderlich.com where we cover Swift itself in great detail.

If you look further down the code, you'll spot the `objects(_)` and `sorted(byKeyPath:)` methods, which are some of the APIs you're going to use throughout this book. `objects(_)` fetches objects of a certain type from disk, and `sorted(byKeyPath:)` sorts them by the value of a given property or key path.

In your code, you ask Realm to return all persisted objects of type `ToDoItem` and sort them by their `isCompleted` property. This will sort incomplete items to the start of the list and completed ones to the end. The method returns a `Results<ToDoItem>`, a generic results type which gives you dynamic access to the result set.

Next up will be updating your view controller to use this new method to fetch and display the to-do items.

Open **Scenes/ToDoListController.swift** and spot the `items` property towards the top of the file. It is an `Optional` type where you'll store the result fetched from Realm.

Next, append to `viewDidLoad()`:

```
items = ToDoItem.all()
```

This code uses your new `all(in:)` method to ask Realm for all persisted `ToDoItems`.

Currently, the app doesn't display any items when launched, since you don't have any data stored. You'll fix that by adding some default to-do items in case the user hasn't created any.

Creating some test data

Open **AppDelegate.swift** and add inside the empty `initializeRealm()` method:

```
let realm = try! Realm()
guard realm.isEmpty else { return }
```

You start by getting an instance of the default Realm by initializing it without any arguments. Then, you check if the Realm is empty using the handy `isEmpty` property. If the Realm isn't empty, you simply return since there's no need to add test data.

Don't worry about the creation of a new Realm in the first line. Initializing a `Realm` object simply creates a handle to the file on disk. Furthermore, this handle is shared across your app, and returned each time you use `Realm()` on the same thread. Therefore, you're not duplicating your data, or consuming any extra memory — all pieces of code in this app work with the same Realm instance and the same file on disk.

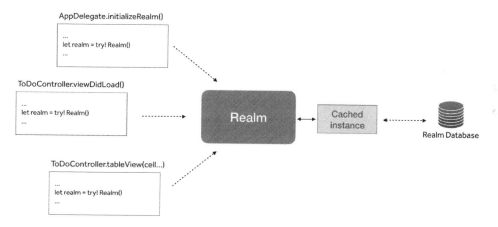

Next, add code to create some test data, right after your `guard` statement:

```
try! realm.write {
  realm.add(ToDoItem("Buy Milk"))
  realm.add(ToDoItem("Finish Book"))
}
```

This quick piece of code persists two objects to disk. And by quick, I mean that it's literally only four lines of code!

You start a write transaction by using `realm.write` and add two new `ToDoItem` objects from within the transaction body. To persist objects, you simply create them as you would any other class, and hand them off to `Realm.add(_)` which adds them to your Realm.

Last but not least, call `initializeRealm` from `application(_:didFinishLaunchingWithOptions:)`. Just before `return true`, add the following:

```
initializeRealm()
```

Build and run the project to see your new code in action:

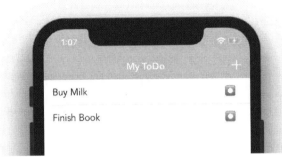

That was easier than expected, wasn't it? To be fair, the starter project *did* include some code to make your life a tad less complicated, but it's clear how easy it is to fetch items from disk and persist new ones when needed.

Open **Scenes/ToDoListController.swift** one more time and look for the `UITableViewDataSource` implementations in the bottom of the file:

- `tableView(_:numberOfRowsInSection:)` uses `items?.count` to return the number of objects fetched in the `items` result set.

- `tableView(_:cellForRowAt:)` uses an index subscript to get the object at the required index path `items?[indexPath.row]` and use its properties to configure the cell.

Additionally, the next class extension defines some delegate methods from the `UITableViewDelegate` protocol that enable swipe-to-delete on table cells. You'll write the code to actually delete items a bit later in this chapter.

Adding an item

Next, you'll add code to allow the user to add new to-do items to their list.

Since this is one of the CRUD operations, let's add the relevant method to the `ToDoItem` class. Open **Entities/ToDoItem.swift** and add right below your `all(in:)` method:

```
@discardableResult
static func add(text: String, in realm: Realm = try! Realm())
    -> ToDoItem {
  let item = ToDoItem(text)
  try! realm.write {
    realm.add(item)
  }
  return item
}
```

`add(text:in:)` lets you create a new `ToDoItem` instance *and* persist it to a Realm of your choice. This is a useful shortcut when you don't intend to use an object outside of the context of the database.

You're already familiar with the type of code above. You create a new `ToDoItem` instance, open a write transaction, and use `Realm.add(_)` to persist the object.

You can now add some UI code to your view controller to let the user input new to-do items and add them to the app's Realm.

Back in **Scenes/ToDoListController.swift**, scroll to `addItem()`, which is a method already connected to the **+** button in your navigation bar. Add inside `addItem()`:

```
userInputAlert("Add Todo Item") { text in
  ToDoItem.add(text: text)
}
```

`userInputAlert(_)` is a `UIViewController` extension method (found in the **Classes** folder of the starter project) that presents a new alert controller on the screen and asks the user to enter some text. Once the user taps **OK**, you'll receive the user-provided text in a closure.

In the callback closure, you use the new method you just created to create and persist a new to-do item to disk: `ToDoItem.add(text: text)`.

Run the project one more time and tap on the **+** button. `userInputAlert(_:_:)` will display an alert on screen and let you enter the text for a new to-do.

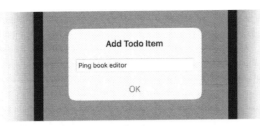

Tapping **OK** will execute your callback and save the new to-do item to disk.

As you might have noticed, the table view still only displays the two items you fetched when initially loading the view controller.

Use Realm Studio to open the app database **default.realm** from the Simulator folders and check its contents. For this, you can use the SimPholders tool as mentioned in Chapter 1, "Hello Realm":

Realm Studio displays a list of all classes stored in your file on the left-hand side and a spreadsheet-like UI on the right side letting you browse all the data persisted in the file:

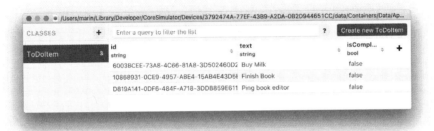

Hey, that new to-do item has been successfully added - you can find it at the bottom of the list!

In fact, if you re-run the project, you'll see it appear in your app as well:

It seems like you need a way to refresh the table view whenever the database changes.

Reacting to data changes

One sub-optimal way to do this is to refresh the table view from `addItem()`. But going down this path means you'll need to refresh the table view from *every* other method that modifies your data, such as when you delete an item, or set its completion status, and so on. Leaving that aside, the real issue is how to refresh the table if you commit a change from another class, which runs somewhere in the background, and is completely decoupled from the view controller?

Fortunately, Realm provides a powerful solution to this. Realm's own change notifications mechanism lets your classes read and write data independently and be notified, in real-time, about any changes that occurred.

Realm's own notification system is incredibly useful, because it lets you cleanly separate your data persistence code. Let's look at an example which uses two classes:

- A networking class which persists JSON as Realm objects on a background queue.

- A view controller displaying the fetched objects in a collection view.

Without Realm and change notifications, you'll need to make one class a delegate of the other (in a way that inevitably couples them) or use `NotificationCenter` to broadcast update notifications.

With Realm, the two classes can cleanly separate their concerns. One will only *write* to the database the other only *reads* and *observes changes*:

With this setup, it would be trivial to do something like test the class that writes objects to the database without creating a view controller. In addition, in the event the app goes offline, the view controller won't care at all about the fact the class responsible for writing objects isn't doing any work at the moment.

Relying on Realm's built-in change notifications lets you separate concerns extremely well and keeps your app's architecture simple and clean.

Let's see how that looks in practice.

Open **Scenes/ToDoListController.swift** and add a new property at the top of the class:

```
private var itemsToken: NotificationToken?
```

A notification token keeps a reference to a subscription for change notifications. You'll be using notifications throughout the book so you'll get to learn all about them, starting in Chapter 6, "Notifications and Reactive Apps".

Continue in `viewWillAppear(_)` where you'll set your notification token:

```
itemsToken = items?.observe { [weak tableView] changes in
  guard let tableView = tableView else { return }

  switch changes {
  case .initial:
    tableView.reloadData()
  case .update(_, let deletions, let insertions, let updates):
    tableView.applyChanges(deletions: deletions, insertions:
insertions, updates: updates)
  case .error: break
  }
}
```

You call `observe(_)` on the to-do items result set, which lets Realm know that you want to receive updates any time the result set changes.

For example, if you add a to-do item, Realm will call your `observe` callback. If you remove a to-do item, Realm will call your callback. If you change a property on one of your to-do items ... yes, you guessed right — Realm will call your callback.

The `observe(_)` callback closure is the place to implement any UI code that will reflect the latest data changes in your app's UI. In the code above, you receive detailed information about what items have been inserted, modified, or deleted. If any changes occurred in your result set, you call the `applyChanges(_)` extension method to apply them on screen, and you also take care of simply reloading the table view with the initial data at the time of observing changes.

> **Note**: The callback is called on the same thread you create the subscription on. In your code above you create the subscription in `viewWillAppear(_)` and is therefore safe to update the app's UI without any extra checks.

That's as far as you'll take this right now. Later on, you'll learn about the notification data in greater detail.

Next, since you start observing `items` in `viewWillAppear(_)`, it makes sense to stop the observation in `viewWillDisappear(_)`.

Add the following to `viewWillDisappear(_)`:

```
itemsToken?.invalidate()
```

`invalidate()` invalidates the token and cancels the data observation.

Run the project again. This time, as soon as you enter a new to-do item, it'll appear in your list with a nice accompanying animation:

Now that you have the table all reactive and animated, you can add the remaining CRUD operations. Thanks to Realm's change notifications, the table will reflect any changes automatically. Isn't that great?

Modifying a persisted object

You just learned how to add new objects to your app's Realm, but how would you modify an object that has already been persisted?

Obviously, you first need to fetch the object from the database and then modify it somehow. In this section of the chapter, you're going to add code to complete (and *un-complete?*) a to-do task.

Open **Entities/ToDoItem.swift** and add a new method below `add(text:in:)`:

```
func toggleCompleted() {
  guard let realm = realm else { return }
  try! realm.write {
    isCompleted = !isCompleted
  }
}
```

`toggleCompleted()` is a new method which allows you to easily toggle the status of a to-do item from incomplete to completed and vice-versa.

Every object persisted to a Realm has a `realm` property which provides you with quick access to the Realm where the object is currently persisted on.

You start by unwrapping the `ToDoItems`' `realm` and start a new write transaction, just like you did before.

From within the transaction, you toggle `isCompleted`. As soon as the transaction has been successfully committed, that change is persisted on disk and propagated throughout your observation to change notifications. You can now add the code to toggle the item whenever the user taps the right button on each to-do item cell.

Switch back to **Scenes/ToDoListController.swift** and add the following method below `addItem()`:

```
func toggleItem(_ item: ToDoItem) {
   item.toggleCompleted()
}
```

This method calls your newly created `toggleCompleted()` on a given to-do item object. You can use `toggleItem(_)` in the code that configures each individual to-do cell.

Scroll down to `tableView(_:cellForRowAt:)` and insert inside the callback closure for `cell.configureWith`:

```
self?.toggleItem(item)
```

When the user taps the cell button, it will call your code back and invoke `toggleItem(item)`, which will toggle that item's status.

That should take care of toggling to-do items in your project.

Run the app one more time and try tapping the status button of some of those to-do items:

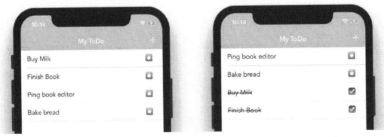

As soon as you modify any of the to-do objects, the view controller is being notified about the change and the table view reflects the latest persisted data.

You'll also notice that items you mark as completed will animate towards the bottom of the list. This is because Realm's `Results` class reorders the objects in the collection according to the sorting you applied when you initially started observing changes. If you look back to `ToDoItem.all(in:)`, you'll see you're sorting the results by their `isCompleted` property — incomplete tasks first, and completed last.

Deleting items

Last but not least, you're going to let the user delete items from their list.

This is quite similar to adding and modifying items: you're going to add a new method on `ToDoItem` and then add the relevant code in the view controller to react to user events.

Thanks to the two `UITableViewDelegate` methods already included in the starter code of `ToDoListController`, the table view already reacts to left-swipes and displays a red **Delete** button:

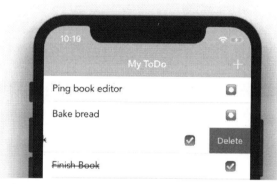

This provides a good starting point for this chapter's last task. Let's get down to business!

Open **Entities/ToDoItem.swift** and add one last method to the extension, below `toggleCompleted()`:

```
func delete() {
  guard let realm = realm else { return }
  try! realm.write {
    realm.delete(self)
  }
}
```

Just like before, you get a reference to the object's Realm and then start a write transaction to perform your updates.

> **Note:** As you'll learn later on, if you try modifying a persisted object without starting a write transaction, your code will throw an exception. You can only modify managed objects inside a Realm write transaction.

Since the class is a Realm object, you can simply call `realm.delete(self)` to delete the current object from the Realm.

Finally, you need to add a few more lines in your view controller to call your new `delete()` method. Back in **Scenes/ToDoListController.swift** add below `toggleItem(_:)`:

```
func deleteItem(_ item: ToDoItem) {
  item.delete()
}
```

Then, scroll down to `tableView(_:commit:forRowAt:)` and append at the bottom:

```
deleteItem(item)
```

This will call your new `deleteItem(_)` method, which in turn invokes the `delete()` method on the to-do item.

Run the app one last time, swipe left on a to-do item, and tap **Delete**:

Just like the previous features you added, the deletion of the object from the Realm is reflected in the table, accompanied by a pleasant animation.

With that last piece of code, your simple CRUD application is complete. You've learned a bit about fetching objects from a Realm file, adding and modifying existing objects, and how to react to data changes and keeping your read and write code separate.

In fact, you already possess the knowledge to create simple Realm apps! However, since working with Realm has so many advantages, you'll want to expand your knowledge as soon as possible. Worry not, we've got you covered. The rest of this book provides everything you'll need to learn about Realm in detail.

Challenges

Challenge 1: Enhance your to-do app with more features

To warm up for the next chapter, work through a few small tasks to polish your to-do application.

Start by modifying the existing code so it only allows the deletion of completed tasks. Way to simulate ticking items off the list!

Finally, add a feature which allows the user to tap a cell and be presented with an alert where they can edit the current to-do item's text. Once they close the alert, the text change will be persisted, and the UI should be updated accordingly.

This chapter didn't go into much detail in regards to the various available APIs, so don't worry too much if you can't figure out how to complete this challenge . You can open the challenge folder of this chapter and peek at the completed solution code. At this point, it's not expected you can figure out everything on your own.

These challenges might not be very complex, but they'll get you writing some simple Realm code to warm up for the grand tour of Realm's object features in the next chapter.

Section II: Creating a Realm Data Model

In this section you are going to learn in detail how to define your database's object schema: simply put, how to define the objects you want to write to and read from disk.

Chapter 3: Object Data Types

You can store a variety of data in a Realm, and in this chapter you will learn about all the supported data types and how to push the limits and create your own types too.

Chapter 4: Schema Relationships

As the old saying goes, no man is an island. Unsurprisingly, that's true not only for people but also for persisted data objects. In this chapter, you will learn how to create object relationships, lists, and reverse links.

Chapter 3: Object Basics and Data types

In the previous chapter, you experienced how it feels to build an app with Realm, and I certainly hope you enjoyed the experience!

Some of the code might have left you wondering "What's exactly going on here?" or "Why did I have to write this specific code and not something else?" Well, that *was* my intention: for you to get a grasp of the easy and clean way of writing Realm-related code, while also sparking your curiosity to learn more and understand the motivation behind the code you've written.

In this chapter, you'll dive deeper into Realm's Swift API and go over many of the available classes and their methods in order to get a solid understanding of Realm's superpowers, as well as some of its limitations.

After working your way through the next few chapters, which focus mainly on in-depth theory, you will move on to building more advanced apps with Realm. But for now, you'll be learning how Realm Objects work and behave, as they are a foundational building block when it comes to understanding Realm as a whole.

Getting started

For this chapter, you will be using an Xcode Playground that's been set up to include the Realm framework and a few utility functions. Since you won't need a UI or other Simulator features, a playground is the fastest and easiest way to experiment and learn.

To get started, open the macOS Terminal app (or another similar app of your choice), navigate to the current chapter's starter project folder, and run the bootstrap script, like so:

```
./bootstrap.sh
```

The bootstrap process will take some time, as it performs the following actions:

- Fetches the Realm source code from Internet.

- Builds all of the required source code.

- And finally, opens the Playground in Xcode.

Next, open Xcode's Debug area to see any output produced by the `print` statements in your Playground:

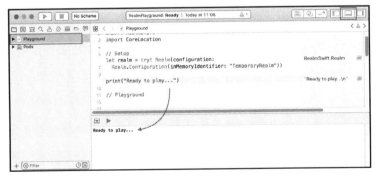

Object basics

Let's start with creating a basic Realm object. Add the following immediately below the `// Playground` comment:

```
class Car: Object {

}
```

This code defines a class, which subclasses Realm's root `Object` class. When your app launches, or in this case, every time the Playground runs, Realm introspects all of the classes in your app and frameworks and finds those classes that subclass Realm's `Object` class. It considers the list of these classes to be your data schema that will be persisted on disk or in-memory.

> ✱ By default, unless you configure Realm otherwise, the framework will assume you'd like to store any and all objects in a single Realm file in your app's **Documents** folder. You will learn about creating different configurations in Chapter 7, "Realm Configurations".

Next, let's add a couple of properties to your newly created **Car** class and a convenience initializer:

```
@objc dynamic var brand = ""
@objc dynamic var year = 0

convenience init(brand: String, year: Int) {
  self.init()
  self.brand = brand
  self.year = year
}
```

You might be wondering why you need to add the `@objc` and `dynamic` modifiers to your property declarations, since you don't have to do this for properties of "normal" classes.

`dynamic`, in combination with `@objc`, makes properties accessible at run time via Dynamic Dispatch. This allows the class to provide a custom, under-the-hood implementation of the data storage of these properties. Realm uses this Swift and Objective-C feature to expose your class' properties as a beautiful and easy-to-access façade that automatically manages reading and writing the actual data to and from disk or memory.

For example, when you access the property brand on your Car class, it doesn't get its value from memory like a usual object, but instead leaves it to Realm to provide you with the actual piece of data.

The same thing happens when you set the value of brand: instead of storing the assigned data in memory, Realm will immediately store that data on disk (or in-memory, depending on the Realm configuration). A simplified schema follows:

To wrap up the Car class, override its default description:

```
override var description: String {
    return "🚗 {\(brand), \(year)}"
}
```

Now, below your definition of the Car class, create a new car and print it:

```
Example.of("Basic Model") {
    let car1 = Car(brand: "BMW", year: 1980)
    print(car1)
}
```

Example.of(_) is a simple helper method provided with the Playground which takes a closure and executes it. You'll use it to separate the code for different examples.

Once the Playground runs, you will see the Car instance description in the output pane:

Currently, the object is not added to a Realm and behaves much like any plain old Swift object. If no other object retains it, it will be released at the end of the closure.

> ✳ Such objects are called **unmanaged** (or detached). As soon as you add an object to a Realm, it will become **managed** by Realm and will implement custom behaviors: it will be stored on disk, it could be modified only in a write transaction, and more.

Your BMW is unmanaged, so as soon as `Example.of(_)` completes executing the closure code, `car1` will be released from memory. You'll look at adding objects to a Realm in more detail in Chapter 5, "Reading and Writing Objects". Then you will get to create as many `Car` objects as you want, and even keep them!

Storage data types

Realm is a multi-platform database and is available for Swift, Kotlin, JavaScript, C#, and more. Thus, it only supports a specific set of data types that can be represented in all of these languages, so you can work with data in a platform-agnostic way.

Now that you have better understanding of object basics, you will look into all of the data types you can store in a Realm and investigate some of the tricks for storing types that aren't supported out of the box.

In this chapter, you will create a newspaper database filled with people of interest. You will have plenty of information to store for each person, but for now, start with an empty class body that extends Realm's `Object`:

```
class Person: Object {

}
```

Object-type properties

Since RealmSwift is a wrapper around the Objective-C Realm framework, there are some aspects of the Swift code that are based on Objective-C *specifics*. One of these oddities is the distinction between *object types* and *primitive types* of data you can store in a Realm object.

Types like `String`, `Date`, and `Data` are sub-classes of `NSObject` in Objective-C, so you can consider them *object types* in Swift as well. Those can be declared as either Optional or non-Optional properties in a RealmSwift Object class, again, because objects in Objective-C can either be `nil` or a memory pointer.

String type

Let's try all object types in action. Add the following code inside your `Person` class:

```
// String
@objc dynamic var firstName = ""
@objc dynamic var lastName: String?
```

You've added two properties:

- `firstName` is a non-Optional `String`, inferred by assigning it a default value of `""`. All non-Optional properties **must** have a default value.

- `lastName`, in contrast, is of type `String?` and does not need a default value. You *could* assign it a default `String` value, but you don't *have* to.

Date type

Add two more properties:

```
// Date
@objc dynamic var born = Date.distantPast
@objc dynamic var deceased: Date?
```

Similarly to the two previous properties, these two are a non-Optional and Optional pair:

- `born` is a date, which every person in the database must have, so it's a non-Optional. Its default value is `Date.distantPast`.

- `deceased` is a date not every person will have, so it's of type `Date?` with no default value.

> ✱ You've probably noticed that `Date.distantPast` isn't a value that would be relevant for *any* of the people on record. This is another oddity in Swift Realm objects that's rooted in their Objective-C inheritance. Due to the fact that `Object` already implements an `init()`, all of your non-Optional properties must have a default value — whether it makes sense or not. The best way to handle this is to always add convenience `init`s that will at least initialize all non-Optional properties with default values.

Data type

The third and final object type you can store is `Data`. Storing data in a database is something that usually won't make sense. You'd usually like to keep the data lean and optimized for speed. Adding `Data` objects will cause the database file to grow unnecessarily, so it's often better to steer clear of this option.

In most cases, storing an image as a file on disk is a better approach than storing said image as `Data` in your database. Add a `Data` property to `Person` to give this option a try:

```
// Data
@objc dynamic var photo: Data?
```

A `Data` property in `Person`'s case could be a downsized thumbnail of the person's photo for easy access. You could pair that thumbnail with another property storing a URL to a photo in the cloud or somewhere on disk.

> ✱ An important limitation to be aware of is that `String` and `Data` properties cannot hold more than 16MB of data. If you need to manage high-resolution images, you will need to store them on disk where there's no such limitation, and store the URL to the file in Realm instead.

Primitive-type properties

To reiterate, what we'll call "primitive types" in this context, in fact, could be objects in Swift. But due to Realm's nature, they are instead represented by primitive types from Objective-C. These types have a slightly different behavior than others:

- They cannot be directly declared as Optional (since primitives cannot be `nil` in Objective-C).

- They can, instead, be wrapped in a generic type called `RealmOptional` to mimic Swift's native Optionals.

Let's look at few examples to get a better grip on this concept.

Bool type

Add the following property to `Person`:

```
// Bool
@objc dynamic var isVIP: Bool = false
```

Adding a non-Optional primitive happens in the same fashion as adding an object type: simply provide a default value and you're all set. The property has to be declared `@objc dynamic` in order for Realm to provide its behind-the-curtain smart storage.

Optional Bool type

> **Note:** In the current 9.3 version of Xcode `RealmOptional` has been broken in playgrounds so you won't get to try the optional code but you can safely use the type in XCode app projects.

If you'd like to add an Optional `Bool` property, you'll have to wrap it in a `RealmOptional` type. That's a very simple type, which bridges the missing support for primitive `Optionals` with regard to Realm's internals.

With `RealmOptional`, you'll have to use its `value` property to get or set its underlying value. Let's look at an optional property called `allowsPublication`. You would declare it like so:

```
let allowsPublication = RealmOptional<Bool>()
```

And you would modify it like so:

```
myPerson.allowsPublication.value = true
myPerson.allowsPublication.value = false
myPerson.allowsPublication.value = nil
```

A `RealmOptional<Bool>` is useful in situations like the one above. The person might have agreed to or declined a publication about them, so you can use `false` and `true` to reflect that in your database. But it's possible the person simply hasn't responded yet, so until they do, you'll have the default value of `nil`.

Last but not least, a `RealmOptional` can also have a default value. Just use its initializer's argument to set one:

```
isVIP = RealmOptional<Bool>(true)
```

Int type variations

To try some of the `Int` types, add these properties to your `Person` class:

```
// Int, Int8, Int16, Int32, Int64
@objc dynamic var id = 0 // Inferred as Int
@objc dynamic var hairCount: Int64 = 0
```

Realm supports `Int`, `Int8`, `Int16`, `Int32`, and `Int64` types to store integer numbers. If you need to specify the size of an integer property, explicitly set the specific type like above: `var hairCount: Int64`.

To add optional properties, you'll need to use the previously mentioned `RealmOptional` wrapper.

Floating point types

`Float` and `Double` types work the same way as the rest of the primitive types. Add these two properties to `Person` to give them a try:

```
// Float, Double
@objc dynamic var height: Float = 0.0
@objc dynamic var weight = 0.0 // Inferred as Double
```

Unfortunately, `CGFloat` isn't supported as this type's representation is platform-dependent, which impedes sharing Realm data between macOS, iOS, Android, or other platforms.

Custom types

Using computed properties when you need some custom formatting is great, but sometimes you need to read and write custom formatted types, or ones that simply aren't supported out of the box.

Storing custom types requires a mechanism to serialize and deserialize data to a supported type. Let's look at two common use cases.

Wrapping CLLocation

> **Note**: Due to the fact Xcode 9.3 broke RealmOptional in playgrounds don't add the code from this section in your playground. You can, of course, use it safely in app projects.

Realm doesn't support `CLLocation` properties, since, like `CGFloat`, it's platform-specific. Fortunately, this type can easily be recreated using a latitude and a longitude, which are both `Double`. You can persist the two `Double` properties in Realm, while exposing a `CLLocation` object to consumers.

Here's how a solution wrapping a `CLLocation` property would look:

```
// Compound property
private let lat = RealmOptional<Double>()
private let lng = RealmOptional<Double>()

var lastLocation: CLLocation? {
  get {
    guard let lat = lat.value, let lng = lng.value else {
      return nil
    }
    return CLLocation(latitude: lat, longitude: lng)
  }
  set {
    guard let location = newValue?.coordinate else {
      lat.value = nil
      lng.value = nil
      return
    }

    lat.value = location.latitude
    lng.value = location.longitude
  }
}
```

And here's the play-by-play:

- By declaring the `lat` and `lng` properties as `private`, they become inaccessible from outside the class.

- By adding a custom getter and setter to `lastLocation`, you publicly expose the two `Double` properties as a `CLLocation` object.

You can wrap any type as long as you can store its data as Realm supported type of data.

Enumerations

Another property type you might want to persist is an Enumeration. Let's add a department to your `Person` class. Inside the class body, add a new enumeration to list all possible values:

```
enum Department: String {
  case technology
  case politics
  case business
  case health
  case science
  case sports
  case travel
}
```

> ✱ The enum doesn't always have to be declared in the class; you'll only do that in the Playground to keep the top namespace clean.

Since `Department` uses a `String` type, all of its case values would have an implicitly assigned raw value matching the case's name. You'll use this raw value to persist the enum options as `Strings` in Realm.

> ✱ For enums that don't have a raw value, you'll need to implement your own method to return a unique value for each case so you can serialize and deserialize them using a type supported by Realm.

Next, add to `Person` a private property for persisting the enum's raw `String` value, as well as the façade property representing the externally exposed `Department` enum:

```
@objc dynamic private var _department =
    Department.technology.rawValue

var department: Department {
  get { return Department(rawValue: _department)! }
  set { _department = newValue.rawValue }
}
```

Realm will persist the private `_department` as a `String` to either disk or memory, while your `Person` class will only expose the `department` property which is of type `Department`. Boom!

Computed properties

You can add computed properties to your class to provide custom formatting or other functionality. Since this kind of properties don't have a setter, Realm will not manage them or try to persist them.

Add two computed properties to `Person`:

```
// Computed Properties
var isDeceased: Bool {
  return deceased != nil
}

var fullName: String {
  guard let last = lastName else {
```

```
    return firstName
  }

  return "\(firstName) \(last)"
}
```

isDeceased is a handy Boolean that checks if the person is deceased and returns a simple true or false value.

fullName implements custom logic to return a properly formatted full name. This will help you keep your UI code simple, since some people in the database might not have a last name. lastName is an Optional value to accommodate for people like Cher or Beck.

Convenience initializers

It makes a lot of sense to always have a custom init for your Object classes, since this adds extra safety to your code, and ensures the object's properties are initialized correctly.

Add a simple initializer to Person to set all of its required properties that need a custom value at creation time:

```
convenience init(firstName: String, born: Date, id: Int) {
  self.init()
  self.firstName = firstName
  self.born = born
  self.id = id
}
```

Notice that these aren't all non-Optional properties, but the remainder have default values already defined.

Default object description

Now that the Person class is *mostly* finalized, let's look at creating some instances and see how to inspect them.

You've done this previously; in the beginning of this chapter (and somewhere around the top of the Playground code) you defined a Car class, and used Example.of(_) to create a Car and dump it to the console.

Car, however, was a somewhat boring Realm object: it featured two lonely String and Int properties, while Person has grown to be a living showcase of Realm's abilities!

Add the following code below the `Person` class:

```
Example.of("Complex Model") {
    let person = Person(
      firstName: "Marin",
      born: Date(timeIntervalSince1970: 0),
      id: 1035)
}
```

This creates a new object named `person`. As mentioned earlier, at this point `person` is not a managed Realm object (also known as a *detached object*). There is no Realm that is actively persisting this object, so as soon as the closure scope ends, the object will be released from memory.

Next, set some values for the object's properties. Below your newly created `person`, add:

```
person.hairCount = 1284639265974
person.isVIP = true
```

As long as the object is not added to a specific Realm, you can modify its properties when and as often as you wish. Once the object is persisted, however, you can only make modifications from within a write transaction. You'll learn more about this in Chapter 5, "Reading and Writing Objects".

For now, let's inspect the current state of the `person` object and look into some interesting details. Append the following to the code inside the closure:

```
print(type(of: person))
print(type(of: person).primaryKey() ?? "no primary key")
print(type(of: person).className())
```

This will print the following to the debug output console:

```
Person
no primary key
Person
```

The first line `type(of: person)` returns the object's type.

The second line of code further uses `type(of:)` and calls the static method `primaryKey()`, which returns the name of the property declared to be the object's primary key. You haven't defined a primary key yet (you will in the next section), so the method returns `nil`.

The third example uses `className()`, which returns the class' name as a `String`. This can be a handy method when you need to work with the name of the class of a given object.

Finally, try the custom description Realm objects provide by default. While still inside the closure, append:

```
print(person)
```

This will print out the object's properties and their values as formatted text:

```
Person {
    firstName = Marin;
    lastName = (null);
    born = 1970-01-01 00:00:00 +0000;
    deceased = (null);
    photo = <(null) — 0 total bytes>;
    isVIP = 1;
    id = 1035;
    hairCount = 1284639265974;
    height = 0;
    weight = 0;
    _department = technology;
}
```

Realm's custom description is a handy way to quickly glance into an object's data in the console. The order in which the properties are defined is preserved while printing the property name-value pairs, so if you're looking for a particular one, keep reading until the end of the list.

> ✱ Don't be confused by the nil values being printed as (null) - that's just another peculiar nod to Realm's Objective-C roots.

A few final points to note before moving on:

• You can see _department — it's a private property, but the class description can access it, so its raw value is printed out.

• You can't see any custom properties like department or others since those aren't managed by a Realm, or stored by one.

With that out of the way, you're ready to look into fine-tuning your Realm objects by providing meta information.

Meta information

We've grouped the few methods you can override on your object's class to provide Realm with more information about your object under the topic **Meta information**. You'll be looking into three static methods that often come in handy in real-life Realm scenarios.

Primary key

You can set one of your object's properties as its primary key. Usually, if your object has an ID or another property that uniquely identifies itself, that is a prime candidate for a primary key.

A primary key is not only a way to uniquely identify an object, but also gives you a way to quickly locate or modify an object in the database. Also note that a primary key is immutable: you can't change an object's primary key's value once an object has been persisted to a Realm.

Time to head back to the Playground and add a primary key to your `Person` class. Add inside the class body:

```
@objc dynamic var key = UUID().uuidString
override static func primaryKey() -> String? {
  return "key"
}
```

This is a common pattern that defines a unique key on a Realm object. You add a `String` property called `key`, or `id`, or `identifier`, or any other name that works for you, and then you override the static `primaryKey()` method and return the name of the primary key property.

The default implementation of `primaryKey()` returns `nil`, as Realm objects don't have primary keys by default.

To avoid using a `String` literal for the return value, you can define a static class constant or use another approach of your choice. In practice, having some pre-defined constants containing the names of the object's properties often comes in handy as you'll need these when you query the database.

Look one more time at the property definition: `var key = UUID().uuidString`. When you create an instance of type `Person`, a UUID (a Swift Foundation class for creating unique values) instance is also created. The `uuidString` property of the UUID is used as the value of `key`.

`uuidString` produces random alphanumeric strings like these:

```
E621E1F8-C36C-495A-93FC-0C247A3E6E5F
8E14BA5A-3375-46FB-9AC5-2B495219C746
89967121-61D0-4874-8FFF-E6E05A109292
...
```

By adding `key` to the `Person` class, you get an automatically-generated unique identifier for each person in your database. After you've created a `Person`, you can retrieve that specific object from Realm using the object's unique primary key.

There's even a special Realm API you can use to quickly retrieve an object by its primary key:

```
let myPerson = realm.object(ofType: Person.self,
  forPrimaryKey: "89967121-61D0-4874-8FFF-E6E05A109292")
```

You'll be learning a lot more about reading objects from the database in Chapter 5, "Reading and Writing Objects".

Other databases and auto-incrementing IDs

Most database platforms, including MSSQL, MySQL, PostgreSQL, SQLite and many others, have the concept of a primary key, just like Realm. And most of those platforms provide a handy mechanism to auto-generate sequential integers for primary keys. It's quick and efficient; as connected clients insert records, the server automatically assigns successive primary keys such as 1, 2, 3 and 4.

A bit of thought will show you that this is a considerable security issue, as an attacker could make informed guesses as to the primary keys of records in a table and try to siphon out data through web interfaces or similar APIs. However, developers keep using this shortcut as an easy way to get a primary key for their table records, despite the security implications.

Another reason auto-incrementing keys have been popular for a long time is that databases like MSSQL or PostgreSQL are usually server-based, where the server acts as the "system of record" and handles the autogeneration of primary keys. Taking this function away from the clients nearly eliminates the possibility of duplicate IDs.

Auto-incrementing primary key values is a rather poor idea for mobile applications, especially ones that use Realm.

Realm powers mobile applications that usually talk to a JSON API or a synchronization service. This means there isn't a "single source of truth" as you'd have in the server-centric "system of record" above.

Instead, choose a value guaranteed to be unique, whether you're passing the object to a JSON API, synchronizing the object to other iOS devices, or even sending the data to Android, Web, Blackberry, or other mobile apps.

Indexed properties

In addition to accessing and modifying records by primary key, you can also choose to create fast-access indexes on other properties of your Realm object.

For example, if your app has two lists in different areas of your app that display the VIP and non-VIP `Person` objects respectively, you might want to add an index on the `isVIP` property to speed up the process of searching the database when querying that specific property. Or, if filtering the database by a `Person`'s first and last names is a common use case, you'd probably like to add indexes on those two properties.

To add an index, you need to override the static `indexedProperties` method. Add the following code to your `Person` class:

```
override static func indexedProperties() -> [String] {
  return ["firstName", "lastName"]
}
```

The `indexedProperties` method is expected to return the names of all properties in your Object you'd like to be indexed.

✱ Adding indexes to your database improves access times when filtering or querying the database, but it also increases the size of the database file and results in a small performance hit when rebuilding the index. Add indexes sparingly and only for those properties you're querying repeatedly in your app.

Other databases and indexes

If you've worked with SQL-based databases in the past, you're probably used to querying the database *constantly* and creating a complex collection of indexes to support a high-performance system.

Realm is quite the opposite of that. Here's why you want to avoid constantly querying the database in Realm:

1. Realm runs on mobile devices, and even though iPhones have become quite powerful, you want to be conservative with a user's CPU cycles and battery drain. Querying the Realm database impacts both these things.

2. In Realm, you have objects that directly point to each other — either as direct object links, or as lists of objects. Following links from one object to another gives you a fixed performance cost and is much more efficient than querying the entire database to find the objects you need, as you would in a traditional SQL application.

Don't stress too much about indexes at this point. Just be aware that they exist, know that they're a bit different than what you might be used to in SQL, and you'll see that you don't actually use them that often in Realm.

Ignored properties

Last but not least, you can simply choose to let Realm ignore some of the object's properties. In a nutshell, you can tell Realm "Hey — here's a perfectly persistable property called so-and-so, but I do **not** want you to do persist that."

That's a perfectly common use case. Realm objects are simply instances of Swift classes, so they can feature any kind of utility methods or properties. You might want to use some of these properties in your ap, but not persist them in a Realm.

There are two ways to have properties ignored by Realm: inaccessible setters, and custom ignored properties.

Properties with inaccessible setters

Realm uses Objective-C class introspection to get the list of your classes' properties and make them "managed". In that sense, any properties that aren't accessible to the Objective-C base Realm class, or that don't have an accessible setter, will be automaticaly ignored.

Let's add a few ignored properties to your `Person` class. First, add a property called `idPropertyName`:

```
let idPropertyName = "id"
```

`idPropertyName` is a `let` constant and its value cannot be changed. It wouldn't make sense for Realm to persist this value, since any `Person` instance you'll create will have this property with this same immutable value.

Now add yet another property; this time, a variable:

```
var temporaryId = 0
```

This property, unlike `idPropertyName`, *does* have a property setter because its value is a variable. It is, however, not dynamic and not accessible by `Person`'s superclass, because it doesn't have the `@objc dynamic` modifiers.

To make sure that Realm ignores this property, look at the debug console and make sure there aren't any `temporaryId` instances in the output of the description of your `Person` instance.

```
Person {
    firstName = Marin;
    lastName = (null);
    born = 0000-12-30 00:00:00 +0000;
    deceased = (null);
    photo = <(null) - 0 total bytes>;
    isVIP = 1;
    id = 1035;
    hairCount = 1284639265974;
    height = 0;
    weight = 0;
    _department = technology;
    key = 11B8C6FE-D659-485A-87B4-2341268649EC;
}
```

Custom ignored properties

Finally, there might be a perfectly fine, Realm-accessible property which you simply don't want to persist in your Realm for any particulary reason. To do this, you'll need to override the static `ignoredProperties()` method, similar to how you used `indexedProperties()`.

Add the following to `Person`:

```
@objc dynamic var temporaryUploadId = 0
override static func ignoredProperties() -> [String] {
  return ["temporaryUploadId"]
}
```

@objcMembers

To wrap up this chapter, you'll look into a Swift modifier that makes Realm code a bit more lean and readable. Frankly, it's a bit tiring to declare all of `Person`'s persisted properties as `@objc`, as it adds extra code and right-indents the actual information, such as the property name and type:

```
@objc dynamic var firstName = ""
@objc dynamic var lastName: String?
@objc dynamic var born = Date.distantPast
@objc dynamic var deceased: Date?
@objc dynamic var photo: Data?
```

As a nod to frameworks such as Realm, which make heavy use of Objective-C introspection, Apple provides the `@objcMembers` modifier which can be applied to *entire* classes or extensions. Setting `@objcMembers` on a class defines all of its members as `@objc`, saving you the trouble of typing `@objc` for each property.

Add this final piece of code to the end of your Playground:

```
@objcMembers class Article: Object {
    dynamic var id = 0
    dynamic var title: String?
}

Example.of("Using @objcMembers") {
    let article = Article()
    article.title = "New article about a famous person"

    print(article)
}
```

You've defined a new class `Article` and used the `@objcMembers` modifier on it. Then, you declared the class properties as `dynamic` only, without needing to explicitly set `@objc` on them. You still need to use `dynamic` for each property you want to persist.

Finally, you added an example in which you instantiate a new `Article`, set its `title`, and print it out. You should see the following output at the end of your console:

```
Using @objcMembers:
_____

Article {
    id = 0;
    title = New article about a famous person;
}
```

The object works as expected!

Apple advices against the overuse of `@objcMembers`, since using dynamic dispatch results in a bit of a performance loss when using Swift classes. For Realm objects however, which *do* need to make use of the Objective-C runtime, using `@objcMembers` is usually justifiable. And the code looks much nicer too!

Challenges

There are quite a few rules to remember when defining your objects: which types can be optional, which cannot, how to define keys and indexes, and more. Don't worry too much about it, as perfection comes from repetition! Before long, you'll be able to define your objects with ease.

Speaking of which, it's time for a quick challenge!

Challenge 1

In this chapter's Playground, add a new `Book` object class that satisfies the following:

- Has an ISBN number (as a `String`), a title, an author name, its bestseller status, and a date of first publishing.

- Could have a date of last publishing.

- Has a convenience initializer to set the ISBN, title, author and first publishing date.

- Has its ISBN number as the book's unique ID, and has an index on its bestseller status.

- Is assigned one of the following classifications using an enum: `Fiction`, `Non-fiction`, `Self-help`.

Finally, create an instance of your newly crafted `Book` class and print it to the debug console to make sure everything works as expected!

Chapter 4: Schema relationships

In the previous chapter, you learned how to design a beautiful and powerful Realm object class. You've mastered your object-type properties and your primitives, learned how to add a primary key and indexes, and other important details.

Your data, however, isn't isolated when in a Realm. You can have many different objects connected to each other in all sorts of useful and meaningful ways.

This chapter will teach you all about building powerful and efficient relationships between objects.

Getting started

For this chapter, you will once again use an Xcode playground that's already been set up to include the RealmSwift framework.

To get started, open the macOS terminal app (or another similar app of your choice), navigate to the current chapter's folder, and run the bootstrap script, like so:

```
./bootstrap.sh
```

This will install Realm from GitHub, build the framework, and finally open the chapter's playground in Xcode.

In this chapter, you'll be working on a simple Car Repair database. You will create several Realm objects in the following schema:

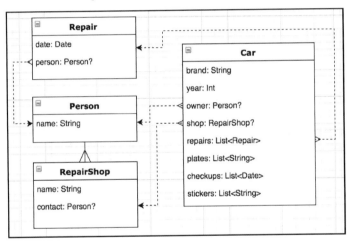

While you're building up the object schema, you will learn everything you wanted to know about object relationships. Let's get started!

To-one relationships

You'll start by looking into what we'll refer to as a **to-one** relationship, also known as an **object link**. This type of relationship allows you to define an object property which points to another Realm object.

You'll begin by creating two objects in your playground: Person and RepairShop. The connection between these will be that each shop (RepairShop) has one contact person (Person).

It's not a good idea to include all of the details for the contact person directly in the shop object, because a single person might be a contact for many shops. Therefore, each person will be a separate object and every shop will simply **link** to a person. This is similar to how object pointers work in memory.

Another benefit of linking to a `Person` rather than storing its information directly in `RepairShop` is data consistency: any change to the linked `Person` will be reflected in its linking object.

Start by adding this simple `Person` object to your playground:

```
class Person: Object {
  @objc dynamic var name = ""

  convenience init(_ name: String) {
    self.init()
    self.name = name
  }
}
```

You won't be adding many data properties to the models in this chapter, as you will focus instead on the relationships between them. Remember that `Person` class from the previous chapter? It was epic!

Now, create the second class which you'll link *to* `Person`:

```
class RepairShop: Object {
  @objc dynamic var name = ""
  @objc dynamic var contact: Person?
}
```

When you create a relationship with another Realm object, its property *must* be of an `Optional` type. In your case, since you're linking to a `Person` object, the `contact` property will be of type `Person?`.

That's pretty much it! Now you can create a `Person` instance and link to it from one or more `RepairShop` objects. That's also the reason it's called a "to-one" relationship: many different objects could point to the same `Person`.

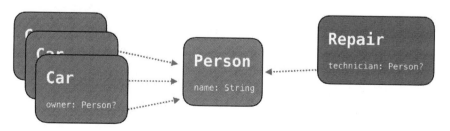

Let's create a few objects which you'll reuse throughout this chapter. At the end of your playground, append:

```
let marin = Person("Marin")
let jack = Person("Jack")

let myLittleShop = RepairShop()
myLittleShop.name = "My Little Auto Shop"
myLittleShop.contact = jack
```

With that chunk of code, you create two people: `marin` and `jack`, and a repair shop called `"My Little Auto Shop"`. (How original!). Finally, you set `jack` as the shop's contact person, which is as simple as assigning `jack` to the `contact` property of `RepairShop`:

```
myLittleShop.contact = jack
```

Realm objects exhibit some of the usual class semantics. In the code above, when you assign `jack` to `contact`, the existing `jack` object isn't copied or retained. The assignment merely sets `contact` to *point* to the `jack` persisted on disk, much like a memory pointer points to a class instance:

The relationship behaves a bit like a `weak` property of a Swift class; if you delete `jack` from your Realm, your shop's `contact` property will become `nil`, as `jack` has been deleted and the object's reference has been lost.

You can modify the `contact` relationship at a later point by assigning a different `Person` object to it, or in the case you don't want to have a relationship at all for `contact`, you can simply assign `nil`:

```
myLittleShop.contact = nil
```

If you want to access a specific value and your data model guarantees a relationship is always set, you can force unwrap related objects. However, the safer and more robust way is to either use `nil` coalescing, which provides a fallback value to print if the original value doesn't exist.

For example, if you needed to print the shop's contact name, you could use the following code:

```
print(myLittleShop.contact?.name ?? "n/a")
```

Or, of course, you can use a guard to unwrap the optional information if it fits better with the rest of your code:

```
guard let name = myLittleShop.contact?.name else { return }
print(name)
```

Finally, since the relationship doesn't manage the life of the related object in any way, it's important to keep in mind that you are responsible for manually creating and deleting all objects.

For example, if myLittleShop closes down and you delete that object from your Realm, that won't cause jack to be deleted. Maybe jack is a contact person for other shops as well, or maybe not - Realm won't make any assumptions about the logic of your app.

If you don't need jack around after deleting myLittleShop, you'll need to delete jack separately.

> ✳ You can only create relationships between Realm objects persisted in the same Realm. You **cannot** create relationships between objects in different files or between a file-based Realm and an in-memory Realm. There's a workaround for these cases, however, which you'll look into later in this chapter.

Let's explore a more complex example by creating another "to-one" relationship. Add a new Car class to keep track of cars in your database:

```
class Car: Object {
  @objc dynamic var brand = ""
  @objc dynamic var year = 0

  // Object relationships
  @objc dynamic var owner: Person?
  @objc dynamic var shop: RepairShop?

  convenience init(brand: String, year: Int) {
    self.init()
    self.brand = brand
    self.year = year
  }

  override var description: String {
    return "Car {\(brand), \(year)}"
```

```
    }
  }
```

Besides having data properties like the brand name and the year in which it was made, Car has two relationships:

- owner is a Person object pointing to the car's owner (or nil if the car is brand new).

- shop points to a RepairShop (or nil in case of a new car).

Your object schema and its relationships should now look like this:

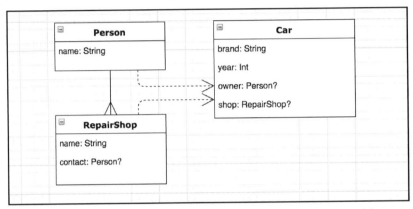

Let's add one more class to push the relationship schema even further. Add a new Realm object class to your playground which will represent a single repair performed at a car shop:

```
class Repair: Object {
  @objc dynamic var date = Date()
  @objc dynamic var person: Person?

  convenience init(by person: Person) {
    self.init()
    self.person = person
  }
}
```

This simple class features the date when the repair was completed (date) and a link to a Person object. This is similar to what you previously did in RepairShop.

Car, Repair, and RepairShip all link to Person. In case of a small shop, it might even be the **same** person for all of these!

Let's try creating some object links before moving on to the next type of relationship.

Add the following code to your playground:

```
let car = Car(brand: "BMW", year: 1980)

Example.of("Object relationships") {
  car.shop = myLittleShop
  car.owner = marin

  print(car.shop == myLittleShop)
  print(car.owner!.name)
}
```

`Example.of(_:_:)` is a method that executes a provided closure code and neatly separates your code examples.

In the example closure above, you set your new car's `shop` and `owner` and then print out a few values.

Give the code a try (or rather, let the playground automatically run when you save your changes) and you'll see the following output in your debug console:

```
 Object relationships:
 _____

 true
 Marin
```

First, you compare `car.shop` and `myLittleShop` and the output is `true`, since the two literally are the same object.

Then, you print the (force-unwrapped) car owner name, which correctly prints `"Marin"` to the console.

To-one relationships as object inheritance

Sometimes you'll need to build some kind of hierarchy between Realm objects, just like you're used to doing with Swift classes. Unfortunately, Realm does not currently support object inheritance out of the box.

The workaround that makes the most sense is to use composition over inheritance.

To guide you in the right direction if you ever stumble upon a similar situation, you'll look into how you would structure different types of vehicles. You would start with the "base" `Vehicle` class (no need to add this to your playground):

```
class Vehicle: Object {
  @objc dynamic year = Date.distantPast
  @objc dynamic isDiesel = false
}
```

Then, you would define the more concrete implementations:

```
class Truck: Object {
  @objc dynamic vehicle: Vehicle?
  @objc dynamic nrOfGears = 12
  @objc dynamic nrOfWheels = 16
}
```

With this solution, creating a new `Truck` object will involve creating a separate `Vehicle`, which is a bit complicated, but as of today, it's the leanest way to have multiple classes all include a base `Vehicle`'s data.

As always, a convenience initializer will greatly simplify your life:

```
class Truck: Object {
...
  convenience init(year: Int, isDiesel: Bool,
    gears: Int, wheels: Int) {
    self.init()
    self.vehicle = Vehicle(year: year, isDiesel: isDiesel)
    self.gears = gears
    self.wheels = wheels
  }
}
```

To-many relationships (for objects)

Besides a simple "to-one" link to a single Realm object, you can also link to a collection of other objects. To continue working on your car repair database, you'll be adding a list of all repairs done on a single car. To do this, you'll need to link your `Car` to a collection of `Repair` objects by using a Realm class called `List`.

`List` is a generic ordered collection, which contains pointers to any number of Realm objects of the *same* type. Lists are very performant and "cheap" in terms of file size because they don't copy or otherwise manage objects; lists merely maintain an ordered collection of object pointers.

Scroll up to your previously created `Car` class and add the following property:

```
let repairs = List<Repair>()
```

Note how this property doesn't need the `@objc dynamic` modifiers you might remember from before, since it doesn't bridge any object or primitive Swift types; instead, it's merely a generic collection implementation specific to Realm that lets you interact with an array-like sequence and access its elements through its methods.

When you create a new `Car` object, `repairs` will be set to an empty `List` of `Repairs`. You can think about it much like an Array of `Repairs`, but specific to Realm. You can then add objects to this collection, query it, move or swap elements, delete elements, and so on.

Let's try out a few examples. Add the following back to the bottom of your playground code:

```
Example.of("Adding Object to a different Object's List
property") {
  car.repairs.append( Repair(by: jack) )
  car.repairs.append(objectsIn: [
    Repair(by: jack),
    Repair(by: jack),
    Repair(by: jack)
  ])

  print("\(car) has \(car.repairs.count) repairs")
}
```

In this block of code, you use two of `List`'s methods:

- `List.append(_)`: Appends a single object to the collection.

- `List.append(objectsIn:)`: Takes a collection of objects and batch appends them all to the list.

In this example, you created some repairs and added them all to `car.repairs`. The last line of code prints the current number of repairs. Your console should have the following output:

```
ℹ Adding Object to a different Object's List property:
_____

Car {BMW, 1980} has 4 repairs
```

The `List` keeps all 4 repairs and preserves the order in which they were appended. Once you persist `car` to a Realm, fetching that `car` back will have its `repairs` collection with the exact same list of repairs, in the exact same order.

Speaking of which, `List` lets you add the same object more than once. Add one more example to give that a try:

```
Example.of("Adding Pointer to the Same Object") {
    let repair = Repair(by: jack)

  car.repairs.append(repair)
  car.repairs.append(repair)
  car.repairs.append(repair)
```

```
    car.repairs.append(repair)

    print(car.repairs)
}
```

You just created a new repair and added it several times to the `repairs` list. When you later print the collection, you can see the same item added several times. Much like other Realm classes, `List` also has a useful custom description when printed:

```
List<Repair> <0x6040002428b0> (
    [0] Repair {
        date = 2018-01-21 23:13:51 +0000;
        person = Person {
            name = Jack;
        };
    },
    [1] Repair {
        date = 2018-01-21 23:13:51 +0000;
        person = Person {
            name = Jack;
        };
    },
    [2] Repair {
        date = 2018-01-21 23:13:51 +0000;
        person = Person {
            name = Jack;
        };
    },
...
```

Managing List elements

Besides `append(...)`, you can also insert objects at specific indices inside the collection:

- `List.insert(_:at:)`: Inserts an object at the given index.
- `List.insert(contetnsOf:at:)`: Inserts a collection of objects at the given index.

Additionally, you can swap elements by using:

- `List.move(from:to:)`

Lastly, you can remove elements from the list by using any of the following:

- `List.removeFirst()`: Removes the first element.
- `List.removeFirst(number:)`: Removes the first `number` elements,
- `List.removeLast()`: Removes the last element.
- `List.removeLast(number:)`: Removes the last `number` elements.

- `List.remove(at:)`: Removes an element at index `at`.

- `List.removeAll()`: Removes *all* elements from the list.

- `List.removeSubrange(bounds:)`: Removes elements in a provided range.

Aggregate functions

There are a few other useful methods of the `List` class worth mentioning.

`min(ofProperty:)` and `max(ofProperty:)` give you the minimum and maximum values of a given property among all objects in a `List`.

These two methods work only on numeric types (such as `Int`, `Float`, `Double`, etc.) and dates. If you consider your `car.repairs` example, you can easily find the oldest and most recent repairs for a car:

```
let firstRepair: Date? = car.repairs.min(ofProperty: "date")
let lastRepair: Date? = car.repairs.max(ofProperty: "date")
```

> **Note:** You'll have to specifically define `firstRepair`'s and `lastRepair`'s type as `Date?` so Realm can infer the return type of these aggregate methods.

Another useful method is `sum(ofProperty:)`. Similarly to `min(ofProperty:)` and `max(ofProperty:)`, this aggregate function produces the sum of a given property for all objects in a list. `sum(ofProperty:)` works only on properties of numeric types and will save you from looping over a list's elements and manually summing up the values.

Finally, there is `average(ofProperty:)` which, in a similar fashion, returns the average value of a numeric property.

Performance

Since lists are a great feature and are very easy to maintain and work with, you'll probably be thrilled to know they are also extremely performant, so feel free to use them as often as needed.

For example, instead of sorting the objects in your database by certain properties whenever a user taps a toggle in your UI, you can pre-sort the objects in two or three different lists. This will eliminate having to do the sorting "live" before actually displaying the objects on screen. For larger datasets, using lists instead of querying the complete database can make a tremendous difference in performance.

To-many relationships (for values)

List isn't only about maintaining a list of links to other Realm objects. A long-requested feature that was added in RealmSwift 3.0, is for List to act like an ordinary Swift array and manage a list of *values*, rather then other Realm objects.

Here's the full list of the types you can store in a List: Bool, Int, Int8, Int16, Int32, Int64, Float, Double, String, Data, and Date (and their optional counterparts).

What does this mean for your shop database?

Let's add a history of all registration plates each car has had. One way to approach this (which you won't implement here) is to create a Plate class containing a single String property and then add a List<Plate> property to the car class.

This approach is completely valid, in the sense that when the database specs change in the future and require you to add more related information to the registration plate, such as which state it was issued in, you can easily add more properties.

As we mentioned earlier though, this section will be about storing actual values in a List, not references to separate objects. Add the following code to your Car class:

```
let plates = List<String>()
let checkups = List<Date>()
```

plates will keep the registration plates history of the car, while checkups will store the dates when the car went through a complete checkup at a service shop. Notice how both properties represent a list of basic object/primitive Swift types, and not any Realm-specific types, which is extremely useful in these kind of situations.

Since List is an ordered collection, you can always access plates.last to get the current registration plate or checkups.first to see when the car underwent a complete checkup.

> ✱ There is one key difference when using List with data values instead of objects. As soon as you remove an element - it's gone. Unlike objects, which still remain in the Realm, values are deleted from the list, memory, and disk.

Let's toy around with some more List related code. Append at the bottom of your playground:

```
Example.of("Adding Primitive types to Realm List(s)") {
    // String
    car.plates.append("WYZ 201 Q")
```

```
    car.plates.append("2MNYC0DZ")

    print(car.plates)
    print("Current registration: \(car.plates.last!)")
}
```

You append two strings to your `plates` list by using one of the `append(...)` method overloads, and then print some output to the console to confirm the data was correctly stored:

```
ⓘ Adding Primitive types to Realm List(s):

List<string> <0x60000004f660> (
    [0] WYZ 201 Q,
    [1] 2MNYC0DZ
)

Current registration: 2MNYC0DZ
```

When you print out the list of values, it really looks much like an ordinary array. Of course, the difference here is that this array-like sequence is automatically persisted for you by Realm.

Note: As of today, Realm incorrectly prints out the data type lowercased, e.g. `List<string>`, `List<date>`, etc. This is a known issue which is reported and being tracked.

Now, to test the `checkups` list, add the following code inside your last `Example.of` closure:

```
// Date
car.checkups.append(Date(timeIntervalSinceNow: −31557600))
car.checkups.append(Date())

print(car.checkups)
print(car.checkups.first!)
print(car.checkups.max()!)
```

Similarly, you can add, move, and delete dates from `checkups`. Unlike lists of objects where you have to specify which property you want to run aggregate methods on, here you can simply call `min()` or `max()` to get the oldest or most recent checkup date.

The precise dates will differ for you but the output should be something along the lines of:

```
List<date> <0x6080000568f0> (
    [0] 2017-01-22 03:04:42 +0000,
    [1] 2018-01-22 09:04:42 +0000
)
2017-01-22 03:04:42 +0000
2018-01-22 09:04:42 +0000
```

Using a list of strings to reference other objects

There is an edge case for using List<String> or List<Int> which is interesting to have a look at in this section.

When you want to create a to-many relationship to other objects, you simply use a List. As mentioned earlier in this chapter, List has a limitation: it only manages links to objects in **the same** Realm file.

When you start working on more complex Realm apps, you will most certainly need to manage a number of different Realm files; some could be pre-built with your app (and therefore read-only), while others could be synchronized with a server or encrypted, and so on.

At some point, you might need objects in one file to point to a single object or a list of objects in another file. You'll examine this scenario shortly.

> **Note:** You are still relatively early in your Realm apprenticeship, so you haven't covered working with multiple Realm files yet. In fact, you aren't even saving the objects you're creating in your playground. In this section, you'll learn how to code the solution and pretend the objects are stored in different files.

Add this new class to your playground:

```
class Sticker: Object {
  @objc dynamic var id = UUID().uuidString
  @objc dynamic var text = ""

  override static func primaryKey() -> String? {
    return "id"
  }

  convenience init(_ text: String) {
    self.init()
    self.text = text
```

```
        }
    }
```

You'll be using this new `Sticker` class to keep track of all bumper stickers an owner might've slapped on their car. (OK, I see how this database might be becoming somewhat too pedantic. This will be the last Realm object you will be adding in this chapter.)

When storing `Sticker` objects in the same Realm file as a `Car` object, you would just add a new list to keep references to sticker objects like so: `let stickers = List<Sticker>()`.

If, however, for some reason you *cannot reference objects directly* (and as discussed, one such reason might be stickers are persisted in a different Realm or in-memory) you'll need a different approach.

Add the following code to your `Car` class:

```
let stickers = List<String>()
```

Instead of linking directly to the `Sticker` objects, you will keep a list of their IDs and use them later to retrieve the objects when needed. Let's see what this code would look like. Append at the bottom of your playground:

```
Example.of("Referencing objects from a different Realm file") {
    // Let's say we're storing those in "stickers.realm"
    let sticker = Sticker("Swift is my life")
}
```

In this example, you create a new `Sticker`, and pretend to store this object in a different Realm file named **stickers.realm**.

Now add the following code to the same closure, pretending to update the main database with cars:

```
car.stickers.append(sticker.id)
print(car.stickers)
```

This will output to the console:

```
 ℹ️ Referencing objects from a different Realm file:

List<string> <0x60c000046ae0> (
    [0] 0C26663C-74BD-4D87-BBAF-120E674A9E79
)
```

This strategy lets you get the list of IDs from one Realm file, while fetching the actual objects from a different one. The process requires an extra lookup when reading those stickers, but nonetheless you have a cross-file reference going on.

What would the code to get those objects from the stickers Realm look like? You will learn everything about querying Realm in Chapter 5, "Reading and Writing Objects", but since you're already here, let's get you started with a little taste!

First, you need to persist your car and sticker objects. Add this code to the same closure from above to add them to the default playground's realm (again, pretend they are stored in different files):

```
try! realm.write {
  realm.add(car)
  realm.add(sticker)
}
```

This will persist the objects in memory and will let you try out the code for looking up relationships via a list of IDs. You haven't yet looked into the APIs to fetch objects, but you can use a few right now to check if that sticker is properly persisted. Immediately after the write closure, add:

```
print("Linked stickers:")
print(realm.objects(Sticker.self)
    .filter("id IN %@", car.stickers))
```

You ask Realm for all objects of type `Sticker` and filter the list to the ones whose `id` property value is found in the list `car.stickers`. That's some quick and easy code!

With these last additions, you finalized the car repair database. You've ended up with a complex database schema, which could well be serving a real-life application.

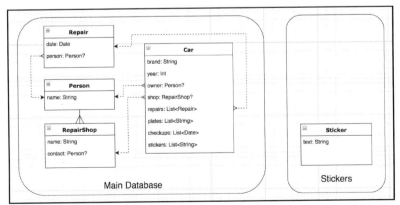

Before you move on to the next chapter and learn more about querying persisted data, you will look into one final type of relationship.

Linking objects

So far, you've learned how to create a relationship from one object to another (or multiple objects, for that matter). But sometimes your code needs to know the reverse: who is linking to a certain object?

It's an interesting issue. When object A links to object B, A is given a "pointer" to B, but B has no clue it's being "pointed" at. This becomes an issue when cleaning up a database cleanup; if there are no objects pointing to object B, you can safely delete said object B to free disk space.

> ✳ As of today, this feature does not work in a Xcode playground, so you will have to run the code for this chapter section in an Xcode project instead.

To get started with the Xcode project for this section, navigate to the project folder **BackLinks-starter** in this chapter's folder, and install the project dependencies:

```
pod install
```

Then open **TestBackLinks.xcworkspace** and run the project. The first time you do this it will take a little while to compile all sources, but eventually you will see a white screen pop in the iPhone simulator. You'll also see an unused value warning for **AppDelegate.swift**. You can ignore this for now, as you'll be using the configuration object shortly.

Open **RealmObjects.swift** to see the stripped down version of the cars database you will use in this section. You'll focus on RepairShop and Car alone. Now switch to **AppDelegate.swift** and create some data to work with. At to the end of your testBackLinks() method, add:

```
let myLittleShop = RepairShop("My Little Shop")
let car = Car(brand: "BMW", year: 1980)
car.shop = myLittleShop
```

You've already mastered this kind of code, so it shouldn't be a problem to follow: you create a shop and a car and link the shop to the car.

Time to persist the objects to the predefined Realm so you can try some new techniques:

```
try! realm.write {
  realm.add(car)
  realm.add(myLittleShop)
}
```

If you run the project now, it should still build and display a white screen in the simulator.

Now `Car` knows that it links to a certain `RepairShop`. But the shop has no idea which cars are being maintained at the shop.

You could, for example, create a `List<Car>` in `RepairShop` and maintain a list of cars manually, but this would be extremely hard to maintain, and could easily fall out-of-sync. Luckily, there is a much easier way via the `LinkingObjects` class.

Switch back to **RealmObjects.swift** and add a new property to `RepairShop`:

```
let maintainedCars = LinkingObjects(fromType: Car.self,
    property: "shop")
```

This property, named `maintainedCars`, is a dynamic collection which automatically provides you with a list of all `Car` objects which have a property called `shop` that point to the current `RepairShop`.

`LinkingObjects` is a bit of a mind-bender, but as long as you remember that it's simply a dynamic collection telling you who links to the current object, you'll be fine. It might make things easier to imagine this as a *reverse relation* between the linked object, and its linking parent(s).

Let's try out your newly created `maintainedCars` property. Switch one last time to **AppDelegate.swift** and add the following at the end of `testBackLinks()`:

```
print("Cars maintained at \(myLittleShop.name)")
print(myLittleShop.maintainedCars)
```

Run the project one final time, and you'll see the result in Xcode's debug console:

```
Cars maintained at My Little Shop:
LinkingObjects<Car> <0x7f86763022c0> (
    [0] Car {
        brand = BMW;
        year = 1980;
        shop = RepairShop {
            name = My Little Shop;
            contact = ;
        };
    }
)
```

`LinkingObjects` is correctly typed as the `Car` type, and prints all cars linking to `myLittleShop`.

Voilà! You've successfully worked through lots of the object relationships that Realm offers. Congratulations!

> **Note:** There is currently an open issue in Realm (Issue 5598 on GitHub) in which accessing a `LinkingObjects` property on a newly persisted object will return empty list. As a workaround, you'll need to re-fetch the object from Realm before correctly accessing the `LinkingObjects` collection.

Designing object schemas

In this chapter, as well as the previous one, you've learned almost everything there is to know about designing object classes and defining relationships between them to create a complete schema.

It does, however, take more than just knowing how to write the code to create complex and performant apps with Realm. It's time for you to gain some experience by working through some real life examples. The next section of this book is all about learning how to read and write objects, and serves as a gentle introduction to using Realm data in simple iOS apps.

Challenges

Challenge 1

To reinforce creating relationships, here's a short exercise you can work through in the Xcode project for this chapter.

You'll be building a small car sales database. Add the following object classes to your project:

- `Sale`, which represents a single sale. It has a date, a value in dollars, and a link to the person who closed the sale.

- `Person` with a `name` as string, a list of sales the person has closed (using `LinkingObjects`), and a list of all of the employee's commissions and bonuses in dollars.

- And finally, `Store`, which represents the business selling cars. It has a name, a list of all cars on sale, and a list of all people working at the store.

Completing this challenge should get you through most of the material you've covered in this chapter and get you ready to finally push your objects to disk in the next chapter: Chapter 5, "Reading and Writing Objects".

Section III: Working with Realm Data

By the end of this section you will have covered all of the Realm basics: defining an object schema, reading and writing data, and last but not least using the database reactive features.

Chapter 5: Reading and Writing Objects

In this chapter, you will learn to create objects, persist them in memory or on disk, and query your Realm in order to fetch them back.

Chapter 6: Notifications and Reactive Apps

This chapter covers one of these special Realm APIs that really makes the database shine compared to all-purpose vanilla databases. Realm notifications are tailored specifically for building dynamic, robust applications and you will learn how to use them in this chapter.

Chapter 5: Reading and Writing Objects

Chapter 4, "Object Relationships", gave you a thorough introduction to designing robust Realm objects and building up a complete object schema that can store complex relational data.

You had a sneak peek into persisting objects and reading them back, but you barely scratched the surface of dealing with stored objects, as you'll realize in this chapter.

In the first half of this chapter you'll look into fetching, querying, and sorting persisted data from Realm. In the second half, you will cover the Realm APIs that let you add, update, and delete objects in your Realm.

Getting started

As usual, you'll work through an Xcode playground that's been set up to include the Realm framework and a few utility functions. In the following chapter, "Notifications and Reactive Apps", you will move on to working on full projects and learning how to use your new Realm superskills to build some incredible iOS apps.

To get started, open the macOS Terminal app (or another similar app of your choice), navigate to the current chapter's **starter** folder, and run the bootstrap script:

```
./bootstrap.sh
```

This will install RealmSwift from GitHub, build the sources, and open the Playground in Xcode. The starter code sets up a Realm for you to work with and creates some test data as well.

The included struct `TestDataSet` features a method `create(in:)` that creates some test objects for you to fetch, filter, and sort throughout the chapter.

> **Note:** If you're curious about the code that creates the test data, open the File Navigator pane on the left hand side of Xcode and open **Sources/Util.swift**.

The object schema is a simplified version of the newspaper database you built earlier in the book. For this chapter, you only need the `Article` and `Person` objects from the original schema:

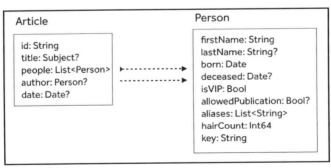

The two objects feature a wide range of properties, as well as to-one and to-many relationships which should keep you busy for the remainder of this chapter.

`TestDataSet.create(in:)` conveniently creates some authors, people of interest, and articles - so you can start poking at the pre-populated Realm right away!

Reading objects

You've already worked with Realm objects in memory, so you know that reading data from their properties is as simple as printing, assigning, or otherwise engaging with, in the usual ways.

The good news is that when working with objects persisted on disk what you learned up until now remains mostly the same. The key skill you need to learn in this chapter is to find the best and fastest route to the object you want to work with. Realm offers a streamlined API for fetching data revolving around the `Results` class.

Realm Results

`Results` is, simply put, an extremely clever API for lazily fetching persisted data.

`Results` mimics a lazy Swift collection, which gives you access to all persisted objects of a certain type in a Realm. You can filter, sort, and randomly access the collection elements.

The key point here, and what makes `Results` so powerful to use, is that the collection is lazy — no actions are performed and no resources are consumed until you access any of the elements.

In that sense, `Results`, which also provides all of the APIs to read data from Realm, is very similar to an ordinary Swift `Array` object. You can use most of the methods you're used to such as `first`, `filter`, `sort`, and more. Additionally, if you do need to work with your objects in the form of an actual `Array`, the conversion from `Results` to `Array` is trivial.

With that said, `Results` is a powerful class so you **do** need to understand the best ways to use it. Luckily, this chapter is *packed* with examples that will show you how to do almost everything you might ever need.

Fetching all objects of a type

Let's start with the simplest `Results` operation: getting all persisted objects of a certain type.

Since your app might be working with several different Realms, the APIs that fetch objects are methods on the `Realm` class. This way, you always know which Realm provides the fetched data.

Your playground already includes a Realm instance. It's initialized at the top of the current code.

```
let realm = try! Realm(configuration:
    Realm.Configuration(inMemoryIdentifier: "TemporaryRealm"))
```

This creates a new temporary Realm in memory. Don't worry, it works much like an on-disk Realm. Since the playground re-runs all of your code each time you modify it, it's a bit quicker to use an in-memory Realm.

The API used to fetch objects from a Realm is `Realm.objects(_)`. The argument it expects is the type of Realm object you'd want to fetch. You can fetch only one type at a time. The good news is that you can navigate to other types if you access any of the object's links or lists.

Without getting into too much detail (yet), let's give this API a try. Append at the bottom of your playground code:

```
Example.of("Getting All Objects") {
    let people = realm.objects(Person.self)
    let articles = realm.objects(Article.self)

    print("\(people.count) people and \(articles.count) articles")
}
```

`people` is of type `Results<Person>` and `articles` of type `Results<Article>`. The two objects (or result sets) do not load or copy the actual people and articles from disk, until you need the actual elements.

Only when you actually use the `count` property will `Results` fetch the metadata of the query; it will know how many objects match what you asked for, but it will still **not** load any data into memory.

> **Note:** Think about a `UICollectionView`'s data source. You need to tell UIKit how many cells to expect, but **not** the data for all of them — only the data for the few items currently visible on screen, and only when UIKit asks the data source for the specific cells.

The code above should neatly output:

```
🛈 Getting All Objects:
─────────────────

5 people and 2 articleS
```

The test data created by `TestDataSet` contains 5 `Person` objects and 2 `Article` objects. `Results.count` returns the number of objects the result set matches.

In case there aren't any objects of the required type, `objects(_)` returns a `Results` that contains **0** elements, as expected.

> ✱ Note that objects in `Results` aren't sorted. Expect `objects(_)` to fetch objects in a random fashion. Once you add objects to your Realm, they'll be stored in the order you added them, but as you use the database and the file is being compacted and optimized, that order might change.

Fetching an object by its primary key

There's actually a second method that allows you to fetch data; you'd use it when you want to get a *single* object by its primary key.

`Realm.object(ofType:forPrimaryKey:)` looks for the one object whose primary key matches the provided key, or returns `nil` if it doesn't find a match.

One of the people in the test data set has a `"test-key"` key, so let's try fetching their object. Append to your playground:

```
Example.of("Getting an Object by Primary Key") {
    let person = realm.object(ofType: Person.self,
      forPrimaryKey: "test-key")

    if let person = person {
      print("Person with Primary Key 'test-key': \
(person.firstName)")
    } else {
      print("Not found")
    }
}
```

As with any `Optional`, if the result is not `nil` you can access the object as usual.

Accessing objects in a result set

Now that you've mastered fetching Realm objects, let's look into how to access them within a result set. Append at the bottom of your code:

```
Example.of("Accessing Results") {
    let people = realm.objects(Person.self)

}
```

This returns all `Person` objects. Lets play with the result set. Inside the example closure, add:

```
print("Realm contains \(people.count) people")
print("First person is: \(people.first!.fullName)")
print("Second person is: \(people[1].fullName)")
print("Last person is: \(people.last!.fullName)")
```

You've just used some of the standard collection features: you're getting the first and last objects in the collection, and also using an indexed subscript to fetch an element at a specific index within the collection.

`first` and `last`, just like their `Array` counterparts, return an Optional result since the collection might be empty. Accessing random elements would also throw an exception if the requested index was out of the collection's bounds, just like a regular collection.

The code above should output:

```
ℹ️  Accessing Results:
_____

Realm contains 5 people
First person is: Klark Kent
Second person is: John Smith
Last person is: Frank Power
```

The exact names that `first`, `last`, and the indexed subscript return, might differ for you, since as mentioned, results aren't sorted automatically. Later in this chapter, you'll learn how to sort your results.

`Results` also features further ways to access its elements - you can use handy collection methods such as `map`, for example. Append the following code inside the last closure to print everyone's first names:

```
let firstNames = people.map { $0.firstName }
  .joined(separator: ", ")
print("First names of all people are: \(firstNames)")
```

You can also get an enumerator to loop over the elements. Add inside the closure:

```
let namesAndIds = people.enumerated()
  .map { "\($0.offset): \($0.element.firstName)" }
  .joined(separator: ", ")
print("People and indexes: \(namesAndIds)")
```

The output from the two examples looks like so:

```
First names of all people are: Klark, John, Jane, Boe, Frank
```

```
People and indexes: 0: Klark, 1: John, 2: Jane, 3: Boe, 4: Frank
```

Results indexes

Since `Results` is a random access collection, it also features a few methods to make working with indexes easier. You've already seen how to access elements by their index in the collection. For the next example, add at the bottom of your playground:

```
Example.of("Results Indexes") {
    let people = realm.objects(Person.self)
    let person = people[1]

}
```

You fetch one of the objects in the result set as `person`. Now, you can also do the opposite — get the index in the collection by providing the object itself. Add to the closure:

```
if let index1 = people.index(of: person) {
    print("\(person.fullName) is at index \(index1)")
}
```

If `person` is found in the `people` collection, `index(of:)` returns its index in the collection; otherwise, it would return `nil`.

Additionally, if you need to find a certain object that matches some custom requirements, you can use `index(where:)` to find the first match. Add:

```
if let index2 = people.index(where: { $0.firstName.starts(with:
"J") }) {
    print("Name starts with J at index \(index2)")
}
```

`index(where:)` takes a closure where you'd define your matching criteria. In that sense, `index(where:)` is a specialization of `filter(_)`, with the difference being it returns an index, and only the one for the first matching element.

Finally, instead of a custom closure, you can use an `NSPredicate`. There are two variations of this method: the former, `index(matching:)`, takes a single `NSPredicate` argument, while the latter takes a predicate format string and a variadic list of arguments: `index(matching:_...:)`.

Let's try the latter. Append this last piece of code:

```
if let index3 = people.index(matching: "hairCount < %d", 10000)
{
```

```
    print("Person with less than 10,000 hairs at index \(index3)")
}
```

Realm takes the "hairCount < %d" format and uses the 10000 argument to build a predicate. It then uses the predicate to find the first matching object in the collection and returns its index.

The completed section code will output something similar to:

```
ℹ️ Results indexes:
————————————————————————
John Smith is at index 1
Name starts with J at index 1
Person with less than 10,000 hairs at index 1
```

Filtering results

You probably have a few concerns about Results. You might be wondering if you'll be forced to use **all** of your Realm-persisted objects without any choice, and how does any of this make sense? You can, of course, filter the objects in a result set to the ones you are actually interested in. Start by adding a new example to your playground:

```
Example.of("Filtering") {
    let people = realm.objects(Person.self)
    print("All People: \(people.count)")
}
```

people, just as before, is a collection of all Person objects persisted in your Realm. But, as mentioned earlier, the collection doesn't really do anything before you access its elements. So you can filter the collection at no cost — nothing is ever loaded before you access the data!

Append inside the current example's closure:

```
let living = realm.objects(Person.self).filter("deceased = nil")
print("Living People: \(living.count)")
```

You start as usual with objects(Person.self) - but this time, you chain another method to the result: filter("deceased = nil"). The filter(_) method takes a predicate format string and will use it to filter the results.

filter(_), in turn, returns Results just like objects(_), which allows you to chain different methods together. The output in the debug console will tell you how many of the persisted Persons are still alive.

```
ℹ️ Filtering:
────────────
All People: 5
Living People: 4
```

Looks like `filter` discarded one of the objects according to your predicate!

There is also a variation of `filter(_)` that, instead of a format string, takes an `NSPredicate` object, providing safer and more robust filtering. Add to the last example:

```
let predicate = NSPredicate(
   format: "hairCount < %d AND deceased = nil", 1000)
let balding = realm.objects(Person.self).filter(predicate)
print("Likely balding living people: \(balding.count)")
```

This time you provide two conditions: the matching objects should both *not* have their `deceased` property set, *and* their `hairCount` needs to be *less than* `1000`.

You can use **most** of the `NSPredicate` syntax you know, but unfortunately not everything's supported. No worries — the next section provides a handy `NSPredicate` cheatsheet you can use as a quick reference.

If you've used `NSPredicate` before, or you are just naturally conscious about the safety of your code, you probably already feel that using strings to query your database is error-prone. You might mistype a property's name, or otherwise unintentionally use a faulty query.

You can use one of the great open source libraries available for building `NSPredicates` in a semantic, type-safe way. In this section, however, you are going to wrap your query in a method to make the code safer and more readable.

Just before the current example code, add a new extension on the `Person` object:

```
extension Person {
   static let fieldHairCount = "hairCount"
   static let fieldDeceased = "deceased"

   static func allAliveLikelyBalding(
      `in` realm: Realm, hairThreshold: Int = 1000) ->
Results<Person> {

      let predicate = NSPredicate(format: "%K < %d AND %K = nil",
         Person.fieldHairCount, hairThreshold,
Person.fieldDeceased)
      return realm.objects(Person.self).filter(predicate)
   }
}
```

`allAliveLikelyBalding(in:hairThreashold:)` builds a predicate and uses predefined constants containing the property names. You will work through a few variations of this code in later chapters; you should experiment with the safety style that fits best in your own project, though.

You can now add this code to the example to try the new method:

```
let baldingStatic = Person.allAliveLikelyBalding(in: realm)
print("Likely balding people (via static method): \
(baldingStatic.count)")
```

> **Note:** Some recommend adding methods like
> `allAliveLikelyBalding(in:hairThreshold:)` via extension directly to the
> `Realm` class to avoid having to pass the Realm as an argument. While this
> approach has its merits, there is a design issue when using multiple Realms.
>
> This method fetches `Person` objects, but if added to the `Realm` class, it could be
> called on a Realm object that doesn't have these objects at all, and you'll end up
> with a runtime crash.

More advanced predicates

In this section, let's try some more complex predicates with `filter(_)`. Add this code to try a predicate matching a list of values:

```
Example.of("More Predicates") {
  let janesAndFranks = realm.objects(Person.self)
    .filter("firstName IN %@", ["Jane", "Frank"])
  print("There are \(janesAndFranks.count) people named Jane or
Frank")
}
```

You just used the IN keyword to match `firstName` from a given list of values to find all people named `Jane` or `Frank`.

Next, let's try BETWEEN to match values in a given range. Add:

```
let balding = realm.objects(Person.self)
  .filter("hairCount BETWEEN {%d, %d}", 10, 10000)
print("There are \(balding.count) people likely balding")
```

Here, you use two numeric arguments for BETWEEN { , } to find people whose hair count is between 10 and 10000 (inclusive).

Let's try some string matching. Add inside your example closure:

```
let search = realm.objects(Person.self)
  .filter("""
          firstName BEGINSWITH %@ OR
          (lastName CONTAINS %@ AND hairCount > %d)
          """,
          "J", "er", 10000)
print("🔍 There are \(search.count) people matching our search")
```

Whoah, that one looks a bit scary. No worries, it's pretty simple! You use a multi-line string literal to neatly format your complex predicate format. Everything between the opening and closing `"""` will be considered a single piece of text.

Focusing on the predicate itself, you filter for:

- Objects having a `firstName` starting with J, e.g. John, Jane, Jim, etc. or

- Objects having a `lastName` containing "er" anywhere in the string, e.g. Tanner, Fuller, Beringham, etc. *and* `hairCount` greater than `10000`.

Sub-query predicates

For even more complex predicates, you can use the `SUBQUERY` predicate function, which allows you to run a separate predicate on each of the objects matching the original predicate. It's a bit of a mind-bender, but hang in there!

Let's have a look at an example. Add this code to your playground:

```
Example.of("Subqueries") {
   let articlesAboutFrank =
realm.objects(Article.self).filter("""
      title != nil AND
      people.@count > 0 AND
      SUBQUERY(people, $person,
        $person.firstName BEGINSWITH %@ AND
        $person.born > %@).@count > 0
      """, "Frank", Date.distantPast)
   print("There are \(articlesAboutFrank.count) articles about
frank")
}
```

The play-by-play of this rather complex predicate is:

1. `title` should not be `nil`.

2. The aggregate property `@count` on the `people` list should return more than `0`, e.g. the `people` list shouldn't be empty.

3. Finally, run a sub-predicate on each of the objects matching the conditions so far.

To execute a sub-query, you use SUBQUERY(people, $person, <predicate>). The first parameter specifies the people collection you run the predicate on, the second assigns a variable name $person to use while looping over the collection, and the third is a predicate. Let's break the sub-query down:

1. It matches people whose firstName starts with Frank.

2. It matches people who were born after Date.distantPast.

3. And finally, by using @count on the SUBQUERY(...) result itself, it filters out all matched objects that don't have any matches for this sub-query.

The output of this example is:

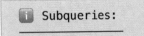 Subqueries:
_____

There are 1 articles about frank

Predicates cheat-sheet

Predicate replacements

- **[property == %d]** filter("age == %d", 30) replaces %d with 30 and matches if column called *'property'* is equal to 30

- **[%K == %d]** filter("%K == %d", "age", 30) replaces %K with 'age' and %d with 30 and matches if column 'age' equals 30

Comparison operators (abbrev.)

- [==] filter("firstName == 'John'") matches values equal to

- [!=] filter("firstName != 'John'") matches values not equal to

- [>, >=] filter("age > 30"), filter("age >= 30") matches values greater than (or equal) to

- [<, <=] filter("age < 30"), filter("age <= 30") matches values less than (or equal) to

- [**IN**] filter("id IN [1, 2, 3]") matches value from a list of values

- [**BETWEEN**] filter("age BETWEEN {18, 68}") matches value in a range of values

Logic operators (abbrev.)

- **[AND]** `filter("age == 26 AND firstName == 'John'")` matches only if both conditions are fulfilled

- **[OR]** `filter("age == 26 OR firstName == 'John'")` matches if any of the conditions are fulfilled

- **[NOT]** `filter("NOT firstName == 'John'")` matches if the conditions is not fulfilled

String operators

- **[BEGINSWITH]** `filter("firstName BEGINSWITH 'J'")` matches if the `firstName` value starts with `J`

- **[CONTAINS]** `filter("firstName CONTAINS 'J'")` matches if the `firstName` value contains anywhere J.

- **[ENDSWITH]** `filter("lastName ENDSWITH 'er'")` matches if the `lastName` value ends with `er`

- **[LIKE]** `filter("lastName LIKE 'J*on'")` matches if value starts with 'J', continues with any kind of sequence of symbols, and ends on 'on', e.g. Johnson, Johansson, etc. In the search pattern a ? matches one symbol of any kind and * matches zero or more symbols.

All operators above can be modified with `[c]` and `[d]` in the following ways: `CONTAINS[c]` for case-insensitive matching, `CONTAINS[d]` to ignore diacritics (i.e. e, è, ê, ë are all considered to be the same character).

Aggregate operators and key-paths (abbrev.)

- **[ANY]** `filter("ANY people.firstName == 'Frank'")` matches if at least one of the objects in the `people` list has a property `firstName` equal to 'Frank'

- **[NONE]** `filter("NONE people.firstName == 'Frank'")` matches if none of the objects in the `people` list has a property `firstName` equal to 'Frank'

- **[@count]** `filter("people.@count == 2")` matches objects whose `people` list contains exactly two elements

Sorting results

Phew! Things certainly got somewhat complex with `NSPredicate`'s advanced syntax. It's time to get back to Realm's own APIs which are simply a joy to use.

In this section, you'll look into a few variations of the `sorted()` method which allows you to sort your queried `Results`. Append to your playground:

```
Example.of("Sorting") {
    let sortedPeople = realm.objects(Person.self)
        .filter("firstName BEGINSWITH %@", "J")
        .sorted(byKeyPath: "firstName")

    let names = sortedPeople.map
{ $0.firstName }.joined(separator: ", ")
    print("Sorted people: \(names)")
}
```

This piece of code fetches `Person` objects starting with the letter `'J'` from your Realm. This time, you used a new method: `sorted(byKeyPath:)`.

Providing a property name to `sorted(byKeyPath:)` sorts the result set by the values for the given property. Realm sorts string properties *alphabetically*, number properties *numerically*, and dates *chronologically*.

The output of the code above is:

> ℹ️ Sorting:
> _____
>
> Sorted people: Jane, John

`sorted()` accepts a second argument called `ascending`, which is set to `true` by default. This orders numbers from smaller to bigger, dates from older to more recent, and so forth. You can reverse the order to descending by setting `ascending` to `false`. Add another example to your existing closure to give that a try:

```
let sortedPeopleDesc = realm.objects(Person.self)
    .filter("firstName BEGINSWITH %@", "J")
    .sorted(byKeyPath: "firstName", ascending: false)

let revNames = sortedPeopleDesc.map
{ $0.firstName }.joined(separator: ", ")
print("Reverse-sorted People: \(revNames)")
```

Sorting the same objects in reverse produces the following output:

> Reverse-sorted People: John, Jane

Note that the first parameter, instead of a property name, can be a keypath — i.e., it can reference a property on an object link. To try this, append to your current example:

```
let sortedArticles = realm.objects(Article.self)
```

```
      .sorted(byKeyPath: "author.firstName")

   print("Sorted articles by author: \n\(sortedArticles.map { "- \
   ($0.author!.fullName): \($0.title!)" }.joined(separator:
   "\n"))")
```

This code sorts all `Article` objects, not by any of their own properties, but by the
`firstName` of a linked `author`.

The list of articles sorted by the author's first name is:

```
Sorted articles by author:
- John Smith: Musem of Modern Art opens a Boe Carter
retrospective curated by Jane Doe
- Klark Kent: Jane Doe launches a successfull new product
```

Finally, `sorted(by:)` lets you sort a result set by multiple keypaths. Append to your
example:

```
let sortedPeopleMultiple = realm.objects(Person.self)
   .sorted(by: [
     SortDescriptor(keyPath: "firstName", ascending: true),
     SortDescriptor(keyPath: "born", ascending: false)
   ])

   print(sortedPeopleMultiple.map { "\($0.firstName) @ \
   ($0.born)" }.joined(separator: ", "))
```

`sorted(by:)` accepts a single parameter, which is a collection of `SortDescriptors`.
`SortDescriptor` is a simple wrapper type which sets a property name to sort on and
whether the order should be ascending or descending.

The code above will sort the list of all `Person` objects:

- First, by their first name in ascending order.

- Then, by their date of birth, while preserving the sorting by name (e.g. the second sort
  rule affects only people which have the same first name).

Your console output should show the following sorted people:

```
Boe @ 1970-01-01 13:53:20 +0000, Frank @ 1970-01-01 08:20:00
+0000, Jane @ 1970-01-01 13:53:20 +0000, John @ 2027-04-03
11:00:00 +0000, Klark @ 1970-01-01 00:00:00 +0000
```

Live results

There is one last aspect of the `Results` class to look into before moving on to write transactions and adding objects to your Realm. Realm result sets always return the latest up-to-date data. Data in `Results` is never outdated.

This means, you never have to reload results from disk or somehow manually refresh in-memory data. This concept might not be entirely obvious to you, so let's try a few examples to get a good grasp of what do live results mean for your code.

Append to the bottom of your playground:

```
Example.of("Live Results") {
    let people = realm.objects(Person.self).filter("key == 'key'")
    print("Found \(people.count) people for key \"key\"")
}
```

The test data set does not include a person with key equal to `"key"`. Thus `people` won't contain any results and the output of the code will be:

```
i  Live Results:
_____

Found 0 people for key "key"
```

Create a new `Person` instance and set its key, then persist it into your Realm instance:

```
let newPerson1 = Person()
newPerson1.key = "key"

try! realm.write {
    realm.add(newPerson1)
}
```

At this point, you know that `people` matches a new object. And since result sets are always up to date, you can simply check the `people.count` property again. Append:

```
print("Found \(people.count) people for key \"key\"")
```

This time the output is:

```
Found 1 people for key "key"
```

You didn't have to, in any way, refresh the results or ask Realm to refetch your results. Every time you ask for `people.count`, you get the count of the objects matching that defined result set.

Let's experiment a bit further. Append:

```
let newPerson2 = Person()
newPerson2.key = "key"
newPerson2.firstName = "Sher"
print("Found \(people.count) people for key \"key\"")
```

This code will still print that only 1 person was found. Since you didn't add `newPerson2` to your Realm, the object isn't part of the persisted `Person` collection, and therefore, not in the `people` result set.

In fact, you can't even add `newPerson2` to the same Realm, as its unique primary key has the same value as `newPerson1`, which has already been persisted. If you try and add `newPerson2`, you'll get a runtime exception saying an object with the given primary key value already exists.

Live results are a very useful feature which you'll use often throughout the rest of the book, and your "real life" code. All apps striving to display real-time data can make use of live Realm results, especially when combined with the built-in Realm change notifications which let you know not only when, but also *what* data changed.

You will get to build your first app using all of these features shortly in Chapter 6, "Notifications and Reactive Apps". And speaking of data changes, you still need to go through a crash course in adding and modifying objects in a Realm.

Writing objects

Any and all modifications to a Realm need to be performed in a write transaction. There are two APIs which you'll learn here that help you perform write transactions.

The former is a method taking a closure. Any changes you add inside this closure are performed in a write transaction:

```
try! realm.write {
    ...perform changes to the realm...
}
```

`write(_)` would throw an error in the rare cases the device is out of free space, or the file is corrupted.

The latter API is a little more flexible, but requires a few extra lines of code. You explicitly start the transaction by using `beginWrite()` and commit it using `commitWrite()`. You can also rollback all changes using `cancelWrite()`, in case things go south.

```
realm.beginWrite()
  ... perform changes ...

// in case you need to rollback the changes
realm.cancelWrite()

// or persist all changes on disk
try! realm.commitWrite()
```

✴ Explicitly adding and removing objects aren't the only actions that count as "modifying a Realm". Once you persist an object, each time you change the value of any of its properties, you modify the object on disk as well, which needs to be performed from within a write transaction.

Adding objects to Realm

You add objects to a Realm by using either of the overloaded `Realm.add(...)` methods:

- `Realm.add(_ object:update:)` persists a single object and all of its links that haven't been persisted yet.

- `Realm.add(_ objects:update:)` batch-persists a collection of objects.

`realm.add(newPerson)` will add `newPerson` to the `realm` Realm. In case an object having the same primary key as `newPerson` already exists in the Realm, an exception will be thrown.

In case you might be adding objects that could already exist in the Realm, you might want to set the second parameter called `update`. `realm.add(newPerson, update: true)` will add `newPerson` to the Realm, but if an object with the same primary key already exists, it will be *overwritten* by the new object.

Cascading inserts

In this example, you'll inspect how one of the coolest features of adding objects works; namely, cascading inserts. Since objects which are persisted cannot point to non-persisted objects, Realm will not only add the object you explicitly provide to `add(_)` but also any non-persisted linked objects.

Append this new example to your playground:

```
Example.of("Cascading Inserts") {
  let newAuthor = Person()
  newAuthor.firstName = "New"
  newAuthor.lastName = "Author"
```

```
    let newArticle = Article()
    newArticle.author = newAuthor
}
```

You create two detached objects: `newAuthor` and `newArticle`. `newArticle.author` links to `newAuthor`. For the moment both objects exist only in memory. Add this code inside the closure:

```
try! realm.write {
    realm.add(newArticle)
}
```

You add `newArticle` to your Realm, and since it references `newAuthor`, that object will *also* be added to the Realm. You can test this easily by adding this code to your example:

```
let author = realm.objects(Person.self)
    .filter("firstName == 'New'")
    .first!

print("Author \"\(author.fullName)\" persisted with article")
```

The important take-away here is that Realm guarantees the integrity of the persisted data by not allowing managed objects to link to non-managed objects so persists any linked object all together.

Querying the Realm for a `Person` with the same name yields a result:

```
ⓘ Cascading Inserts:

Author "New Author" persisted with article
```

Updating objects

Now that you know how to add objects, you're probably wondering how to modify them later on. It's simpler than you think: just change their properties as you usually would, and Realm will take care of the rest!

Add a new example which fetches an already persisted `Person` and prints some of its current data:

```
Example.of("Updating") {
    let person = realm.objects(Person.self).first!
    print("\(person.fullName) initially - isVIP: \(person.isVIP),
allowedPublication: \(person.allowedPublicationOn != nil ? "yes"
: "no")")
}
```

This should print to the console:

```
ℹ️ Updating:

Klark Kent initially – isVIP: false, allowedPublication: nO
```

Next, update `person` with some new data by adding:

```
try! realm.write {
    person.isVIP = true
    person.allowedPublicationOn = Date()
}

print("\(person.fullName) after update – isVIP: \(person.isVIP),
allowedPublication: \(person.allowedPublicationOn != nil ? "yes"
: "no")")
```

All changes in the closure you provide to `Realm.write(_)` are being instantly transferred to disk, and any that are outside of that closure will raise an exception. The output this time is:

```
Klark Kent after update – isVIP: true, allowedPublication: yes
```

Deleting objects

Last but not least, once you don't need certain objects, you are welcome to delete them from your Realm. Any objects currently linking to the deleted ones will set their linking property to `nil`. If those objects are linked from any `List` properties, they will be removed from the lists in question.

Let's try a few examples to get an understanding of how to get rid of objects. Append to your playground:

```
Example.of("Deleting") {
    let people = realm.objects(Person.self)

    print("There are \(people.count) people before deletion: \
(people.map { $0.firstName }.joined(separator: ", "))")
}
```

This will output:

```
ℹ️ Deleting:

There are 7 people before deletion: Klark, John, Jane, Boe,
Frank, , NeW
```

Using `Realm.delete(_)`, you can delete a single object or a collection of objects. Append:

```
try! realm.write {
  realm.delete(people[0])
  realm.delete([people[1], people[5]])
  realm.delete(realm.objects(Person.self).filter("firstName
BEGINSWITH 'J'"))
}

print("There are \(people.count) people after deletion: \
(people.map { $0.firstName }.joined(separator: ", "))")
```

In this last chunk of code you do three deletes:

- A single object, which you grab at index 0 from `people`.

- A collection of objects with the specified indexes 1 and 5.

- And finally you delete the objects fetched by a `Results` using a predicate.

Since the `people` result set represents live data, printing it again without any refresh would output the expected result:

```
There are 3 people after deletion: New, Frank, Boe
```

Finally, there's one last method you can use which deletes *all* objects in the Realm. Add inside the last example closure:

```
print("Empty before deleteAll? \(realm.isEmpty)")

try! realm.write {
  realm.deleteAll()
}

print("Empty after deleteAll? \(realm.isEmpty)")
```

`Realm.deleteAll()` simply purges all data from the Realm and `Realm.isEmpty` is at your disposal to prove it. A great API for whenever you need a fresh start!

The last output added to the console should confirm this:

```
Empty before deleteAll? false
Empty after deleteAll? true
```

Challenges

This was a long and theory-heavy chapter, and I bet you're longing to write some code yourself. To try out some of the APIs covered in this chapter, you will work through a series of tasks related to reading and writing objects in your playgrounds's Realm.

Challenge 1

Write code to:

1. Create an article with any author, and add a `Person` named `Jim` to its `people` list.

2. Print a list of all articles that have a person whose first name is `Jim` in its `people` list.

3. Write the opposite of the above, printing all articles that *don't* have a person whose name is `Jim`.

4. Print a list of all articles that have at least one person in their `people` list.

5. Print a list of all people sorted by their `hairCount` (from least to most); for the ones who have the same hair count, order them by `firstName` alphabetically.

6. Rename any people named `Jim` to `John`.

Chapter 6: Notifications and Reactive Apps

In the previous chapter, Chapter 5, "Reading and Writing Objects", you finally learned how to interact with your app's Realm in detail: how to create new objects, persist them to disk, and of course, fetch them back from Realm, with either a simple fetch by primary key or more complex queries.

You are probably eager to use the in-depth knowledge you soaked up working through the last few chapters in practice, and rightfully so.

There is good news and bad news, at this point, though. The good news is that, by the end of this chapter, you'll be able to fire up the iPhone Simulator with a new app you worked on. The bad news, if you could call it that, is that you'll have to work through a bit more theory before you get to that point.

In this chapter, you'll learn about Realm's built-in notification APIs. Realm features a rather clever system of detecting any changes, regardless of the thread or process responsible for those changes, and deliver notifications to any observers.

In the second half of this chapter, you'll work on a simple chat app which will help you learn the basics of building reactive apps using Realm notifications.

Change notifications

One of the core features of the Realm database is the idea that data is *never* outdated. The clever way Realm maps in-memory objects used in your app code, to data persisted on disk, guarantees that your data is fresh.

This is also one of the reasons why Realm is such a great platform for mobile applications; it's been designed to answer the data management needs of modern mobile applications.

Despite everything you've learned so far, a tiny piece of the puzzle is still missing. Even if you always access the latest up-to-date data, you still need to know *when* the data has been changed so you can update your app's UI accordingly. You still have no way to mirror changes in your persisted Realm data directly to your UI. You'll need some kind of API to notify you whenever the data has changed.

Fortunately, Realm has a lightweight notification system which is designed to solve this exact problem. It keeps you in the loop about *when* your data changes, and even more importantly - gives you precise fine-grained data about *what* was changed. It lets you decouple your model persistence code and the presentation code for your UI. Realm serves as a dispatch between the two:

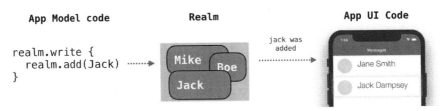

Realm provides notifications on three levels, going from more granular to less:

- **Object level**: You can observe a single object for property changes.

- **Collection level**: You can observe a collection of objects — a list, results, or linking objects property — for changes happening on any of its elements or the collection itself.

- **Realm level**: You can observe changes on an entire Realm, as a notification is sent after each successful write transaction.

You'll learn how to use each of these options soon - but first, let's go through some details you should keep in mind for this chapter.

Notification details

There are a few things to keep in mind when using Realm's notifications mechanism, especially regarding threads and Apple's own run loop:

1. **Threads**: You'll be notified about changes made to your data from any of your app's threads, or even other processes. The notification handler will be called **on the same thread** where you subscribed for the notifications.

2. **Run loop**: Realm uses Apple's run loops to deliver change notifications. Therefore, you can subscribe for notifications only from a thread that has a run loop installed. By default, the main thread has a run loop, but any threads you create (either via spawning new threads or using Grand Central Dispatch) won't have one. You'll learn how to install a run loop and subscribe for changes in a background thread later in this book.

3. **Notifications granularity**: Realm dispatches change notifications to all interested observers after each successful write transaction. Since those are delivered using the subscribing thread's run loop (which might sometimes be busy with other work) it might happen that another change is performed in the Realm before the notification is delivered. In that case, Realm will aggregate the changes and deliver them together.

4. **Persisted objects only**: Realm allows you to observe changes on persisted objects only, i.e. they need to be added to a Realm.

5. **Notification tokens**: Subscribing for notifications returns a *token* object. Notifications are delivered on the particular subscription until you call `invalidate()` on the token object, or the token object is *released* from memory. For example if it's retained by a view controller's property and the controller is deinitialized.

All of these notes will make much more sense going through the next few chapters, where you'll get to work on some more advanced projects. Keep the list above as a quick reference and let's get some examples running so you can finally write some code.

Getting started

As usual, this chapter includes a Playground pre-configured with Realm.

To get started, open the macOS Terminal app (or another similar app of your choice), navigate to the current chapter's **starter** folder, and run the bootstrap script, like so:

```
./bootstrap.sh
```

This will install and build the project, and eventually open the playground in Xcode. As soon as the playground opens you'll see its start page:

Notifications and Reactive Apps

This section provides several asynchronous examples that work best when executed individually.

Table of contents:

- Observing an Object
- Observing a Collection
- Collection Changes
- Avoid notifications for given tokens
- Realm-wide notifcations

> **Note:** If you don't see the rendered text but instead see raw source code, you can enable rendering. From the Xcode main menu choose **Editor ▸ Show Rendered Markup**.
>
> Also, if for some reason you see an error along the lines of `no such module 'Playground_Sources'`, this is probably Xcode acting up. Run the bootstrap script one more time like so `./bootstrap.sh clean`. Your playground should build and work without any issues.
>
> Additionally, as a last resort, while the playground is active, go to the File Inspector on the right side panel, switch the **Platform** under **Platform Settings** to macOS, and then back to iOS.

In this chapter, you'll be working on a multi-page playground. Since the APIs you'll be covering are asynchronous, it's much easier to have the different examples run separately from each other. Every new playground page will work as if you restarted a simulator with a different example, giving you a clean slate.

The object schema for the current playground is the newspaper database you're probably already quite familiar with from previous chapters. You'll be looking into people of interest and articles about them one final time.

Observing an object

Select the playground page named **Observing an Object**. You'll see the familiar setup code that creates an in-memory Realm. Each of the playground pages features this code in order to set up a clean Realm for this section's examples.

Since you have a fresh Realm, your first step will be to create and persist an `Article` object to it. Append to the playground:

```
let article = Article()
article.id = "new-article"

try! realm.write {
  realm.add(article)
}
```

You just created an article and added it to the playground's Realm. Now let's see how to subscribe for changes on `article`. Add:

```
let token = article.observe { change in

}
```

`Object.observe(_)` is the API that lets you observe changes on a single Realm object. The provided closure is the notification handler; Realm will call the closure *every time* a change occurs for a specific object. The `change` closure argument includes detailed information about what properties have been changed, and in what way.

Inside the `observe(_)` closure, add:

```
switch change {
case .change(let properties):
  break
case .error(let error):
  print("Error occurred: \(error)")
case .deleted:
  print("Article was deleted")
}
```

`change` is of type `ObjectChange`, an enumeration with three cases:

- `.change(properties)`: When a property value has been modified. `properties` is of type `[PropertyChange]` and provides information about which properties have been changed, along with the changed values, old and new.

- `.error(error)`: When an error has occurred.

- `.deleted`: Emitted once the object has been deleted and you can no longer observe it.

The most interesting and useful of the following is the `.change` case, which lets you know that you need to update your app's UI with the latest data.

Let's handle changes on the observed article. Insert the following into the `.change` case just above `break`:

```
for property in properties {
  switch property.name {
  case "title":
    print(" 📝 Article title changed from \(property.oldValue ??
"nil") to \(property.newValue ?? "nil")")
  case "author":
    print(" 👤 Author changed to \(property.newValue ?? "nil")")
  default: break
  }
}
```

You loop over the list of changed properties (`properties`) and react differently for different properties: if the title changes, you print " 📝 `Article title changed ...`". If the author changes, you'll print: " 👤 `Author changed to ...`".

Besides iterating over the property list, you can also use `contains(where:)` to look for a specific property by its name. Immediately after the `for` loop (e.g. just before `break`), append this code to try it out:

```
if properties.contains(where: { $0.name == "date"}) {
  print("date has changed to \(article.date)")
}
```

The notification token object is assigned to `token` in the very first line of this example's code. The playground will hang onto the `token`, but if you're subscribing for notifications in an app, like in your view controller or view model, make sure you're retaining that token somehow. Making it a property on your view controller is often times the easiest way to do that. Inspect the token by adding at the bottom of the playground code:

```
print("Subscription token: \(token)")
```

The sole purpose of a `NotificationToken` object is to control the notification subscription lifetime. The only method this class exhibits is `invalidate()`, which both releases the token and cancels the subscription.

Now that you have the notification closure set up, let's try and modify one of the article's properties. Add to the playground:

```
try! realm.write {
  article.title = "Work in progress"
}
```

Look at the console, where you'll find a message waiting for you:

```
ℹ️ Observing an Object:
─────────────────────
Subscription token: <RLMObjectNotificationToken: 0x6000002c0850>
📝 Article title changed from nil to Work in progreSS
```

In this particular example, reacting to that simple data change probably doesn't feel like a big gain. What really makes a difference is that you'll be notified on any change happening from anywhere in your app - be it from the same thread, a different one, or even from a completely different process.

You can easily confirm that by using GCD. Create an asynchronous task on a background queue:

```
DispatchQueue.global(qos: .background).async {
    let realm = try! Realm(configuration: configuration)
}
```

Inside the task's closure, you create a Realm object by using the same configuration parameter that is being used for the main playground Realm. There's more about configurations in the next chapter, "Realm Configurations".

Any change you perform inside of this closure will be committed on a background queue. Try it by adding into the closure:

```
if let article = realm.object(ofType: Article.self,
    forPrimaryKey: "new-article") {
    try! realm.write {
        article.title = "Actual title"
        article.author = Person()
    }
}
```

You fetch the article you worked on previously by its primary key and update both its `title` and `author` properties.

After you finish adding the code, let the playground run and you'll see the notification handler being called a second time:

```
📝 Article title changed from Work in progress to Actual title
👤 Author changed to Person {
    firstName = ;
    lastName = (null);

    ...
}
```

That wasn't difficult at all, was it?

Observing a collection

Now let's move to the next level and look at observing collections of persisted objects.

As mentioned earlier, a collection of objects is any of the following: a list of objects, a filtered and/or sorted result set, or a linking-objects property.

Since each of these different collection types serves a different purpose, you would probably end up observing them with different goals in mind. Leaving practical examples aside for now, let's figure out how collection notifications work and how to use them.

A notification triggering a collection change might be one of the following:

- **Inserting** or **deleting** an object that belongs to a list or is fetched in a result set.

- **Moving** an object to a different index via List's move() method, or by being sorted to a different index in results. This removes the object from its old index and inserts it at a new position, producing two separate changes.

- **Modifying** the value of a property for an object that's part of to the collection.

- **Modifying** the property of an object linked from an object that's part of the collection.

- **Modifying** the property of an object belonging to a list property of an object that's part of the collection.

To play around with some code, open the next page of the playground by selecting **Observing a Collection** in the File navigator:

Add the following code to the playground to get started:

```
let people = realm.objects(Person.self)
  .sorted(byKeyPath: "firstName")

let token = people.observe { changes in
  print("Current count: \(people.count)")
}
```

You fetch the test data set of `Person` objects, sorted by their `firstName` property. You then call `observe` on the result set and provide a closure as a notification handler.

`observe(_)` works in almost the exact same way as for a single object. You pass it a closure and it returns a notification token you can use to control the notification subscription's lifecycle. The difference here is that the closure parameter isn't of type `ObjectChange`, but of type `RealmCollectionChange` instead.

When you start observing a collection, a notification is immediately emitted to notify you about the collection's initial state. You'll see the following in your console:

```
ⓘ Observing a Collection:

Current count: 5
```

Let's quickly do some tests and trigger a few notifications on `people`. Add:

```
try! realm.write {
    realm.add(Person())
}
```

Your console output should show:

```
Current count: 6
```

Since `people` is a results collection of all `Person` objects persisted in your Realm, when you add a new `Person` your notification handler is triggered, since that counts as a modification to your `people` result set.

Add the same code one more time:

```
try! realm.write {
    realm.add(Person())
}
```

That calls your handler a second time:

```
Current count: 7
```

Finally, to check if collection notifications work exactly like object notifications (spoiler alert: *they do!*), append this code to add yet another person, but this time, from a background thread:

```
DispatchQueue.global(qos: .background).sync {
    let realm = try! Realm(configuration: configuration)
    try! realm.write {
```

```
      realm.add(Person())
    }
  }
```

Everything seems to be working just fine, so let's move on to testing one last feature: cancelling subscriptions.

For this exercise you'll need to run some asynchronous code. Add a delayed task to invalidate your notification token:

```
DispatchQueue.global().asyncAfter(deadline: .now() + 1) {
    token.invalidate()
}
```

One second from now, you call `invalidate()` on `token`, which will immediately cause Realm to stop delivering notifications regarding `people`. You can try this by making yet another change to your data two seconds from now — that is, a second after the subscription has been cancelled. Add:

```
DispatchQueue.main.asyncAfter(deadline: .now() + 2) {
    try! realm.write {
      realm.add(Person())
    }
    // does not produce a notification
}
```

As the comment in the code block suggests, your notification handler won't print anything in the console for this last change. Notifications have been cancelled like a third-rate TV show in its fourth season.

Collection changes

So far, you've experimented quite a bit with collection notifications, but the real interesting part is the changes parameter of the notification handler.

The fine-grained change information gives you the opportunity to update only the specific items in your UI that reflect the changed data. Think about a table view. When the item representing row number 2 has changed, you don't need to reload the entire table, do you? You only need to refresh the cells that represent the changed items in the your data model.

Open the **Collection Changes** page in your playground and at the bottom append the following code to create an article:

```
let article = Article()
article.title = "New Article"
```

```
try! realm.write {
  realm.add(article)
}
```

Your article currently doesn't link to any people of interest, but you'll add some later on in this section. Let's set up a notification handler first. Add one on the `article.people` list property:

```
let token = article.people.observe { changes in
  switch changes {
  case .initial(let people):
    print("Initial count: \(people.count)")
  case .update(let people, let deletions, let insertions, let
updates):
    print("Current count: \(people.count)")
    print("Inserted \(insertions), Updated \(updates), Deleted \
(deletions)")
  case .error(let error):
    print("Error: \(error)")
  }
}
```

You can already get a sense for the possible cases for `changes`'s value:

- `.initial(collection)` is the notification Realm emits when you initially observe collection changes. This notification isn't triggered by a collection change *per se*, but it provides you with the initial state so you can initialize your UI.

- `.update(collection, deletions, insertions, updates)` is a notification triggered by any changes in the collection. The last three parameters are of type `[Int]` and represent the indexes in the collection that have been *deleted*, *inserted*, or *updated*. Remember that moving an object between indexes will produce one entry as insertion at the new position and one entry as deletion at the old one.

- `.error(error)` is triggered if Realm fails to produce a valid changeset. Once a subscription errors, it will cancel observation of further changes.

In your notification handler, you print `people`'s count and the provided changeset. This will give you an idea of what information is sent upon each change in your collection. Start by adding some objects:

```
try! realm.write {
  article.people.append(Person())
  article.people.append(Person())
  article.people.append(Person())
}
```

You can see the notification handler's output in the console:

```
ℹ Collection Changes:

Initial count: 0
Current count: 3
Inserted [0, 1, 2], Updated [], Deleted []
```

You see the count changing to 3, while the inserted array lists the indices where the new objects were added in: 0, 1, and 2.

Now, modify the value of one of the linked Person objects:

```
try! realm.write {
    article.people[1].isVIP = true
}
```

This also triggers a change notification:

```
Current count: 3
Inserted [], Updated [1], Deleted []
```

Try bundling a few changes in a single write transaction by adding:

```
try! realm.write {
    article.people.remove(at: 0)
    article.people[1].firstName = "Joel"
}
```

Your console should show:

```
Current count: 2
Inserted [], Updated [2], Deleted [0]
```

Hopefully that output set off some alarms!

You clearly updated the people element at index 1 (from above: people[1].firstName = "Joel"), but Realm reports that an object at index 2 was updated. Is that a bug? What do you think?

When your Swift code runs, each line executes in turn:

```
46
47  try! realm.write {
        article.people.remove(at: 0)
49      article.people[1].firstName = "Joel"
50  }
```

You first remove the object at index 0, which shifts the person at index 2 to index 1. Then, you modify index 1 which is the object that just moved from position 2.

The changeset that Realm provides is of the indices changed since *the last* change notification you received. In that sense, what you should do to reflect the changeset in your app's UI is to remove the table cell at what used-to-be index 0 and then refresh the cell that used-to-be at index 2.

At first sight, that might seem like a bit of a mind bender, but you won't have to do much manually. Realm's changesets fit very easily with UIKit's API so the changes are almost automatically applied to your UI. There's more about this later in this chapter.

To wrap up with testing collection changes, delete all people from the list and see the corresponding indices of all people left in the list being purged:

```
try! realm.write {
   article.people.removeAll()
}
```

Ignore notifications for token

One last feature you're going to cover in this section of the chapter is the ability to choose which tokens will be notified for changes. Simply put, when you commit changes to the database, you can decide if you want to notify *all* observers or just *some* of them.

This feature is mostly used for what is referred to in the Realm docs as "*UI-driven-writes*". Imagine the following situation: you have an ON/OFF switch somewhere in your app's UI. When a user toggles the switch, your code persists the new state to Realm.

In this situation, since UIKit automatically toggles the switch state, you don't want to be notified about that change by Realm - the UI is already up to date! However, there might be other processes in the background, or other parts of the UI that are still interested in a notification about that particular change.

Let's dive into an example: you'll create multiple subscriptions on the `people` collection and will then trigger some writes and choose which tokens are notified.

Open the playground page called **Avoid notifications for given tokens**. Create subscription number 1, which you'll consider to be the subscription which usually updates the app's UI:

```
let people = realm.objects(Person.self)
let token1 = people.observe { changes in
  switch changes {
  case .initial:
    print("Initial notification for token1")
  case .update:
```

```
      print("Change notification for token1")
    default: break
    }
  }
```

Then, create another subscription that observes the same collection. Let's say it updates some auxiliary UI or other data in the background:

```
let token2 = people.observe { changes in
  switch changes {
  case .initial:
    print("Initial notification for token2")
  case .update:
    print("Change notification for token2")
  default: break
  }
}
```

Now let's say you're adding an object from a background process, so your state is already up to date. You want to notify **only** subscription number 1 so it updates your UI.

You'll use `Realm.beingWrite()` and `Realm.commitWrite(withoutNotifying:)` to start and commit a write transaction and, by using the `withoutNotifying` parameter, choose which observers will get notified and which won't. Add:

```
realm.beginWrite()
realm.add(Person())
try! realm.commitWrite(withoutNotifying: [token2])
```

In this example, the subscription for `token2` will not receive a change notification and the output in the console will be:

```
 Avoid notifications for given tokens:

Initial notification for token1
Initial notification for token2

Change notification for token1
```

Observing an entire realm

Finally, you'll look briefly into observing changes on an entire Realm. Open the **Realm-wide notifications** playground page and create a new subscription:

```
let token = realm.observe { notification, realm in
  print(notification)
}
```

This code subscribes to any change, on any object, in the given Realm. In fact, Realm sends a Realm-wide change notification upon committing each write transaction, so you don't actually need to make any changes. An empty `write(_)` call will do the trick.

Add the following:

```
try! realm.write { }
```

This will invoke your notification handler and you'll see the following in the console:

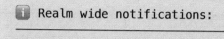
```
   Realm wide notifications:
   ───────────────────────────

didChange
```

The `notification` closure parameter can be one of two enumeration cases:

- `.didChange` is sent after each write transaction.

- `.refreshRequired` is sent in case you've disabled auto-refreshing data (always up-to-date objects) for your Realm. This notification will let you know every time a write transaction was committed so you can refresh your app's UI accordingly.

Realm-wide notifications aren't very useful when you're looking for fine-grained information about specific changes. However, Realm-wide notifications are much lighter to observe; they are sent upon committing each write transaction regardless of what data was changed. If you have multiple Realms containing numerous objects, this might be a case to observe Realm-wide notifications.

With that behind you, you've learned almost everything there is to know about Realm's notification system. A few edge cases and their solutions will pop up later in the book while you're working on more advanced projects.

Reactive apps

Reactive systems exhibit several key features: reacting to changes as they occur, using a message-based workflow, having the ability to scale, and more. Realm allows you to easily implement many of these, which you'll examine by quickly building a chatter app (somewhat like Twitter) with Realm, using Realm notifications.

To get started, open the **Chatter-starter** folder in this chapter and install the project's dependencies by running in the terminal:

```
pod install
```

Open `Chatterz.xcworkspace`. The starter app features two tabs: one is the Stats tab that displays how many messages are currently stored in Realm, and the other tab displays all messages in a table view.

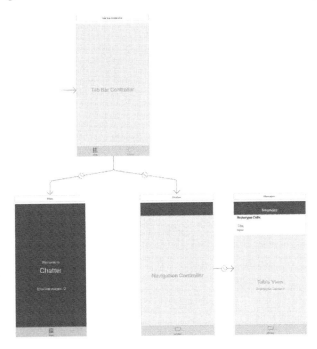

Neither of the screens does much right now. It'll be your task to add the code to connect everything up.

> **Note:** This project uses a mock networking API via the `ChatAPI` class. The networking part itself isn't essential in this chapter, but the API is designed so it mimics real-life API design. Good news though, the last chapter in this book leads you through building a real chat application with Realm Cloud!

Writing messages to the database

To get started, open **AppDelegate.swift** and check the code in `application(didFinishLaunchingWithOptions:)`. You create a `ChatAPI` instance and use the `connect` method, which will "connect" to the server and periodically fetch new messages in JSON format. From inside the closure, you call `persist(messages:)` and pass any new messages returned by the API.

Add `print(messages)` to the `persist(messages:)` method, run the project and wait a bit. You'll see the new messages being printed in the console over time:

```
[("Ray", "anyone around?"), ("Derek", "I\'m outta here"),
("Derek", "Bye"), ("Josh", "I have a question")]
[("Paul", "Bye"), ("Paul", "testing testing ... 1, 2, 3"),
("Ray", "anyone around?"), ("Sam", "hello everyone")]
...
```

In `persist(messages:)`, you'll add the code to store the received JSON as `Message` objects in the app's Realm. But first, start by adding the following code to it:

```
SyncManager.shared.logLevel = .off
```

This code turns off any sync-related debug messages from Realm. This will help you keep your console clean and tidy. Now add the following:

```
DispatchQueue.global(qos: .background).async {
    let objects = messages.map { message in
      return Message(from: message.0, text: message.1)
    }
}
```

In order to never block the main thread, which handles your app's UI, while performing heavy work such as converting JSON to objects, you switch to a background thread. In this simple app, you just use a basic GCD background queue. In later projects, you'll explore more advanced solutions.

Inside the `DispatchQueue` closure, add the following code to persist the messages:

```
let realm = try! Realm()
try! realm.write {
   realm.add(objects)
}
```

Your app will now persist all new messages received from the ChatAPI class to the default Realm. If only all tasks in life were so easy to complete!

Reacting to database changes

Your app's setup is pretty much finished: you have a mock network API receiving JSON data, and you just wrote the code to persist the received messages as Realm objects. Next, you'll work on the app's UI; more specifically, you'll react to batches of new messages being added to Realm.

Open **StatsViewController.swift** and add the following to `viewDidLoad()`:

```
let realm = try! Realm()
let messages = realm.objects(Message.self)
```

You get the default Realm and fetch all `Message` objects. In the Stats screen, you'll display the number of messages, so you don't need to filter or sort `messages`.

To observe the messages collection, you'll use the `observe(:)` method discussed earlier, meaning you'll need to store the returned token. Add a new property to the `StatsViewController` class:

```
private var messagesToken: NotificationToken?
```

You'll store the observation token in `messagesToken` so that the view controller retains the token. This is handy, because as soon as you dismiss the view controller, the view's life cycle will take care of releasing the token object from memory. This will in turn cancel your notification subscription.

Speaking of which, back in `viewDidLoad()`, add the following code to observe the messages result set:

```
messagesToken = messages.observe { [weak self] _ in
  guard let this = self else { return }

  UIView.transition(with: this.statsLabel,
    duration: 0.33,
    options: [.transitionFlipFromTop],
    animations: {
      this.statsLabel.text = "Total messages: \(messages.count)"
    },
    completion: nil)
}
```

You subscribe for change notifications from the `messages` result set. In the provided notification handler, you update `statsLabel` with a nice flip animation. Build and run the project to see your label updating every time a new batch of messages is added to your Realm:

You are probably questioning this section's title right now. Is this *really* a reactive app? It sure is! Let's analyze the few lines of code you added here:

- You react to data changes instead of polling the database.

- You use message-based architecture, as "*write*" code is completely decoupled from read code.

- The stats screen performance remains similar regardless of how many messages are stored in the database.

- The write transaction is performed on a background queue, so it never affects the UI responsiveness.

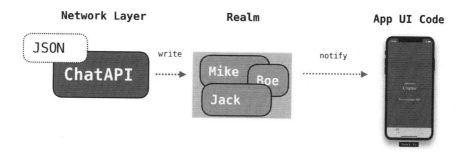

You have to admit, Realm's built-in superpowers are pretty remarkable!

Collection changes updates

Now let's get some fine-grained notifications updates. The Chatter tab is currently empty, but the table is already configured. You'll only need to wire up some Realm objects and everything should work!

Open **ChatViewController.swift** and add the following property to store the result set your view controller will use:

```
private var messages: Results<Message>?
```

Next, scroll down to viewWillAppear(_) and add:

```
let realm = try! Realm()
messages = realm.objects(Message.self)
  .sorted(byKeyPath: Message.properties.date, ascending: false)
```

This code fetches the sorted messages from your Realm and retains the result set in the messages property.

You'll use `messages` to finalize the table view's data source methods. Find `tableView(_:numberOfRowsInSection:)` and replace the current code with:

```
return messages?.count ?? 0
```

This will define the amount of table rows presented to be equal to the number of messages. You'll also need to fill in some details for each table cell to display the messages on screen. Scroll down to `tableView(_:cellForRowAt:)`.

Immediately before the line `return cell` insert:

```
let message = messages![indexPath.row]
let formattedDate = formatter.string(from: message.date)
```

You get the message corresponding to the current table row, and a formatted date using a formatter already included in the starter code. Now you can finally set all of the cell's outlets:

```
cell.contentView.backgroundColor = message.isNew ?
highlightColor : .white
cell.textLabel?.text = message.isNew ? "[\(message.from)]" :
message.from
cell.detailTextLabel?.text = String(format: "(%@) %@",
formattedDate, message.text)
```

The cell has a different background depending on whether the message has been marked as new. It also features the message author, date, and content.

To add live updates, you'll use a notification subscription. Just as before, you'll retain the token in your view controller. Add a new property to your view controller:

```
private var messagesToken: NotificationToken?
```

And add the subscription back in `viewWillAppear()`:

```
messagesToken = messages!.observe { [weak self] _ in
  self?.tableView.reloadData()
}
```

Any time there are changes to the `messages` collection, you'll reload the table view's contents, guaranteeing that the user always sees the latest data on the screen.

To save resources, you'll stop listening for notifications as soon as the user leaves the screen. There is no point in updating the UI if nobody can see it. (There's a "falling tree in the forest joke" somewhere here, but let's keep the focus on Realm notifications.)

$[=

Inside `viewWillDisappear(_)`, add:

```
messagesToken?.invalidate()
```

Every time the user selects a different tab, you cancel the subscription. Then, when the user opens Chatter again, the code in `viewWillAppear(_)` will recreate the subscription. This is a common pattern you should use, especially with navigation controllers, since the navigation stack can contain a bunch of view controllers that aren't currently visible. There's no point in keeping notification subscriptions for these.

Finally, let's add the code to handle a cell tap, and mark the message as read. Append to `tableView(_:didSelectRowAt:)`:

```
let message = messages![indexPath.row]

let realm = try! Realm()
try! realm.write {
  message.isNew = false
}
```

Build and run the project. You'll see the messages pouring in as the app fetches new batches from the API. Tap any row to see how it changes its appearance:

Challenges

Challenge 1

The current code, somewhat brutally, reloads the entire table view whenever anything has changed in the collection. You probably already have some ideas for a more graceful way to solve this problem.

Before you start, check the code in **Helpers/UITableView+RealmChanges.swift**. An extension on UITableView adds a method called applyChanges(...) which accepts three arrays: deletions, insertions, and updates. The method uses the built-in UITableView methods to insert, delete and reload table rows at the required index paths. And not only that, but it will perform the updates with animations too!

In this challenge, rewrite the code in ChatViewController while using the indices provided in the notification handler. For the .initial case, just reload the table data, for .update, take the three arrays of indices, and use the applyChanges(...) method to update the table.

When you finish the notifications code, add one last user interaction. In **ChatViewController.swift**, scroll down to tableView(_:commit:forRowAt:) and write the needed code to get the message for the given index in the collection and delete it from the Realm.

This will help you test fine-grained table updates. Swipe left on a table row and delete it to see it disappear with a neat animation!

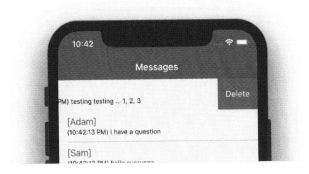

Section IV: Intermediate Realm Apps

By this point in the book you've covered everything you need to build simple applications. In this section you'll move on to developing more complex solutions which address real-life app needs.

Chapter 7: Realm Configurations

In this chapter you will learn how to configure your app's Realm, enable or disable features, and put your Realm where it belongs.

Chapter 8: Multiple Realms and Shared Realms

Apps often need more that one Realm to segregate different types of data or simply isolate read-only from mutable records, plain accessible from encrypted data, and more. You'll develop an app that showcases using Realms in a number of locations like the app's bundle, the documents folder, and a shared container.

Chapter 9: Dependency Injection and Testing

Without going into app architecture specifics, this chapter will introduce you to some best practices when it comes to decoupling classes and easily covering your database code with tests.

Chapter 7: Realm Configurations

In the previous chapter, "Notifications and Reactive Apps", you learned how to observe the contents of a Realm and receive notifications of any changes performed on it. Even earlier than that, you learned how to persist objects to a file and fetch them back.

However, you skipped the topic of **actually opening the Realm file** itself. Every example you've worked on until now had Realm already pre-configured and ready-to-go.

In this chapter that covers Realm configurations, you'll take a step back (or is it one forward?), dig into working with the `Realm` class itself, and learn about how to configure Realm using `Realm.Configuration`.

You'll learn how to work with different Realm files on disk and in-memory, as well as how to use advanced features such as data encryption.

This chapter will follow the format of the previous one: you'll start with a playground to explore the configurations API, and move on to working on a complete iOS app later on to practice some of the more advanced features unavailable in playgrounds.

Opening a Realm

So far, you've seen two different ways to open a Realm in this book. The first one is opening the default realm file for your app:

```
let realm = try! Realm()
```

Besides this method, you've probably noticed the following code included in some of the starter playgrounds:

```
let realm = try! Realm(configuration:
  Realm.Configuration(inMemoryIdentifier: "TemporaryRealm"))
```

The `configuration` parameter is a `Realm.Configuration` struct which toggles a set of features for the specific Realm you're trying to open. In the case above, you enable in-memory storage (as opposed to persisting to a file on disk) by providing an `inMemoryIdentifier`.

Sharing a Realm instance, or making a new one?

Every time you've worked with Realm in this book, you created a new local constant: `let realm = try! Realm()`. If you're coming from a Core Data background or similar ORMs, you've probably been taught to create a single instance and share it throughout your code.

Realm works differently, and arguably, smarter. Realm keeps a map of all currently active Realms in your app. Then, any time you would try to create a new Realm, you'll actually get a *shared* instance **if** you're already actively using it from another spot in the same thread. This lets Realm provide several runtime optimizations:

- Most importantly, calling `Realm()` returns the same shared instance for each file, regardless of which thread you created the `Realm` instance on. Objects and Realm instances are confined to the thread where they were created, so sharing them across threads is not possible. Realm already takes care of clever caching of Realm instances on a per-thread basis and returns them as needed.

- Realm will provide several safety measures when you call `Realm(configuration:)`. For example, you'll get an error if you are trying to open the same file with different encryption keys, or if the file doesn't exist.

> ✱ It's counter-productive to share a Realm instance across multiple parts of your code - an instance is confined to the thread it was created on and once you have a

complex enough app you'd certainly like to perform some of the heavy work in the background.

As a rule of thumb, try to always create a local `Realm` instance via `Realm(configuration:)` as it'll help you keep your code thread-safe and make sure you always get a Realm for the specific thread you're working on. This is part of Realm's multi-threading strategy, designed to aid you in creating safe, concurrent code.

Working with configuration options

To get started with this chapter's playground, open the macOS Terminal app (or a similar app of your choice), navigate to the current chapter's **starter** folder, and run the bootstrap script, like so:

```
./bootstrap.sh
```

The script will take some time while it builds the playground and `RealmSwift`, but after a few moments, it will launch Xcode and you will face an empty playground.

For this chapter, you'll use a simplified version of the newspaper database with two objects: `Person` and `Article`. We won't cover any of the model code as you should already be familiar with it from previous chapters, but if you still want to peek at it, the files are in **Playground/Sources**.

Configuration options

The list of `Realm.Configuration` options include:

- **fileURL**: Used to create a file-backed Realm (e.g. where Realm persists data to disk).

- **inMemoryIdentifier**: Used to create an in-memory Realm (e.g. where Realm does *not* persist data to disk).

- **syncConfiguration**: Enables real-time server data syncing, you'll learn a bit more about that in the last book chapter.

- **encryptionKey**: An encryption key used to either create new or open an existing encrypted file.

- **readOnly**: Lets you open a Realm in read-only mode.

- **objectTypes**: A list of Realm objects you'd like to persist in the given Realm (instead of all objects in your app, which is the default).

- **schemaVersion**: Sets the specific database schema version your code uses.

- **migrationBlock**: A closure you can provide to migrate a Realm schema, if needed.

- **deleteRealmIfMigrationNeeded**: Deletes the realm file before opening if it was created with a previous version of the app. Useful while you're developing and your classes evolve constantly or in production if you don't want to keep around old app data.

- **shouldCompactOnLaunch**: A closure you can provide that defines if Realm should try compacting the file before opening it.

You will cover many of these options in this chapter, and will look into the rest in some of the later chapters of this book.

Default configuration options

Let's first examine what kind of options you get when you create a new `Realm.Configuration`. Append to your playground:

```
Example.of("New Configuration") {
    let newConfig = Realm.Configuration()
    print(newConfig)
}
```

This example creates a new configuration and prints it to the console:

```
ⓘ New Configuration:
────────────────────

Realm.Configuration {
    fileURL = file:///var/folders/.../
com.apple.dt.playground.stub.iOS_Simulator.Playground-472FDDF4-3
FD0-4B3D-8008-6AD6BD000BAD/Documents/default.realm;
    inMemoryIdentifier = (null);
    encryptionKey = (null);
    readOnly = 0;
    schemaVersion = 0;
    migrationBlock = (null);
    deleteRealmIfMigrationNeeded = 0;
    shouldCompactOnLaunch = (null);
    dynamic = 0;
    customSchema = (null);
}
```

This information provides you with a pretty clear idea of what's enabled by default. The only option populated with a meaningful value is fileURL, which points to a file called **default.realm** in the current container's **Documents** folder. For apps working with a single Realm file, that's often a fine choice.

For the time being, the takeaway is that Realm will figure out a path for your default Realm file on its own, as long as you don't care about the precise location.

To help you avoid creating a new configuration every time you want to access the default file, Realm.Configuration has a special shared static instance. Add:

```
Example.of("Default Configuration") {
  let defaultConfig = Realm.Configuration.defaultConfiguration
  print(defaultConfig)
}
```

After carefully reviewing the output, you'll notice that the options of defaultConfiguration are identical to the defaults you got by creating a new configuration via Realm.Configuration().

Using defaultConfiguration has several benefits: it's a configuration you can access throughout your app's code, and it's the one used by Realm's initialization by default. So every time you write the following code, you are opening a Realm using the Realm.Configuration.defaultConfiguration configuration:

```
let realm = try! Realm()
```

This creates an opportunity for you to alter the shared config with custom-tailored options for your app. For example, the default schema version is 0 but once you release the next version of your app, you'd want to change that to 1. Will you then have to adjust every occurrence where you create a Realm instance? Not necessarily. You can modify the default configuration like so, instead:

```
var config = Realm.Configuration.defaultConfiguration
config.schemaVersion = 1
Realm.Configuration.defaultConfiguration = config
```

With this code in place, every time you call let realm = try! Realm(), the return Realm will be using your customized default configuration.

> **Note**: The examples in this book often use try! for brevity but this doesn't mean in any way that you can't handle errors thrown by Realm in your production code. If you need to learn more about error handling in Swift check out the Swift Apprentice book from raywenderlich.com at: https://bit.ly/2ue5EH3.

In-memory Realms

You might keep a Realm in-memory (vs. on disk) for different reasons. In this book, you'll mostly do this to either improve performance (especially in a playground), or to provide a clean slate for your unit tests.

`inMemoryIdentifier` is just like a file path: it gives your Realm a unique identifier, so objects persisted on it are contained in that specific Realm. Let's create two in-memory Realms to try this. Append to your playground:

```
Example.of("In-Memory Configuration") {
  let memoryConfig1 = Realm.Configuration(
    inMemoryIdentifier: "InMemoryRealm1")
  print(memoryConfig1)

  let memoryConfig2 = Realm.Configuration(
    inMemoryIdentifier: "InMemoryRealm2")
  print(memoryConfig2)
}
```

The Realms you'll later create with the identifiers `InMemoryRealm1` and `InMemoryRealm2` will be managed in-memory and will have an identical object schema, featuring `Person` and `Article` objects. The two configurations give you access to two *separate* containers. Add this code inside the latest example to add some objects to `InMemoryRealm1`:

```
let realm1 = try! Realm(configuration: memoryConfig1)
let people1 = realm1.objects(Person.self)

try! realm1.write {
  realm1.add(Person())
}
print("People (1): \(people1.count)")
```

> **Note:** When adding/modifying objects in a Realm, you always have to use a write transaction - whether it's an in-memory Realm or one persisted on disk.

The newly-created person is persisted to `realm1`, that uses the `InMemoryRealm1` identifier provided in its config. Let's make sure this object wasn't persisted in your second in-memory Realm by adding the following code:

```
let realm2 = try! Realm(configuration: memoryConfig2)
let people2 = realm2.objects(Person.self)
print("People (2): \(people2.count)")
```

As expected, the new object is found only in the first Realm, as both Realms are uniquely identified by the provided `inMemoryIdentifier` of their respective configurations:

```
People (1): 1
People (2): 0
```

Realms in a custom location

You can create a Realm file in any writable path. This section will cover different common locations, and what are the benefits each of them offers.

Documents folder

The default configuration uses a file called **default.realm** in your app's (or playground's) **Documents** folder. That's a great default name, but you might want to have a custom name. Let's explore this option. Add the following example to your playground:

```
Example.of("Documents Folder Configuration") {
  let documentsUrl = try! FileManager.default
    .url(for: .documentDirectory, in: .userDomainMask,
      appropriateFor: nil, create: false)
    .appendingPathComponent("myRealm.realm")

  let documentsConfig = Realm.Configuration(fileURL:
documentsUrl)
  print("Documents-folder Realm in: \
(documentsConfig.fileURL!)")
}
```

You use the default `FileManager` to call `url(for:in:appropriateFor:create:)` which returns the URL of the **Documents** folder. You then use `appendingPathComponent(_)` to *append* a file name to the folder's URL.

The example you just added will output the path to **myRealm.realm** in the current **Documents** folder when running in the Simulator or in a playground. This path points to an ordinary file on your computer's disk so you can open it like any other file (for example by using Realm Studio to inspect the data it contains):

```
Documents-folder Realm in: file:///var/folders/.../
com.apple.dt.playground.stub.iOS_Simulator.Playground-472FDDF4-3
FD0-4B3D-8008-6AD6BD000BAD/Documents/myRealm.realm
```

> ✱ When you call `Realm(configuration:)`, Realm will check if a file exists at the given `fileURL`. Otherwise, it will create an empty Realm file and open it.

Storing files in the **Documents** folder gives your app a couple of free features: the files are automatically backed up to the user's iCloud storage, and can also be easily backed up by the user using iTunes, making the files easily accessible.

However, Apple traditionally recommends storing your app's files in the **Library** folder, and not the **Documents** folder. Let's look into that option next.

Library folder

If you don't want to automatically back up your app's Realm files to iCloud, you'd probably want to use the **Library** folder. Luckily, you can re-use the same method you used to get the path to the **Documents** folder. Add to your playground:

```
Example.of("Library Folder Configuration") {
    let libraryUrl = try! FileManager.default
        .url(for: .libraryDirectory, in: .userDomainMask,
            appropriateFor: nil, create: false)
        .appendingPathComponent("myRealm.realm")

    let libraryConfig = Realm.Configuration(fileURL: libraryUrl)
    print("Realm in Library folder: \(libraryConfig.fileURL!)")
}
```

Let the playground run one more time, and you'll see the path to **myRealm.realm** in the current container's **Library** folder.

App Bundle folder

If you have a Realm file bundled with your app and want to open it and fetch some of its stored objects, you can use the `Bundle` class to access the app's resources folder. Just remember — the app's bundle is *read-only*; you can't add new files to it or modify existing ones.

Furthermore, since the playground doesn't have a bundle, you can't test this right now, but you'll give this a try in the iOS app project later in this chapter. Just for your reference, this is what opening a bundled Realm file looks like:

```
let bundledURL = Bundle.main
    .url(forResource: "bundledRealm", withExtension: "realm")
let bundleConfig = Realm.Configuration(fileURL: bundledURL)
```

Shared container

Another common location for storing Realm files is a folder shared between your iOS app and one of its extensions. You'll work through a project which shares data between a Today extension and an iOS app in the chapter "Multiple Realms / Shared Realms".

Unfortunately, you won't be able to try this in a playground as well, but here's a code snippet for your reference:

```
let sharedURL = FileManager.default
  .containerURL(forSecurityApplicationGroupIdentifier:
    "group.com.razeware.app")!
  .appendingPathComponent("Library/shared.realm")
let sharedConfig = Realm.Configuration(fileURL: sharedURL)
```

Using `containerURL(forSecurityApplicationGroupIdentifier:)` allows you to get a shared local URL, which both the extension and the app can access via the specified group identifier. Once you create a configuration and Realm with this URL, you'll be able to read and write objects just like any other Realm, on both targets.

Encrypted realms

Data encryption is one of Realm's most overlooked features. All you need to do is add an encryption key to your configuration, use it to open a Realm and BAM! Realm will do all of the heavy lifting of encrypting, decrypting, and keeping your sensitive data secure.

Realm makes creating and working with encrypted data incredibly simple. You set the `encryptionKey` property on your configuration with the desired key to encrypt and decrypt the file and Realm automatically does the rest for you.

The first time you open your encrypted file, Realm will create it on disk and will encrypt it with the given key. Any time in the future you'd like to read or write data you need to use the same configuration with the same encryption key.

Realm uses a 64-byte key to encrypt your data. You can derive these bytes from a string password or any other way you wish to generate them.

When you try opening a Realm file with an invalid key, Realm will throw an error that you can catch and handle (do not add this code to the playground):

```
var cryptoConfig = Realm.Configuration()
do {
  cryptoConfig.encryptionKey = Data(...)
  let cryptoRealm = try Realm(configuration: cryptoConfig)
  print(cryptoRealm)
} catch let error as NSError {
  print("Opening file failed: \(error.localizedDescription)")
}
```

In your `catch` block, you have the chance to present some custom UI; you can ask the user to re-enter their password, or present them with an error. You'll get to do just that later in this chapter when you work on an iOS project that manages some encrypted data.

Read-only Realms

There's a difference between opening a file which you simply *cannot* modify (located in a read-only folder or current user not having sufficient access rights) and letting Realm know that you do not *intend* to write to the file.

When enabling the read-only option for a Realm, you'll:

- Get an exception as soon as you try to start a write transaction.

- Allow Realm to optimize for performance, since it knows it will not trigger any change notifications for that particular configuration.

Let's give the above a spin in the chapter's playground. Add a new example:

```
Example.of("Read-only Realm") {
  let rwUrl = try! FileManager.default
    .url(for: .documentDirectory, in: .userDomainMask,
      appropriateFor: nil, create: false)
    .appendingPathComponent("newFile.realm")

  let rwConfig = Realm.Configuration(fileURL: rwUrl)
}
```

You are already familiar with this type of code: you create a URL to a local file in the **Documents** folder and create a new configuration called `rwConfig`. Configurations allow reading and writing by default.

Next, add inside the example's closure the following code to create a new Realm and add some objects to it:

```
autoreleasepool {
  let rwRealm = try! Realm(configuration: rwConfig)
  try! rwRealm.write {
    rwRealm.add(Person())
  }
  print("Regular Realm, is Read Only?: \
(rwRealm.configuration.readOnly)")
  print("Saved objects: \(rwRealm.objects(Person.self).count)
\n")
}
```

The default configuration lets you add a new object to the Realm every time the playground runs:

```
 Read-only Realm:

Regular Realm, is Read Only?: false
Saved objects: 3
```

> **Note**: You need the `autoreleasepool` to explicitly make sure there aren't dangling handlers to the Realm instance left after the code completes.

Let's try the read-only option next. After the first `autoreleasepool`, add:

```
autoreleasepool {
   let roConfig = Realm.Configuration(fileURL: rwUrl, readOnly:
true)

   let roRealm = try! Realm(configuration: roConfig)
   print("Read-Only Realm, is Read Only?: \
(roRealm.configuration.readOnly)")
   print("Read objects: \(roRealm.objects(Person.self).count)")
}
```

The `roRealm` Realm will only let you read objects from it. If you try writing into it, you'll end up with an exception.

Object schema

By default, Realm will inspect your app's Realm objects and will basically define your entire database schema based on these inspected objects. Let's examine how these schemas look like. Append to your playground:

```
Example.of("Object Schema - Entire Realm") {
   let realm = try! Realm(configuration:
     Realm.Configuration(inMemoryIdentifier: "Realm"))

   print(realm.schema.objectSchema)
}
```

This code will print the full schema of your Realm. If you're overwhelmed by the amount of information, worry not. Let's look into a portion of it:

```
 Object Schema - Entire Realm:

[Article {
  id {
    type = string;
    indexed = YES;
    isPrimary = YES;
    ...
  }
  title {
    type = string;
    indexed = NO;
```

```
    isPrimary = NO;
    ...
  }
...
```

`Realm.schema.objectSchema` contains a description of all objects stored in a Realm, including the list of all data properties which are persisted along with their meta information. Scroll through the schema dump and notice that it includes the two objects defined in your playground: `Person` and `Article`.

Let's say you want to only persist `Person` objects in some Realm. You can do that by adding the `objectTypes` option to your configuration, listing all objects you're interested in persisting for that specific Realm.

Add this final example to your playground:

```
Example.of("Object Schema - Specific Object") {
    let config = Realm.Configuration(
        inMemoryIdentifier: "Realm2",
        objectTypes: [Person.self]
    )

    let realm = try! Realm(configuration: config)
    print(realm.schema.objectSchema)
}
```

Let the playground run one more time and inspect the console output. You'll notice that, this time around, `objectSchema` contains only the `Person` object meta information, skipping the `Article` object.

This is indeed quite a brief introduction to object schemas, but have no fear as you'll learn how to work with multiple files and schemas in the next chapter, Chapter 8, "Multiple Realms / Shared Realms".

This wraps up your usage of a playground for this chapter. You will now use your new-found knowledge about Realm in a real-life project.

My ToDo

In the last section of this chapter, you'll get to work with different configurations in an iOS app. The project is a simple ToDo app - something you may already have built on your own! That's why you'll start with a working app and extend it with features specific to using Realm configurations.

Getting started

Open up the macOS Terminal app or a similar app of your choice and navigate to the current chapter's **MyToDo-starter** folder.

Install the project dependencies by running the following in the starter folder:

```
pod install
```

When installation is done, open **MyToDo.xcworkspace**.

As mentioned earlier, the project already has some basic functionality implemented and includes mostly UI, non-Realm specific code (including a build warning that you will clear while working through the chapter).

Build and run the project and you'll be able to add new todo items by tapping the + button, delete items by swiping on a table row, and change an item's status by tapping the indicator on the right side of each row:

The project currently uses a single Realm file called **mytodo.realm** located in the **Documents** folder, where the app stores the todo items. Here's a peak into the app's **Documents** folder where you can see the file, its meta information, and Realm's server management folder.

Throughout the rest of this chapter, you'll work on adding two new features to your app:

- You'll start by adding some pre-bundled todo items. When the user runs the app for the first time, they'll see what the UI looks like and can start using the application.

- You will then add a feature allowing the user to encrypt the contents of their todo list by migrating the existing data to an encrypted Realm file.

The final setup will look like this:

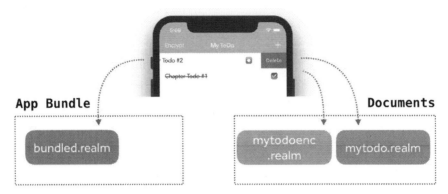

Working with a pre-bundled Realm

You can use a pre-populated Realm file bundled with your app in different ways. For example, you could use the data in read-only mode when you need a data set that the user will not modify. You can still update the file when you release new app versions. Another common method is to use the bundled file as a starting point for the file your app will use.

The starter project already includes a pre-populated Realm file. In this exercise, you'll check for the existence of plain Realm file or an encrypted one. If neither is present, you'll copy the pre-populated file to the **Documents** folder. You will do this in your `AppDelegate` before any UI code reads objects from the app's Realm file.

Open **AppDelegate.swift** and find the `TodoRealm` enumeration at the end of the file. This enumeration lists the paths to the three Realm files you'll be using in this project.

- `plain`: The *unencrypted* todo Realm, which uses a file called **mytodo.realm** located in the app's **Documents** folder.

- `encrypted`: The *encrypted* todo Realm, which uses a file called **mytodoenc.realm** located in the app's **Documents** folder.

- `bundle`: The pre-populated starter Realm bundled with the app.

Append inside `setupRealm()`:

```
if !TodoRealm.plain.fileExists && !
TodoRealm.encrypted.fileExists {

}
```

In the piece of code above, you check if the plain or encrypted files are present. If neither file is found, that means the user is starting the app for the *very first time*, so you'll need to copy the starting file from the app bundle into the **Documents** folder. Inside the curly braces of the `if` statement, add:

```
try! FileManager.default.copyItem(
   at: TodoRealm.bundle.url, to: TodoRealm.plain.url)
```

To test this new feature, you'll need to *first delete the app* from the Simulator or your device (to simulate an app's first run). To do that, tap and hold the app icon until it starts to jiggle and then tap the top-left "X" icon to delete it.

Run the project again, and you'll notice the app already features some classic todo items for you to complete as soon as it launches:

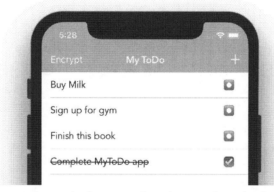

Good job! In this example you had a taste of working with multiple files at different locations. Since Realm files are just "normal" files, you only needed `FileManager` methods to check if files were present and to copy them around.

The Realm SDK also features some extra file APIs, on top of what you can already do with `FileManager`. You will look into these in the next section.

Encryption and copying Realm data

Run the project one more time and notice the button on the left hand side of the navigation bar:

Currently, you don't see much happening when you tap **Encrypt** - you shortly see the root view controller and then the app navigates back to the list controller. You are now going to add the code to allow the user set a new password and encrypt the existing file.

Open **Scenes/SetupViewController.swift** and scroll to `viewDidAppear(_)`. The existing code calls `detectConfiguration()` which simply sets the default configuration to the plain file URL and then calls `showToDoList()`, which sends the user back to the todo list screen.

You'll need to replace the current code with one that checks if `setPassword` is set to `true`. Otherwise, you'll ask the user to set a password to encrypt the Realm file.

Replace the contents of `viewDidAppear(_:)` with:

```
super.viewDidAppear(animated)
if setPassword {
  encryptRealm()
} else {
  detectConfiguration()
}
```

The skeleton for `encryptRealm()` is already included in `SetupViewController`. To keep focus on Realm-related code, you already have the code to pop an alert on screen and ask the user to set a new password.

What you'll do next is to take that password and use it to create an encrypted copy of your Realm file. That should keep those todos safe from prying eyes!

Creating an encrypted file copy

The project includes a handy extension on `String` that provides you with a byte representation of a given string. These bytes can be used directly as an encryption key with Realm! It's a useful extension that you can re-use in your own projects if you want to use text passwords as encryption key. The extension adds a `sha512` computed property on all `Strings`.

> **Note:** The code that hashes the password and exports the hash as bytes is located in **Classes/String+sha512.swift**. It isn't strictly relevant to Realm but you might want to take a look for your own interest.

Inside `encryptRealm()`, insert the following inside the `userInputAlert(...)` callback closure, below the `// copy to a new location...` comment:

```
autoreleasepool {
  let plainConfig = Realm.Configuration(
    fileURL: TodoRealm.plain.url)
  let realm = try! Realm(configuration: plainConfig)
  try! realm.writeCopy(
    toFile: TodoRealm.encrypted.url, encryptionKey:
password.sha512)
}
```

> **Note**: You wrap the code in an `autoreleasepool` block to make sure that all objects and references to your Realm are released once you're finished copying the Realm file.

You use `TodoRealm.plain.url` to create a new config called `plainConfig`. This config allows you to open the plain Realm file. Once you create a Realm with this new configuration, you use its `writeCopy(toFile:encryptionKey:)` method to create a copy which is encrypted with the given key.

Now that you have the encrypted version of the Realm file, you can delete the exiting unencrypted version of it. Since there are multiple meta files and folders created alongside a single Realm file, you'll need to delete them all:

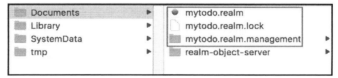

To completely clean the **Documents** folder of old artifacts, you'll need to find all items starting with `mytodo.` and delete them. This, again, involves some handy methods of the `FileManager` class.

While still inside the callback closure, append:

```
do {
  // Delete old file
  let files = FileManager.default.enumerator(
    at: try Path.documents(), includingPropertiesForKeys: [])!

  for file in files.allObjects {
    guard let url = file as? URL,
      url.lastPathComponent.hasPrefix("mytodo.") else { continue
}
    try FileManager.default.removeItem(at: url)
```

```
    }
  } catch let err {
    fatalError("Failed deleting unencrypted Realm: \(err)")
  }
```

The code will enumerate over the **Documents** folder and delete files and folders with names starting with "mytodo.".

With the the task of creating an encrypted copy of your Realm file complete, you can send the user to the list controller. Append one last line inside the callback closure:

```
self?.detectConfiguration()
```

Opening an encrypted file

In detectConfiguration(), you'll add a check to confirm there is an encrypted file, prompting the user for a password if necessary. Replace the contents of detectConfiguration() with:

```
if TodoRealm.encrypted.fileExists {
  askForPassword()
} else {
  Realm.Configuration.defaultConfiguration =
    Realm.Configuration(fileURL: TodoRealm.plain.url)
  showToDoList()
}
```

With this code, you check if an encrypted version of the Realm file exists and if so, call askForPassword(). If there's no encrypted file, the app continues using the default configuration with the plain Realm and navigates to the list screen.

The code already includes an askForPassword() method which asks the user for a password and passes it along to openRealm(with:), which is where you are going to perform the real work.

First, you'll need to create a configuration with encryption enabled and set it as the default Realm configuration. Insert into openRealm(with:):

```
// Add password to the default configuration
Realm.Configuration.defaultConfiguration = Realm.Configuration(
  fileURL: TodoRealm.encrypted.url,
  encryptionKey: password.sha512
)
```

You're using the sha512 extension on String that was mentioned earlier to convert the text password to bytes and create your new encrypted configuration.

> **Note:** You're changing Realm's `defaultConfiguration`. This means every new Realm instance created without a provided configuration will use this encrypted configuration.

Now, you can try and open the encrypted file and see if the given password is valid. Append:

```
// Try to open the Realm file
do {
  _ = try Realm()
  showToDoList()
} catch let error as NSError {
  print(error.localizedDescription)
  askForPassword()
}
```

In the do block, you open the default Realm, which is the encrypted one at this point. If the operation is successful (e.g. if it doesn't throw), you navigate to the list view controller.

In the catch block, you print the error for debug purposes and ask the user to enter their password again by calling `askForPassword()`.

With this last piece of code, the complete encryption workflow has been finalized. Run the project one more time and tap on **Encrypt**. This time around, you'll be presented with an alert box asking you to set a new password to encrypt the todo list:

Enter a password of your choice (or use the good ol' "123456" like I did) and tap **OK**. This will copy the plain file into its new, encrypted location as **mytodoenc.realm**, and delete the old plain version.

After a successful encryption, the app will ask you to enter a password to use to open the file. Failing to provide a correct password will result in the app asking for it indefinitely, while providing the correct password will present you with the todo list scene, using your brand new encrypted Realm.

Peeking into the app's **Documents** folder, you'll be able to see that **mytodo.realm** and its companions are gone and only the encrypted file is present:

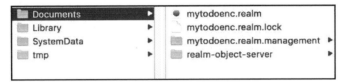

I bet you can come up with a list of new features to add to this todo app, such as decrypting the list, introducing different users while maintaining their own todo list with their own password, and more.

For now, though, your work here is done. You've learned a ton about using Realm in this chapter, and you've successfully worked through ever-more-complex examples. Now is probably a good time to take a break and review the last couple of chapters, since the next few chapters will see you working on a serious project that makes use of everything you've learned so far, as well as introducing you to more new APIs!

Chapter 8: Multiple Realms / Shared Realms

In the previous chapter, "Realm Configurations", you learned quite a lot about working with Realm files. In fact, the amount of knowledge you gained in the previous chapters of this book has already put you at the head of the pack when it comes to using Realm.

In this chapter, you're going to make use of your existing Realm skills while learning some new ones. You're going to use multiple configurations, read and write data, use notifications to build reactive UI, and explore new topics like sharing data between your app and a Today extension.

Last but not least, you're going to touch on a topic which is often pushed to the sidelines within the iOS community — creating your own project tooling. In this chapter, as in previous ones, you're going to use a pre-populated Realm file bundled with your app. This time around, you're also going to code your own tool to produce this pre-populated file for you.

The project you're going to work on is going to span over this and the next chapters and is called **Flash Cards**. The completed app allows its users to memorize words and expressions in the Spanish language, download extra sets (from a mocked server API), and set a word they'd like to actively learn each day via a Today extension.

Here's how the completed app will look at the end of next chapter. From left to right: a list of card sets to practice, a practice session scene, and the Today extension showing the selected word of the day:

I hope you're excited about the work that lies ahead. Let's get started!

Getting started

To get started with this chapter, open up the macOS Terminal app or a similar app of your choice and navigate to the current chapter's **starter** folder.

Install the project dependencies by running:

```
pod install
```

Open the project's workspace and browse through it. It features two tabs: one to browse and play the installed learning sets, and another to show the list of available words and select the word of the day from that list.

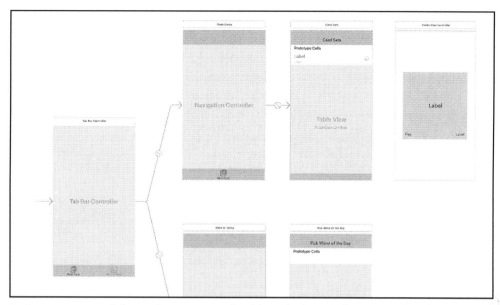

Right now, none of the app's screens work, although the Xcode project already includes a substantial amount of starter code. Most of the code is responsible for some non-Realm related features or mocking some of the features you're going to develop throughout the next two chapters. You're going to work on adding code to the relevant places to interact with Realm and complete the app functionality.

The demo project uses a basic MVVM architecture, with no special handling of navigation. Here are the key areas of the project, and the folders where you can find the relevant source code.

Main app folder structure:

- **Entities**: All Realm objects the app is going to read/write over several different files.

- **Models**: Data model classes which interact with Realm. `CardsModel` reads/writes flash cards, `SettingsModel` reads/writes the app settings to Realm, and so forth.

- **Scenes**: The source files to power a "scene": view controllers, view models, and additional view classes.

The scenes used are follows:

- **FlashCardsSets**: The list of available card sets.

- **FlashCards**: The screen displaying flash cards from a selected set.

- **WordOfToday**: The list of words from which the user can select the current word of the day to practice via the Today extension.

The interaction between classes looks like this for each of the scenes in the project:

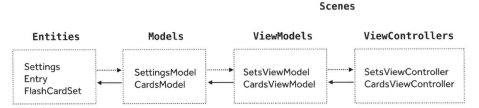

Besides the main app, the project contains two more targets:

Today extension

- **FlashCardsTodayExt** contains a single view controller of FlashCard's Today extension available via the iOS Notification Center.

Tooling

- **FlashCardsTooling** is a class which generates the prepopulated Realm files to bundle with the app for distribution.

Even if somewhat challenging, you'll quickly figure out the setup of the FlashCards app. Feel free to take a moment and scan the source code provided in the Xcode project before you move on to working through this chapter's exercises.

A Realm provider

When you're building a real-life application, you'll likely find yourself working with multiple Realm files. Once you've worked with multiple Realm files for a while, you'll find yourself coming up with some centralized class or struct to give you simplified access to all Realm files your code needs.

For this chapter, you're going to create a struct called `RealmProvider` to easily give you access to the app's Realms. Feel free to reuse it in your project and develop it further to better fit your use cases.

> **Note:** A common issue is error handling. Like any file-based operation, every time you open or write to a Realm file, the operation might fail. Fortunately, Realm fails in a few very limited cases - if there's not enough disk space, insufficient memory, or if there's a file corruption caused by another process.

The project will work with a total of six Realm files, but only four will be used in the main app. Their object schemas and locations are as follows:

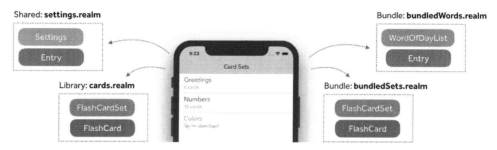

Note how some of the objects are part of more than one Realm file. This is often the case when you need to copy data between files. For example, you'll be copying the bundled data from its read-only location in the app bundle folder to a read-write file in the app's **Library** folder. More about this shortly.

Before diving into action, you'll put together the basics of the central struct that will give you access to all of your Realm files. Open **FlashCards/Models/RealmProvider.swift**. The struct is defined, but its body is empty; it's a blank canvas to boldly paint on. Add a few initial lines of code:

```
let configuration: Realm.Configuration

internal init(config: Realm.Configuration) {
  configuration = config
}
```

`RealmProvider` will basically be a wrapper around `Realm.Configuration`. You'll initialize it with a configuration and it will provide you with a Realm instance created by using said configuration. Add a `realm` computed property to do that:

```
var realm: Realm {
  return try! Realm(configuration: configuration)
}
```

> ✱ An easy approach to error handling in this case would be to replace `try!` with `try?` and change the property type to `Realm?`, returning a `nil` value in the rare case the there's not enough space on disk or the file has been corrupted by another process. Another approach would be to have a throwing `realm()` method instead of a property.

A `RealmProvider` wrapper offers several benefits compared to working directly with Realm instances or configurations:

- You have a centralized place to manage your Realm configurations.

- You can pass it across threads (unlike Realms).

- You can predefine a list of provider instances for each of the Realm files your app needs.

- Finally, you can add some initialization code to the predefined provider accessors, for example, to make sure a given Realm contains default data, or to check the integrity of the data in a Realm upon first access.

Flash cards Realm provider

Let's add some pre-defined providers to `RealmProvider`. You'll start with a Realm containing the app's flash cards database. Add the following code to your `RealmProvider` struct:

```
private static let cardsConfig = Realm.Configuration(
  fileURL: try! Path.inLibrary("cards.realm"),
  schemaVersion: 1,
  deleteRealmIfMigrationNeeded: true,
  objectTypes: [FlashCardSet.self, FlashCard.self])

public static var cards: RealmProvider = {
  return RealmProvider(config: cardsConfig)
}()
```

A private property named `cardsConfig` of type `Realm.Configuration` provides access to **cards.realm**, located in the **Library** folder. It features the `FlashCardSet` and `FlashCard` objects:

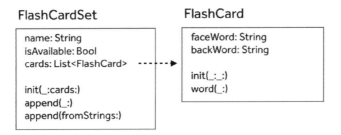

A public static property named `cards` provides access to a lazily-initialized `RealmProvider`. This way, your code can access `RealmProvider.cards.realm` to work with the underlying Realm and pass `RealmProvider.cards` around between objects and threads as needed, since the Realm is created *on demand*.

Bundled sets Realm provider

Next, you'll add one more provider, which you'll use to access the bundled card sets Realm. Add to `RealmProvider`:

```
private static let bundledConfig = Realm.Configuration(
  fileURL: try! Path.inBundle("bundledSets.realm"),
  readOnly: true,
  objectTypes: [FlashCardSet.self, FlashCard.self])

public static var bundled: RealmProvider = {
  return RealmProvider(config: bundledConfig)
}()
```

Just as in the previous provider, you define a private configuration `bundledConfig`, which you can adjust when needed, and a public static property `bundled` to access the provider. **bundledSets.realm** is bundled with the app, so you can use the `Path` class as in previous chapters to get the path to the bundle folder.

The object schema for this file is the same as for **cards.realm**, since **bundledSets.realm** contains the initial data you'll copy when the user first runs the app.

Copying initial data between Realms

In the previous chapter, "Realm Configurations", you created an app workflow where you copied a bundled file to the **Library** folder on first launch of your app. This is a sensible approach if you need to copy the bundle data only once or replace any existing file completely multiple times.

In this chapter, you'll take a different approach which will allow you to iteratively bundle more initial data on top of any existing data. After each app update, you'll copy *only* the new pieces of data to the app's working file.

Open **AppDelegate.swift** and add to the empty `setupRealm()` method:

```
let cardsRealm = RealmProvider.cards.realm
let bundledSetsRealm = RealmProvider.bundled.realm
```

You use your new `RealmProvider` struct to get the bundled and so-called "working" Realm. Now you can check: are there any card sets found in the bundled file, but not in the working file? If so, copy them over.

Add immediately after the last piece of code:

```
var setsToCopy = [FlashCardSet]()
for bundledSet in bundledSetsRealm.objects(FlashCardSet.self)
  where cardsRealm.object(
```

```
      ofType: FlashCardSet.self,
      forPrimaryKey: bundledSet.name) == nil {

      setsToCopy.append(bundledSet)
  }
```

For each `FlashCardSet` object in `bundledSetsRealm`, you confirm whether or not it exists in `cardsRealm` and add the ones that aren't present in both to `setsToCopy`. Next, you'll simply copy all objects from `setsToCopy` over to `cardsRealm`.

Add after the `for` loop:

```
guard setsToCopy.count > 0 else { return }

try! cardsRealm.write {
  for cardSet in setsToCopy {
    cardsRealm.create(FlashCardSet.self, value: cardSet, update:
false)
  }
}
```

You use `Realm.create(...)` to create new `FlashCardSet` objects in `cardsRealm` by copying their data over from the existing objects from `bundledSetsRealm`.

This short and sweet code will ensure that any new sets that appear in the bundled file (e.g. via an app update from the App Store) will be copied over to the working file upon application start.

Run the application and you'll see the empty, uninviting sets list in the Flash Cards tab of the app. However, upon closer inspection, you'll see that a **cards.realm** file is created in the app's **Library** folder and, even more spectacularly, it contains the copied data from the bundled file. You can find the URL to your Realm file by printing its configuration (e.g. `cardsRealm.configuration.fileURL`):

An easy win, which you'll follow up with some great code to display the practice card sets on screen.

Wiring up the sets scene

At this point, you'll need to slightly modify the mocked model and view models to get your Flash Cards tab up and running.

CardsModel is the model class that reads entities from **cards.realm**, which is where you'll start replacing some mock code from the starter project with real code.

Open **Models/CardsModel.swift** and modify sets() to use your new provider struct instead of the default Realm.

Replace:

```
let realm = try! Realm()
return realm
```

With:

```
let provider = RealmProvider.cards
return provider.realm
```

Instead of initializing a Realm directly, you use the centralized provider for this purpose. Wrap up your changes by modifying setWith(_).

Replace:

```
let realm = try! Realm()
return realm
```

With:

```
let provider = RealmProvider.cards
return provider.realm
```

> **Note:** I'll bet you can see an opportunity to store the provider in a property of the model and reuse it across its methods. That would make absolute sense and you'll do exactly that — in the next chapter.

Great job! You've altered the cards model to use your new provider instead of directly creating a Realm. Your model will now read and write objects from/to **cards.realm** and will power your scene with some Realm data.

In fact, if you look into **Scenes/FlashCardsSets/SetsViewModel.swift**, you'll find that SetsViewModel already features code to load sets from the model class. SetsViewController also already includes the code to use your simple view model, so you should be all set and ready to go!

Run the project one more time to see the available sets on screen:

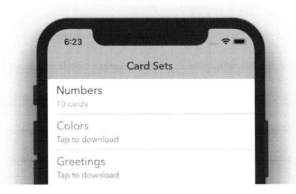

> ✴ The key point in this section is using the centralized provider–factory instead of sharing Realm instances or creating them ad-hoc.

Well done so far! Tap on **Numbers** and take a little break from coding. Swipe left and right to browse the card set, and tap on a card to flip it and learn the corresponding Spanish word.

Word of Today scene

Next, you'll modify a few files to get the Word of Today scene running. To access the word list, you'll need a new provider. Open **RealmProvider.swift** and add it to the `RealmProvider` struct:

```
private static let wordOfDayConfig = Realm.Configuration(
  fileURL: try! Path.inBundle("bundledWords.realm"),
  readOnly: true,
  schemaVersion: 1,
  objectTypes: [WordOfDayList.self, Entry.self])

public static var wordOfDay: RealmProvider = {
  return RealmProvider(config: wordOfDayConfig)
}()
```

The **bundledWords.realm** Realm file, accessible via the `wordOfDay` property, features two objects: `WordOfDayList` and `Entry`.

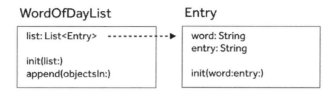

WordOfDayList is a simple ordered list of Entry objects, where each entry is a pair of a word in Spanish and its details, including its English translation and example usage in a sentence.

Just as in the previous section, you'll add some code to the respective model class first. Open **Models/WordOfDayModel.swift** and replace the mock code in words() with:

```
let wordOfDay = RealmProvider.wordOfDay
return wordOfDay.realm.objects(WordOfDayList.self).first!.list
```

You use RealmProvider.wordOfDay to access the Realm and return an ordered list of Entry objects. you'll use this list to feed the table view in the Word of Today scene.

Peek into **Scenes/WordOfToday/WordOfTodayViewModel.swift**. WordOfTodayViewModel loads the list of words from the model class, and WordOfDayTableViewController displays this list in a table view. Run the app and tap the **Word of Today** tab bar option. You'll see a list of words, of which you can pick one as the "Word of the Day" to practice:

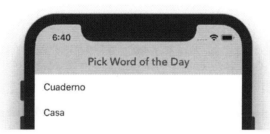

Using a RealmProvider type of struct makes it easy to wire up these models. You might wonder if things might be more difficult if you wanted to use a Realm file from a different process outside of your app. You're going to give that a try in the next section and see for yourself. Spoiler alert — it's a piece of cake.

Today Extension

In the previous chapter, "Realm Configurations", you briefly explored the possibility of using a shared app container to share a Realm file between an app and its extensions. Seems like now would be the perfect time to give this option a try! The FlashCards project includes a Today app extension which you can add to the Simulator's (or your device's) Notification Center. To test the app extension, select the respective Xcode target called **FlashCardsTodayExt**:

Run that scheme and you'll be presented with the extension's view controller:

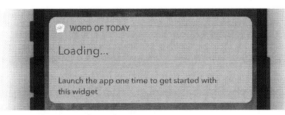

In the extension's UI, you'll display the currently selected word of the day, its translation, and example usage in a sentence. To do this, you'll first need to complete the Word Of Today scene and wire up the extension view controller.

Set the Word of Today in the app

Select the **FlashCards** target in Xcode and open **RealmProvider.swift** to add yet another provider:

```swift
private static let settingsConfig = Realm.Configuration(
  fileURL: try! Path.inSharedContainer("settings.realm"),
  schemaVersion: 1,
  objectTypes: [Settings.self, Entry.self])

public static var settings: RealmProvider = {
  if let realm = try? Realm(configuration: settingsConfig),
    realm.isEmpty {
    try! realm.write {
      realm.add(Settings())
    }
  }
  return RealmProvider(config: settingsConfig)
}()
```

Unlike your other providers, you added a bit of custom code for `settings`. Since the code is executed just once at the very first time `settings` is accessed, this is a great place to check if the Realm contains at least one `Settings` object, and create a default if there isn't one.

settings.realm contains `Settings` and `Entry` objects. Every time the user selects a word of the day, you'll copy its `Entry` object from **bundledWords.realm** into **settings.realm**.

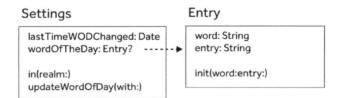

The settings Realm file is located in a shared container so it can be accessed from both the main app and the Today extension. You briefly saw how to get a path to a realm in the app's shared container previously, but if you need a refresher, check out the code in `Path.inSharedContainer(_)`.

> ✳ By abstracting all of the different configurations inside `RealmProvider`, you transparently offer the same API regardless whether the file is read-only, located in the bundle or documents, or shared via app group sharing.

In the following section, you'll adjust the word of today view model so it can be used by the view controller to update the currently selected practice word. When the user picks a word, such as an `Entry` object from **bundledWords.realm**, you'll copy it over to **settings.realm** which is also accessible by the extension.

Open **Models/WordOfDayModel.swift** and add to the currently empty `updateWordOfDay(word:)`:

```
let settings = RealmProvider.settings
guard let appSettings = Settings.in(realm: settings.realm)
  else { return }
```

`Settings.in(realm:)` returns the `Settings` object from a given Realm; it's a static method provided by the `Settings` class. You can now modify the app's settings. Append:

```
appSettings.updateWordOfDay(with: word)
```

updateWordOfDay(with:) is another handy method on the Settings class. It copies the given Entry and updates the last-updated date. The method features mostly code you've written over and over again in previous chapters so we won't cover it in detail here. Same goes for tasks like fetching objects or modifying persisted objects, or similar tasks which you covered many times in previous chapters.

With WordOfDayModel completed, you should add a few finishing touches to the view model as well. WordOfTodayViewModel has two mocked methods that you'll adjust for real use.

Open **WordOfTodayViewModel.swift** and add to updateWord(to:):

```
model.updateWordOfDay(word: word)
```

The view model's updateWord(to:) will simply pass the given word to the model's updateWordOfDay(word:) method as there is no data to re-format or other business logic to implement in the view model.

The second method to modify is isCurrentWord(_), which will check if a given word is the currently set word of the day. Replace the code in isCurrentWord(_) with:

```
return appSettings.wordOfTheDay?.word == word.word
```

Finally, you'll add a few finishing touches to the Word Of Today view controller. Open **WordOfDayTableViewController.swift**, scroll to tableView(_:didSelectRowAt:) and add to that method:

```
let newWord = viewModel.word(at: indexPath.row)
viewModel.updateWord(to: newWord)
```

Every time the user selects a row in the table, you use the view model to get the word at the selected index and then to set it as the current word of the day.

Another method that could use a bit of love is tableView(_:cellForRowAt:). Add to its end, just before return cell:

```
if viewModel.isCurrentWord(word) {
  cell.accessoryType = .checkmark
  tableView.selectRow(at: indexPath,
    animated: true, scrollPosition: .none)
}
```

Select the **FlashCards** scheme, run the app again and give the Word of Today scene a try. You'll see all words as listed in **bundledWords.realm**. Each time you select a word from the list it will update your **settings.realm**'s contents.

For example, tap on **Cuaderno** to select it as the word of the day, then open **settings.realm** in the app's shared container folder (use SimPholders and Realm Studio as mentioned earlier in the book). You'll see that it now contains one Entry object linked from Settings and the entry word is ... *Cuaderno*.

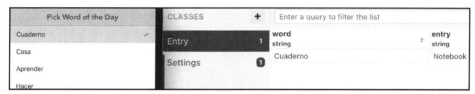

Next step will be modifying the app extension to work with your new shared Realm file.

Finalize the Today extension

Open **FlashCardsTodayExt/TodayViewController.swift**, and you'll notice that the extension's view controller looks similar to a "normal" iOS view controller: you have UI outlets and a viewDidLoad() method to set up your interface.

Additionally, the class conforms to the NCWidgetProviding protocol which defines several optional methods, one of them being widgetPerformUpdate(completionHandler:) - a method which the system will periodically invoke on its own accord to ask your class if it would like to update the widget's UI with new data.

This is the perfect spot to add a bit of code to read the entry from **settings.realm** and check if it's been changed since the last time the widget was updated.

Without going too deep into widget development, you'll add the code relevant to working with the shared **settings.realm** file and complete the Flash Cards extension.

First, you'll check if the word has been updated by comparing the current entry in the settings with the current text displayed in the widget's UI. It's a bit decadent to grab that value straight from the UI, but you're focusing on the relevant Realm code, so it's OK in this case.

Add to widgetPerformUpdate(completionHandler:):

```
guard
  let appSettings = Settings.in(realm:
RealmProvider.settings.realm),
  let wordOfTheDay = appSettings.wordOfTheDay,
  wordOfTheDay.word != word.text else {

}
```

This rather lengthy `guard` statement fetches and unwraps the current app settings object from `RealmProvider.settings`, grabs the current `wordOfTheDay`, and finally compares it to the currently displayed word.

Somewhat *magically*, fetching data from a shared Realm file was indeed a matter of a single line of code. Due to the fact that `RealmProvider` is shared between the app and extension code, you reuse the same provider struct. `RealmProvider.settings` points to the same app group shared container and therefore to the exact same **settings.realm** file.

If any of the `guard` conditions fail, you can safely let Notification Center know that there's no need to refresh the widget. You do that by calling the `completionHandler` closure. Insert into the `guard`'s body:

```
completionHandler(.noData)
return
```

In the other case, where there's a new word available since the last time the widget refreshed, you'll update the UI accordingly by calling the completion with a different parameter. Append at the bottom of `widgetPerformUpdate(completionHandler:)`:

```
updateUI(word: wordOfTheDay.word, details: wordOfTheDay.entry)
completionHandler(.newData)
```

`updateUI(word:details:)` updates the widget's two labels with the latest word of the day. You're off and running with your Spanish lessons — *¡Bueno!*

Switch to the **FlashCardsTodayExt** extension target and run to see your widget displaying your latest pick:

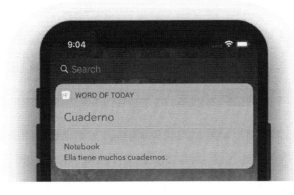

Tooling

The final part of the project you're going to work on in this chapter is the target called **FlashCardsTooling**. Like previous chapters, Flash Cards uses some pre-populated Realm files bundled and distributed with the app.

You can create these pre-populated files manually in Realm Studio by defining the object schema and manually inputting all of the data. However, it is more practical to create a tool to create these files automatically.

You'll often need to convert data from other formats such as JSON, CSV, or plain text into objects and store them as Realm files to bundle them with your app. In this case, having a tool to read the input format and re-create the output upon request is priceless.

For this chapter, you're going to code the tool to create the two files bundled with Flash Cards:

- **bundledSets.realm**: contains the available sets for the app.

- **bundledWords.realm**: which contains the word of the day entries.

Open **FlashCardsTooling/Tools.swift**. You'll see the list of words at the top of the file. In this project, the data is included in the source file, but in real-life apps you might be reading data from a file located on a Git server, a local file checked out on the build machine, or anything else that works for your setup.

First of all, add a static method which will be called at app startup. This method will detect whether or not you're running the `FlashCardsTooling` target. If that's the case, you generate the output files and exit.

Add the new method to the `Tools` class:

```
static func runIfNeeded() {
  guard ProcessInfo.processInfo.environment["SIMULATOR_UDID"] !=
"",
        ProcessInfo.processInfo.environment["TOOLING"] == "1"
else {
      return
  }
}
```

The code in `runIfNeeded()` ensures two conditions are met:

- The environment variable `SIMULATOR_UDID` is set, meaning the app is running in the Simulator. (In Swift 4.1 which is not yet out as of the time of this writing you can use `#if targetEnvironment(simulator)`.)

- `TOOLING` is set to `1` which is an environment variable set by the `FlashCardsTooling` target.

`FlashCardsTooling` defines the `TOOLING` environment variable so you don't need to do that yourself. If you're curious about how it's set: In Xcode, go to **Product ▶ Scheme ▶ Edit Scheme** and under the **Run** action, you'll see any custom variables with the option to add more:

When you run the project with the main app target, the app will launch as usual and `Tools.runIfNeeded()` will return as soon as it's called, having no effect. Anything you append after the `guard` in `runIfNeeded()` will be executed *only* when you're running the `FlashCardsTooling` target.

Append to `runIfNeeded()`:

```
createBundledWordsRealm()
```

`createBundledWordsRealm()` will enumerate over the pre-defined word list and create **bundledWords.realm** so you can bundle it up with your app for distribution.

Scroll down to `createBundledWordsRealm()` and add:

```
let conf = Realm.Configuration(
  fileURL: try! Path.inDocuments("tooling-bundledWords.realm"),
  deleteRealmIfMigrationNeeded: true,
  objectTypes: [WordOfDayList.self, Entry.self])
let newWordsRealm = try! Realm(configuration: conf)
```

`conf` is a Realm configuration that uses a file called **tooling-bundledWords.realm** in the **Documents** folder. You use this configuration to create `newWordsRealm`, which is the Realm you'll populate with words.

Now append:

```
let list = wordsList().map(Entry.init)
```

You get the pre-defined list from `wordsList()` and map each item in that list as an `Entry` object. Next, you add the list to the Realm you just created:

```
try! newWordsRealm.write {
  newWordsRealm.deleteAll()
  newWordsRealm.add(
    WordOfDayList(list: list)
```

```
    )
  }
```

Finally, print a friendly message to the console including the full path to the output file. Append:

```
print("""

*
* Created: \(newWordsRealm.configuration.fileURL!)")
*
""")
```

To wrap up the `Tools` class , add two more lines to `runIfNeeded()`:

```
createBundledSetsRealm()
exit(0)
```

`createBundledSetsRealm()`, in a similar way to what you've done above, creates the flash card sets using the list of sets included in the app source code. The working code is already provided in this case as it's very similar to what you just did.

Last but not least, you terminate the app by calling `exit()` with a status code of `0` (success), since you don't want to actually start the iOS app when running the tools target.

Fantastic work! That concludes the task of creating the tool to generate the pre-populated Flash Cards files. Now to actually invoke `Tools.runIfNeeded()`.

Open **AppDelegate.swift**. At the very beginning of `application(_:didFinishLaunchingWithOptions:)`, before the call to `setupRealm()`, insert:

```
Tools.runIfNeeded()
```

This will invoke the main entry point to the `Tools` class you just wrote, right before letting the app do anything else. And in case you're running the `FlashCardsTooling` target, it will produce the the two Realm files and quit the app.

Run `FlashCardsTooling`, let it finish running, and check the Xcode output console for the path to the generated files:

```
*
* Created: file:///Users/RayWenderlich/Library/Developer/
CoreSimulator/Devices/3792474A-77EF-43B9-A2DA-0B2D944651CC/data/
Containers/Data/Application/43E54F19-8FBF-466C-8296-
E2CF347E944C/Documents/tooling-bundledWords.realm")
*
```

```
  *
  * Created: file:///Users/RayWenderlich/Library/Developer/
  CoreSimulator/Devices/3792474A-77EF-43B9-A2DA-0B2D944651CC/data/
  Containers/Data/Application/43E54F19-8FBF-466C-8296-
  E2CF347E944C/Documents/tooling-bundledSets.realm
  *
```

You can grab the two files from the specified locations and simply drag them into any Xcode project to bundle them with the app.

> **Note:** When bundling files with your app, you only need to copy the **XXX.realm** file. You don't need the lock file or the management folder.

Having the tooling as part of the actual project allows you to share the Realm object classes so the files and app object schema never gets out of sync.

What's next for Flash Cards?

You spent this chapter exploring the idea of using a central structure to manage access to multiple Realms and sharing code between project targets and processes.

The project implements a light MVVM architecture matching the size and complexity of the app. However, you're probably experienced with shipping larger apps, and are interested to learn how to scale the code you've written in this chapter.

This, and further topics, are what you're going to look into in the next chapter, "App architecture and tests". You'll revise the Flash Cards code and organize the setup around dependency injection to allow for more flexibility and testability of the app.

Challenges

Phew, that was a long and intense chapter. Great job!

There's no challenge for this one. Instead, take a short breather before tackling the work in the next chapter; perhaps think about some ways you might improve the Flash Cards project. After you've rested up, flip the page (or swipe left) to dive deeper into rearchitecting and scaling up your app.

Chapter 9: Dependency Injection and Testing

In this chapter, you're going to touch on two important topics: how to use **dependency injection** to improve the architecture of your Flash Cards apps, and how to write both synchronous and asynchronous tests powered by Realm.

This chapter won't delve into topics such as test driven development, but will instead focus specifically on tips and tricks for testing classes that use Realm objects and depend on Realm-specific functionality such as change notifications. The intent is not to impose a single style for writing tests, but instead to guide you as you implement what suits you best in your own projects.

You'll start by writing some test code and reiterating over the model and view model classes as you go to make them more flexible and testable along the way.

Realm test extensions

To facilitate writing tests that rely on Realm, you'll add a couple of extensions. First of all, you won't use the four Realm providers already defined in `RealmProvider` in your tests. In fact, you won't be using on-disk Realms at all. To run tests more efficiently and to avoid test artifacts, you'll use a separate, ephemeral, in-memory Realm for every test.

Creating separate providers for your test target would be tedious, not to mention that this would create a maintenance overhead since you would need to create two providers per `RealmProvider`. To avoid this scenario, you'll add a method which clones existing providers and returns an in-memory copy of them. This will preserve the object schema and other details you still want to have while making a suitable copy for testing.

To get started, open the macOS Terminal app (or another similar app of your choice), navigate to the current chapter's starter project folder, run `pod install` and open the newly created Xcode workspace.

> **Note**: If you worked successfully through the last chapter you can just keep working in your existing Xcode project.

Open **FlashCardsTests/TestExtensions.swift** and add the new `RealmProvider` extension we just mentioned:

```
extension RealmProvider {
  func copyForTesting() -> RealmProvider {
    var conf = self.configuration
    conf.inMemoryIdentifier = UUID().uuidString
    conf.readOnly = false
    return RealmProvider(config: conf)
  }
}
```

`copyForTesting()` gets the configuration of the current provider and converts it to an in-memory configuration by setting its `inMemoryIdentifier` (which also automatically sets `fileURL` to `nil`). You set the identifier to a unique UUID string to make sure each test runs in isolation. You also disable read-only mode so you can add mocked data to your tested Realm before running any tests.

Speaking of adding some test data - since you'll be doing that for every test case, it's going to be quite handy to add a method to automate opening a write transaction and adding objects to the Realm.

Add one more extension to the same file:

```
extension Realm {
  func addForTesting(objects: [Object]) {
    try! write {
      add(objects)
    }
  }
}
```

`Realm.addForTesting(objects:)` is a method you'll use in each test's setup to add some data to the test Realm. It simply saves you few lines of code, but given the number of unit tests a project usually has — the savings easily add up!

You're ready to write some tests!

Testing the cards scene

Let's get started with arguably the easiest part you'll test in Flash Cards: the cards scene. This is where the user can practice a selected deck of flash cards and involves these classes:

- **CardsViewController**: Sets up the needed gesture recognizers and updates the UI based on the user's input. You won't cover UI testing in this chapter.

- **CardsModel**: A simple wrapper that abstracts querying objects from Realm. Writing tests for it would mean repeating the same code in your test and compare the output, which provides no actual value. Besides that, what you would be really testing here would be Realm's underlying implementation, which is already well-tested.

- **CardsViewModel**: Implements the business logic for this scene. It formats the model output to be displayed on screen and provides methods to interact with the model. This would be a perfect candidate for some unit tests!

You won't need a Realm instance in your tests to test the cards scene view model. That's why, as mentioned earlier, this is the easiest piece you'll test. Let's get started with it.

The app's `SetsViewController` pushes `CardsViewController` onscreen and injects its view model - `CardsViewModel`. Neither of these classes have direct dependency on any specific Realm.

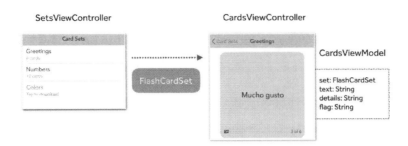

> **Note:** Passing the `FlashCardSet` object freely between classes is possible since everything here happens on the main thread where the object originated from; from the controller's `viewDidLoad()` code, through the method that handles table cell taps, as well as the navigation itself.

In a test case scenario, creating a new detached `FlashCardSet` will be good enough to run tests on your view model. This will further speed up your tests since Realm won't have to create an entire in-memory Realm to hold the object you're using for testing:

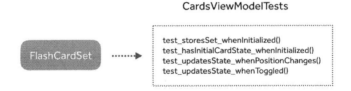

All right, I hear you — you get it. Let's add some tests!

Updating CardsViewModelTests

Open **FlashCardsTests/CardsViewModelTests.swift** and you'll see the list of tests you'll need to implement. You'll test if the view model:

- Stores the set when initialized.

- Returns the card's initial state when initialized.

- Updates its state when the user advances through the practice deck.

- Updates its state when the user flips a card.

Note: This chapter doesn't enforce any particular testing methodology - the app code is up and running so you will mostly simply cover it with tests to get accustomed to writing Realm-based tests. The starter test suite includes a number of failing tests, which you will turn into passing tests.

All of these tests need a `FlashCardSet` object to provide to the view model you'll be testing. To automate this task, you'll add a method to create a fake `FlashCardSet` object whenever you'll need one. Add a new method to the `CardsViewModelTests` class:

```
private func testSet(_ setName: String = "") -> FlashCardSet {
    return FlashCardSet(setName, cards: [FlashCard("face",
"back")])
}
```

The method creates a detached `FlashCardSet` object with the provided name, and features a single flash card with the text "*face*" on its front and "*back*" on its back.

Next up - replace the contents of `test_storesSet_whenInitialized()` with:

```
let setName = "testSet"
let vm = CardsViewModel(set: testSet(setName))
```

You create a new set named `testSet` and a new view model `vm` with the newly created card deck. You can now simply assert your test case on the view model object. Add:

```
XCTAssertEqual(vm.set.name, setName)
```

This will check if the view model stores the given set in its `set` property. Since Realm objects behave largely like any plain Swift object when not persisted, you can very easily create them, pass them around, and write tests for them. Let's flesh out the second test case. Replace the contents of `test_hasInitialCardState_whenInitialized()` with:

```
let vm = CardsViewModel(set: testSet())
```

In this test, you don't care about the set itself or its name, so you just get one with an empty name and pass it to the view model directly.

What you want to test this time is whether the view model correctly returns the face of the first card upon initialization. You'll also want to confirm it correctly returns the current progress through the deck. Add:

```
XCTAssertEqual(vm.text, "face")
XCTAssertEqual(vm.details, "1 of 1")
```

Hopefully by this point you've been convinced that testing `CardsViewModel` and using Realm objects for this is quite easy, and rather similar to testing a standard Swift object. In fact, it is so easy that you'll complete the remainder of the `CardsViewModel` tests in the challenges section at the end of this chapter on your own.

For the time being, run the two tests you just wrote by going to **Product ▸ Test** or using the **Command + U** shortcut. You should see your two tests pass successfully in Test Navigator:

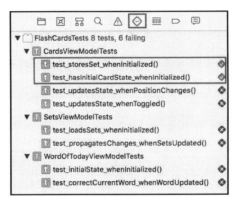

Testing the sets scene

So far, you've added few unit tests that take in some mock values and produce output. You're now going to write some more involved tests. In your scene that shows the list of available sets, your view model depends on Realm notifications to dynamically update the data. You have to either:

- Mock the Realm framework in order to test view models that rely on notifications and other advanced Realm features.

- Write tests that depend on Realm's notifications

> **Note:** It's somewhat debatable whether tests that depend on Realm's notification mechanism are unit tests or integration tests. Regardless, you will go that way in order to test your view models in this chapter.

Having created the test extensions in the beginning of this chapter, you've probably already guessed that you'll be going for the second option: mock data in a temporary Realm and test your classes by having them use it.

Dependency injection

To make your tests work, you'll need to alter your code slightly to provide a way to inject test Realm providers into your models and view models.

In your tests, you'll create a test provider and pass it over to your view model, which in turn is going to pass it over to the model itself, like so:

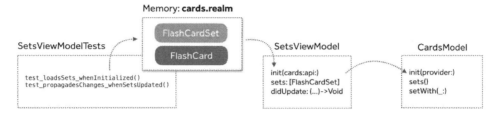

This way, the view model and model classes don't know what kind of Realm they're using for storage. They simply receive a provider and use it, passing it along to classes they own as needed.

When the app is running, the view model and model will still receive the provider they need from a different object. Depending on your architecture, this might be the view controller for the current scene, a navigator object that presents your scenes, a scene coordinator, or something else entirely.

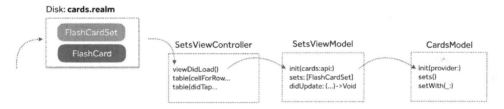

You can also use a default provider for your app runs, while injecting a test provider when under test. You'll follow this approach in this chapter.

Updating CardsModel

You'll start with the cards model to add a custom initializer that will let you inject a Realm provider.

Open **Models/CardsModel.swift** and add at the top of `CardsModel`:

```
private let provider: RealmProvider

init(provider: RealmProvider = .cards) {
```

```
    self.provider = provider
}
```

The new `init(provider:)` initializer takes a single parameter called `provider` with a default value of `.cards`. This allows you to use the pre-defined `RealmProvider.cards` when not providing any Realm (e.g. the default argument), but provides the benefit of providing an external Realm for other situations, such as our testing scenario.

Also, since `RealmProvider` is a plain struct, you can use it and pass it around across thread boundaries. Should your model need to do some heavy lifting and switch to a different thread, it can always access the `provider` property to get a thread-safe Realm instance.

To wrap up the model class, you'll need to make **two more changes**. Revisit both `sets()` and `setWith(_ name: String)` and **delete the following line** in both:

```
let provider = RealmProvider.cards
```

This removes the explicit internal dependency on `RealmProvider.cards` and lets the code use the provider injected to it in its `init(provider:)` initializer.

`CardsModel` is now more flexible and testable. You can reuse it, not only in your iOS app and test suite, but also in app extensions, watchOS apps and tvOS apps, and you can always provide it with a different `RealmProvider` appropriate to what you need to do.

Updating SetsViewModel

You'll make some similar changes to `SetsViewModel`. The class currently just creates a new model upon initialization. You'll need to change it to allow for external injection of the Realm provider.

Open **Scenes/FlashCardSets/SetsViewModel.swift** and start by changing the existing `model` property to:

```
private let model: CardsModel
```

This will require you to set a model from within any initializer of your class, instead of creating it on-the-fly when initializing the property. Add a new parameter to `init(api:)` so it looks like this:

```
init(cards: RealmProvider = .cards, api: CardsAPI) {
```

Then, insert at the top of the init's body:

```
model = CardsModel(provider: cards)
```

The new parameter `cards` is a Realm provider, which you immediately use to create a `CardsModel` model. You won't store the provider in the view model itself as it doesn't interact directly with Realm. You wouldn't want it to go around the model, would you now?

These are all of the changes needed in `SetsViewModel`. The rest of the code uses `model` to fetch and observe Realm objects so it'll work out of the box with the injected provider.

Updating SetsViewModelTests

Last but not least, it's time to add some tests in `SetsViewModelTests`. Open **FlashCardsTests/SetsViewModelTests.swift** and you'll find two tests for you to work on.

Start with the first test by replacing the contents of `test_loadsSets_whenInitialized()` with:

```
let testCards = RealmProvider.cards.copyForTesting()
let setName = "testSet"
```

You create a test copy of the default `.cards` provider by calling `copyForTesting()`, which you created earlier in this chapter. `testCards` is an empty, unique, in-memory Realm which you can mess around with freely during this test.

Speaking of, let's add a bit of sample data:

```
testCards.realm.addForTesting(objects: [
  FlashCardSet(setName, cards: [FlashCard("face", "back")])
])
```

You use `addForTesting(objects:)`, which you created earlier, to open a write transaction for your newly created Realm and add a single card set with one card.

Next, create the view model and inject the test Realm provider:

```
let vm = SetsViewModel(cards: testCards, api: CardsAPI())
```

This creates a view model instance which uses the test Realm instead of the default one. You're ready to run some assertions to test the initial state of the view model.

As the test name suggests, you'll test if the view model loads the list of card sets when it's initialized.

Add:

```
XCTAssertEqual(vm.sets.count, 1)
XCTAssertEqual(vm.sets.first?.name, setName)
```

You just added code to confirm `vm.sets` contains the set from the test Realm, and if the name of the first one matches the name you used earlier. If these two tests pass, you should feel confident the test is successful.

Asynchronous tests for Realm notifications

Moving on to the next test which tests if the view model invokes its callback whenever a new card set is downloaded.

This test, yet again, is a bit more complex than earlier tests because this time you'll have to *wait* for Realm's asynchronous change notifications to deliver the change before you can test your assertions.

Replace the contents of `test_propagatesChanges_whenSetsUpdated()` with:

```
let testCards = RealmProvider.cards.copyForTesting()
let setName = "testSet"
testCards.realm.addForTesting(objects: [
  FlashCardSet(setName, cards: [FlashCard("face", "back")])
])
let vm = SetsViewModel(cards: testCards, api: CardsAPI())
```

This is pretty much the same setup you used for the previous test, so we won't cover it in detail. You start off with a single set with one card and a view model instance `vm` ready to go.

Let's flesh out the test itself. First of all, since this is an asynchronous test that will monitor events over time, you'll need somewhere to store the results while the test runs. To do that you'll use a simple `String` array. Add the following:

```
var results = [String]()
```

You'll also be using `XCTestExpectation` from Apple's `XCTest` framework. The expectation class will help you *wait* for certain conditions to be fulfilled in your test before moving on to the part where you test your assertions.

Create an expectation by adding to the test:

```
let expectation = XCTestExpectation()
expectation.expectedFulfillmentCount = 3
```

expectedFulfillmentCount tells the expectation that it will be fulfilled when three events are recorded. These three events will be data changes that you'll trigger in the view model. Keep going for now; this code will make much more sense once you've completed it.

Any time the card set changes, the view model class calls its didUpdate closure property. This is where you'll add your test code to record any updates, along with the details about each of them.

Add a change handler to the view model:

```
vm.didUpdate = { del, ins, upd in
  let result = [del, ins, upd].reduce("", indicesToString)

}
```

didUpdate provides three parameters: the indexes of objects that have been deleted, inserted, and updated. You take these three arrays and reduce them to a single string using the indicesToString function defined at the top of the file.

indicesToString is used by the reduce method to convert the arrays to a string representation — one you can safely store and use in your assertions when it's time to do so.

result is a string in the format of "[1] [2,3] [5]" describing the three arrays passed to didUpdate and their values.

While still inside the change handler, append the following code to record the result:

```
results.append(result)
expectation.fulfill()
```

You store the updated indexes in results and call expectation.fulfill(), which tells the expectations the expected events have happened. This way, when the view model calls didUpdate three times, your test expectation will know it's time to wrap things up.

It's now time to add code to trigger the changes described above. Start by adding one more card set, below your vm.didUpdate closure:

```
DispatchQueue.main.async {
  testCards.realm.addForTesting(objects:
    [FlashCardSet(setName + "New", cards: [FlashCard("face",
"back")])]
    )
}
```

This code schedules a task on the main queue to add one more FlashCardSet object to the test Realm.

Inside your `DispatchQueue.main.async` closure, just after the code from above, add code to delete all data models in your test Realm:

```
try! testCards.realm.write {
  testCards.realm.deleteAll()
}
```

Since the view model calls `didUpdate` once with its initial state, these two changes will increase the count of recorded events to 3.

Next, add the code that *actually* waits for the expectation to be fulfilled:

```
let waitResult = XCTWaiter().wait(for: [expectation], timeout:
1.0)
```

Here you use the `XCTWaiter` class which holds the execution of the test until the expectation is fulfilled. `XCTWaiter` is a handy class from Apple's `XCTest` framework which temporarily stops the execution of the current code, without blocking the current thread. `XCTWaiter` periodically checks on the state of the expectation so when your asynchronous code increases the fulfillment count to 3, `XCTWaiter` will take care of resuming the execution of the test.

That means that you can simply add your assertions after the last line of code and they'll be evaluated when the time is right.

Finish up your test by appending:

```
XCTAssertNotEqual(waitResult, .timedOut)
XCTAssertEqual(results[0], "[][][]")
XCTAssertEqual(results[1], "[][1][]")
XCTAssertEqual(results[2], "[0,1][][]")
```

That's a lot of assertions! Let's break it down:

- First, you check `XCTWaiter`'s result. If you never record the 3 fulfillments after the set timeout, you'll receive a `.timedOut` result.

- You check if the first recorded change set is empty [] [] []. This is the initial state the view model emits.

- Next, you check if the update for your inserted set was recorded [] [1] [].

- And finally, when you delete all sets, you expect two deletions at indexes 0 and 1 and no updates or inserts: [0,1] [] [].

Working with `XCTWaiter` is a bit of a mind-bender the first time around, but once you grasp it, testing asynchronous code becomes a blissful experience.

This API can be priceless, especially when testing code based on Realm notifications that are delivered asynchronously and out of your control.

Run your test suite by going to **Product ▸ Test** or using the **Command + U** shortcut to confirm your new tests pass successfully:

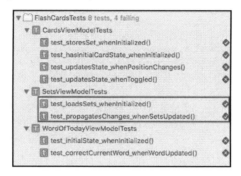

Testing Word of Today scene

You're going to complete this chapter by revising the remaining model and view model classes and completing the tests for the Word of the Day view model.

Let's start by adding Dependency Injection to `WordOfDayModel` and `SettingsModel` as the view model you'll test uses both.

Updating SettingsModel

Open **Models/SettingsModel.swift** and add a property to store the injected provider and a new and shiny initializer to facilitate the injection of a `RealmProvider`. Add to `SettingsModel`:

```
private let provider: RealmProvider

init(provider: RealmProvider = .settings) {
  self.provider = provider
}
```

Now clean up the `appSettings` getter by **deleting the following line**:

```
let realm = try! Realm()
```

As soon as you remove that line of code, Xcode will complain that `realm` is an unresolved identifier. Replace `realm` with `provider.realm` to use the injected provider's Realm. You should be all good and error-free!

Updating WordOfDayModel

Another model class which needs a caring touch is `WordOfDayModel`. You'll need to inject two different providers, which is quite similar to injecting a single one.

Open **Model/WordOfDayModel.swift** and add to the top of `WordOfDayModel`:

```
private let settings: RealmProvider
private let wordOfDay: RealmProvider

init(wordOfDay: RealmProvider = .wordOfDay,
     settings: RealmProvider = .settings) {
  self.wordOfDay = wordOfDay
  self.settings = settings
}
```

You store the two providers and, just as before, you'll get rid of the defaults in the model's methods.

Scroll down to `updateWordOfDay(word:)` and **delete the line**:

```
let settings = RealmProvider.settings
```

Do the same for the `words()` method and **delete the line**:

```
let wordOfDay = RealmProvider.wordOfDay
```

This will let the code use the injected `settings` and `wordOfDay` instance properties instead of a the instance internally created previously.

The model updates are complete! You can continue altering the view model for the scene.

Updating WordOfDayViewModel

Open **Scenes/WordOfToday/WordOfTodayViewModel.swift** to make the required changes to the view model.

Currently, the view model creates default settings and word-of-today data models. Much like before, you'll alter the code to allow for Dependency Injection before moving on to writing the tests for the view model.

Start by adding two parameters to `WordOfDayViewModel.init` like so:

```
init(wordOfDay: RealmProvider = .wordOfDay,
     settings: RealmProvider = .settings) {
```

Then, at the top of `init(wordOfDay:settings:)`, initialize the first model:

```
model = WordOfDayModel(wordOfDay: wordOfDay, settings: settings)
```

And immediately after, modify the `model` property on the top of the class to resolve the Xcode error:

```
private let model: WordOfDayModel
```

That takes care of one of the models, but you're still using the internal `SettingsModel` instance. Back in `init(wordOfDay:settings:)` find this line:

```
appSettings = SettingsModel().appSettings
```

Replace it with:

```
appSettings = SettingsModel(provider: settings).appSettings
```

This will initialize `SettingsModel` with the injected provider and use it to fetch the proper app settings.

Updating WordOfTodayViewModelTests

You can finally add some tests for the Word of Today view model. Exciting!

Open **FlashCardsTests/WordOfTodayViewModelTests.swift** and you'll see there are two tests for you to write. You'll complete one of them now, and the other in the challenges section on your own.

Let's start with `test_correctCurrentWord_whenWordUpdated()`. This test will verify that calling `WordOfTodayViewModel.updateWord(_)` correctly updates the app's settings via `SettingsModel`.

Let's start by adding the setup code. Replace the contents of `test_correctCurrentWord_whenWordUpdated()` (the second test) with:

```
let testWOD = RealmProvider.wordOfDay.copyForTesting()

testWOD.realm.addForTesting(objects: [
  WordOfDayList(list: [Entry(word: "word1", entry: "entry1")])
])
```

This code creates a test copy of the `testWOD` provider and adds a single `WordOfDayList` object with a single `Entry` attached to it. These will do just fine for the purpose of testing the update logic.

To create a test settings provider append:

```
let testSettings = RealmProvider.settings.copyForTesting()
let appSettings = Settings()

testSettings.realm.addForTesting(objects: [appSettings])
```

This code creates a test copy of the settings `RealmProvider` and inserts an empty `Settings` object to its Realm.

With the two providers ready, you can create the view model you wish to test:

```
let vm = WordOfTodayViewModel(wordOfDay: testWOD,
    settings: testSettings)
```

With that done, the setup is finalized and you can add some assertions to confirm the initial state of the view model:

```
XCTAssertEqual(appSettings.lastTimeWODChanged, Date.distantPast)
XCTAssertNil(appSettings.wordOfTheDay)
```

These two asserts confirm that the initial app settings returned are indeed the unmodified default values for `wordOfTheDay` and `lastTimeWODChanged` of the `Settings` class.

Next, you'll call `updateWord(to:)` to set the current word of the day. Add:

```
let testWord = testWOD.realm.objects(WordOfDayList.self)
[0].list[0]
vm.updateWord(to: testWord)
```

You set the current word to the first (and only) `Entry` in the list of words and call `updateWord(to:)`. This should make the view model immediately update the word of the day stored in the settings Realm.

Finally, add code to finalize your test, confirming the updates have been saved successfully:

```
XCTAssertEqual(appSettings.wordOfTheDay?.word, testWord.word)
XCTAssertEqual(
    appSettings.lastTimeWODChanged.timeIntervalSinceReferenceDate,
    Date().timeIntervalSinceReferenceDate, accuracy: 0.5
)
```

You get the current value from `appSettings` and compare it to the value you initialized `testWord` with.

With that, this simple test is completed. Run your test suite one more time by going to **Product ▸ Test** or using the **Command + U** shortcut.

You should see all but three tests pass successfully:

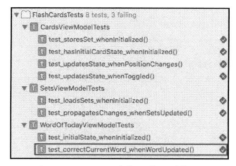

Great job! In this chapter, you've experienced first hand how easy it is to write both synchronous and asynchronous tests with Realm. The key points to take away from this chapter are:

• Test your own logic, and not Realm's as it's already well-tested and used by millions of users world-wide.

• "Dumb" models and view controllers result in easier testing of the view models, where you'd usually put the logic of an MVVM app.

• Using a central provider structure to abstract the retrieval of certain dependencies is helpful when writing tests that needs specific test-versions of these dependencies.

In general, testing Realm-based code probably won't change the way you build your own test suite. With the experience from this chapter, you should be able to write solid tests for your Realm-based project, for whatever architecture your heart desires.

> **Note:** Mocking Realm itself for your unit tests is a matter of preference. If you would like to mock Realm and remove the Realm dependency from your test suite, you can mock the key methods such as `objects(_)`, `filter(_)`, etc. The risk is the amount of code you'll have to add and maintain over time to stay in parity with Realm's own behavior, especially when a great solution such as in-memory Realms exist.
>
> The only benefit I personally see in mocking Realm is that the Realm dependency adds to the time that your CI server needs to install, build, and test your app. That would be where you'll need to decide for yourself if it's worth mocking the entire Realm framework.

Challenges

In this challenges section, you'll work on completing the Flash Cards test suite. There are two empty tests in the cards view model test class and a final one to flesh out in the Word of Today view model test class.

Challenge 1: Completing the missing tests

CardsViewModelTests

Open **FlashCardsTests/CardsViewModelTests.swift** and scroll down to find the two tests that are still empty.

Start with `test_updatesState_whenPositionChanges()`. In this test you'll confirm that the view model's `text` and `details` properties return correct values after every time you advance through the card deck.

For the test's setup, create a `FlashCardSet` with two `FlashCard` objects (consult the existing code in the test case) and finally create a view model using the test set.

To conduct the test in `test_updatesState_whenPositionChanges`:

- Add assertions that confirm the view model's `text` returns the face of the first card, and `details` returns "1 of 2".

- Call `advance(by: 1)` on the view model.

- Assert that `text` returns the face of the second card, and `details` returns "2 of 2".

- Call `advance(by: 1)` one more time.

- Add assertions to check the view model correctly goes back to the first card and returns the correct values for `text` and `details`.

With that test done, move on to `test_updatesState_whenToggled`; get a test set by calling `testSet()` and initialize a `CardsViewModel` with it.

In this test, you're going to verify that the view model correctly returns the text of the face or back of the current card when flipped over. Write the test consisting of the following steps:

- Check if `vm.text` returns the current card face.

- Call the `toggle()` method on the view model.

- Verify `text` returns the back of the flash card.

- Call `toggle()` one more time.

- Verify `text` return the face again.

These tests should sufficiently cover `CardsViewModel`, but feel free to add more tests if you have any other ideas!

Testing Word of Today

You've already added one test to `WordOfTodayViewModelTests` but now you're going to add one more as an exercise. To get started, open **FlashCardsTests/WordOfTodayViewModelTests.swift** and find the `test_initialState_whenInitialized()` method.

In this test, you'll confirm the Word of Today view model returns all defined entries and the word's order matches.

To complete the test's setup, follow these steps:

- Get a testing copy of `RealmProvider.wordOfDay`.
- Create a `WordOfDayList` object with two `Entry` objects.
- Add the above objects to the test provider.
- Create a `RealmProvider.settings` copy for testing.
- Create a Word of Today view model using the providers from above.

You can now create proper assertions to ensure that:

- The `wordCount` view model property returns the correct number of words.
- The first returned entry by `word(at: 0)` is the same word you stored first to the test provider's Realm.

In case you are feeling stuck at any point, feel free to consult the completed project in the **challenge** folder for this chapter. And again, if you feel like adding more tests to the test suite — more tests can never hurt, so go wild!

Section V: Advanced Realm Apps

In this section, you will continue exploring more complex projects powered by Realm. The apps you'll build in these three chapters will offer you patterns to use directly into your own projects when you need to build your multi-threading strategy and/or schema migrations.

Chapter 10: Effective Multithreading

In this chapter, you will explore three different solutions to the same problem and get to compare the results in the Simulator or your device to gain some insights on the impact of each code change.

Chapter 11: Beginning Schema Migrations

You will learn how to build a schema migration to handle upgrades of your app's database from one version of the app to the next. You will experiment in a playground to grasp the basics of migrations.

Chapter 12: Advanced Schema Migrations

In this chapter, you will work on a project which builds three different versions of the same app. This setup will give you the chance to work on all the migration steps between each app version and simulate all app updates as well.

Chapter 10: Effective Multi-threading

In the previous chapter, you went deeper into integrating Realm efficiently and safely into your application's architecture. The really convenient side of Realm is that it doesn't force you into any particular architecture. Realm offers an extensive toolset for persistence and data modeling, and it's up to you to decide *how* you wish to structure your usage of it.

Speaking of architecture, a lot of the issues you would experience with database ORMs and/or other databases are rooted in asynchronous, multi-threaded code. Accessing your data from concurrent threads in an efficient and safe manner is, unsurprisingly, not very straightforward and quite error-prone.

Realm saves you from the hassles of over-thinking concurrent threads, since it's been planned with a deeply integrated multi-threading strategy which makes concurrent access to the database a walk in the park.

In previous chapters, you've already tried some simple code to read and write data with Realm using Grand Central Dispatch on various queues. For apps that have relatively simple needs, such as fetching JSON every now and again and adding that data to Realm on a background queue, GCD dispatch queues are definitely the way to go.

For these simpler scenarios, Realm already takes care of mostly everything behind the scenes, so you usually won't ever need to think about multi-threading. Unless your app writes multiple times per second, you aren't likely to hit any performance issues.

Realm threading

Before you can work on this chapter's project (or pretty much any real-life Realm app) you need to understand Realm's strategy for multi-threaded database access.

Realm lets you work on the same database from multiple threads concurrently. That means no matter which thread you'll be accessing Realm on, you'll always be able to read and write the latest data without taking any extra steps to ensure the integrity of the data.

> **Note**: To put this in perspective for folks coming from Core Data or other similar databases: you won't have to explicitly configure a different context or duplicate the database manually when working with multiple threads. Realm handles everything behind the scenes for you, so you can simply read and write objects on any of your threads.

Working with Realm on the main thread

For simple queries, like showing `List` items in a table view, you'll usually fetch the results on the main thread. The performance of this varies largely based on the size of your data set, but for a reasonable amount of ordered items in a `List`, there is usually no apparent performance hit.

Reading data on the main thread (as you've done throughout the chapters of this book) results in simpler code, as you can directly use the fetched Realm objects to update your app's UI. All lifecycle methods and most UIKit delegates in your view controller are called on the main thread, so objects you fetch in `viewDidLoad()`, `viewWillAppear(_)`, or `tableView(_:cellForRowAt:)` can be used right away to update the UI.

The same goes for simple updates of the persisted data. Fetching an object from a reasonably-sized set of data by its primary key and updating some of its properties, can be safely done on the main thread without any noticeable performance penalty.

Working with Realm in a background thread

Thanks to Realm's multi-threading model, you can work with your database from any thread in your application, safely and efficiently.

When you're working with data not needed for UI purposes, you should do it from a background queue to reduce the workload on the main thread of the application, and clear it for rendering the app's UI onscreen.

A good example is an app that periodically fetches JSON from a server and stores these results in a database. If the fetched JSON refers to images from the web, you would need to fetch those in the background as well. A simple JSON-based app might include:

- Displaying List items in a table view on the main thread.

- Periodically converting fetched JSON to Swift objects and persisting those on a background thread.

- Fetching referenced images, storing them on disk, and updating the database with their local file paths as they are downloaded on a background thread.

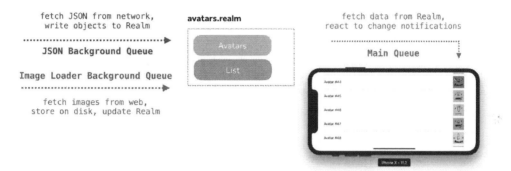

When you open your Realm file from a new thread, its snapshot of the database contains all changes, including the latest successful write transaction.

At the beginning of each run loop, the Realm snapshot accessible from the current thread will be refreshed automatically and will contain all changes committed from other threads. Realms are also refreshed upon each successful write transaction, such as after a Realm.write(_) block completes, or after a successful call to Realm.commitWrite().

You can disable auto-refreshing in special cases where you'd like to improve the performance of your app. For example, if you use a Realm instance to only add data, you don't need the auto-refresh capability. All you need to do is set the Realm's autorefresh property to false.

Moving objects between threads

One of the limitations of Realm, which is an intentional trade-off made for performance considerations, is that Realm instances and Realm objects cannot be used across threads.

You can read from and write to your Realm files from any thread in your app, but you *cannot* create a Realm instance in one thread, and use that same instance on a different thread. Once an object is persisted or fetched from disk, that specific reference of it is confined to the thread it originated from.

Trying to use a Realm instance or one of its fetched objects from a different thread leads to an immediate crash.

For that reason, it's best practice to always initialize a new Realm to get a new instance for the current thread it's needed on. As mentioned earlier, this initialization won't create a new instance of Realm every time, but rather return a cached instance per-thread as needed.

When you do need to pass an object across thread boundaries, you have two options:

• Pass an object's primary key across threads and re-fetch the object from the thread-specific Realm in your other thread. Since primary keys are strings or numbers, they're safe to pass around thread boundaries.

• Alternatively, you can use Realm's `ThreadSafeReference` class, which creates a thread-safe reference that can be freely passed between thread boundaries and resolved on the target thread. You create this reference by simply using `let ref = ThreadSafeReference(to: myRealmObject)` and resolve it in your other thread by using `let myRealmobject = realm.resolve(ref)`.

Whichever option you use, moving objects between threads requires some extra work, so minimizing that practice in your code would be beneficial and reduce the thread-specific code's footprint.

> **Note**: When using the `ThreadSafeReference` option, note that you *must* resolve the created reference at *most* once. Creating a thread-safe reference will keep the Realm retained and prevent it from deallocating, until you resolve it. For that reason, prefer using `ThreadSafeReferences` for short-lived scenarios.

Getting started with Sensors

In this chapter's project, called **Sensors**, you'll work on an app that reads air quality sensors at great speeds and tries to persist the readings to a Realm file.

> **Note**: The app reads mock sensor values for test purposes only, as the focus is on working with Realm and threads.

Sensors implements a relatively simple setup to read and write data. The key focus points of the provided starter project are as follows:

- **API/SensorAPI.swift**: Provides a class that lets you subscribe to a sensor and repeatedly get readings via a callback.

- **Scenes/SensorsViewModel.swift**: Provides the sensors scene's view model and, once initialized, subscribes to three different sensors. The view model accepts a `DataWriterType`-conforming writer in its initializer, which provides it with the ability to write sensor readings as they come from the API. The view model calls the writer numerous times per second.

  The view model also manages various statistics using a class that grabs the current amount of samples stored in the database every second, checks the file's size, and calculates the average values of the latest `10,000` readings.

- Throughout this chapter, you'll be mostly working with the classes in **Models/ DataWriter**, where you'll implement three different writing strategies and see the respective changes in the app's performance.

Without further ado, navigate to this chapter's starter project folder and run `pod install` as usual to install the project dependencies. Once the install process completes, open the workspace file and peek around.

The app's storyboard includes a menu scene which offers a choice of three writing strategies and a sensor scene which will subscribe to the mock sensors and display the running stats:

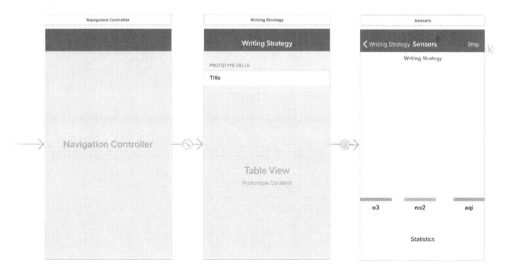

Once you start the app, it'll present you with the three options you'll be implementing for writing data into your Realm:

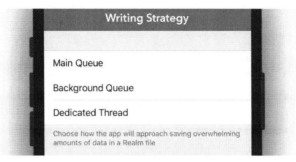

You can tap one of these to navigate to the sensor scene, but since none of the writer classes are implemented yet, the scene doesn't do anything.

Implementing the data writers

Throughout the course of this book, you've worked on projects that didn't need to write large amounts of data to disk. If you don't need to write huge amounts of data, you can safely write to your Realm file from any thread (including the main thread) as write transactions are usually quite fast.

Let's implement Sensor's first data writer class, without caring much about threads at this point.

Writing on the current queue

Open **Models/DataWriter/DataWriterMain.swift** where you'll find, inside your DataWriterMain class, an empty stub of the only required method of DataWriterType called write(sym:value:).

In all writers you'll implement, write(sym:value:)'s role will be to save the received sensor reading to the app's Realm file. A RealmProvider similar to previous chapters is already included in the starter project:

Add inside DataWriterMain's write(sym:value:) method:

```
let realm = RealmProvider.sensors.realm
guard let sensor = realm.object(ofType: Sensor.self,
  forPrimaryKey: sym) else { return }
```

This code gets a reference to the app's Realm and fetches the Sensor object for the given symbol (in your app, the mock sensors provide readings for o3, no2, and aqi).

You can now add the reading to the readings list of the fetched sensor. The Sensor class wraps the functionality of adding readings in a method called addReadings(_). addReadings(_) accepts a list of Reading objects and adds them to a list property on the sensor object. Append:

```
try! realm.write {
    sensor.addReadings([Reading(value)])
}
```

This code should persist the current sensor reading to the database. Run the project and select **Main Queue** in the main menu.

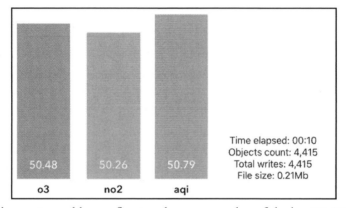

The app displays animated bars reflecting the average value of the last **10,000** readings of each sensor. It also provides additional statistics for:

- How long the app has been running.

- How many objects are currently persisted in the database (they're cleared every time you start the project).

- How many writes were performed in total.

- How large the current Realm file is.

> **Note:** This sample app is in no way a measure of Realm's performance. The numbers produced are only interesting in comparison with other writers of the same app; e.g. they can only serve as a comparison between different implementations, not of Realm in general, nor in comparison to other databases.

While playing around with the app, you'll get a feeling of how the performance changes by altering the code or the execution environment.

For example, when I run the project in the Simulator from Xcode, I get `4,415` objects written in about `10` seconds, and the file grows to a size of `0.21`MB. Exact numbers vary across multiple runs and can be off by a long shot on your hardware.

When I tried the project on a physical iPhone SE device, I got `1,094` objects written in the same time and the file grew to a mere `0.08`MB. When I let the app run longer until it got to `4,415` persisted objects (like in the Simulator run), the file size was `0.16`MB.

Comparing these numbers reveals that:

1. The performance, naturally, varies across devices. If you are measuring the performance of your app (or Realm in general), all results will be relative to the certain context you run in.

2. Files containing the same number of objects will not necessarily be of the same size. The file size depends on many factors and conditions under which the data was written to disk. Realm tries to automatically compact the data and minimize the file's size, but usually, if objects are burst-written, the file will grow faster than if the same amount of objects were written at a slower pace.

What about using asynchronous writing? Try offloading the code execution of `write(sym:value:)` using Grand Central Dispatch. Wrap your existing code in a `DispatchQueue.main.async` block, e.g. :

```
DispatchQueue.main.async {
   ... existing code ...
}
```

Using this code, you schedule the writing of the readings as asynchronous tasks, instead of immediately starting a write transaction to persist the object in a more synchronous fashion. This allows Grand Central Dispatch to provide much more performant execution of these intense write bursts.

When I try the updated project on an iPhone SE device, the number of written objects in `10` seconds increases from `1,094` to `1,899`, while the file's size stays low at `0.1`MB.

Good job — with this change you almost doubled your app's performance!

Writing on a background queue

You achieved some performance gains by using asynchronous tasks with GCD, but the main queue is *still* a serial queue, and it can only do so much in terms of running through an overwhelming pile of tasks.

Another serious problem with the previous solution is that overloading the main queue with non-UI related work can potentially impair the responsiveness of your app.

You're probably already thinking of how using GCD can solve this, which you'll explore in this very section. Open **Models/DataWriter/DataWriterGCD.swift** and you'll find another empty class conforming to the `DataWriterType` protocol. You'll use this class to further experiment with GCD in this section.

Start by adding a dedicated dispatch queue to the class to avoid having to use `DispatchQueue.global(qos:)` every time you need to schedule tasks. Add a new `DispatchQueue` property to the `DataWriterGCD` class:

```
private let writeQueue = DispatchQueue(label: "background",
   qos: .background,
   attributes: [.concurrent])
```

The queue has a `.background` quality of service that's lower priority than the main queue and is a concurrent queue. You can now use the queue and complete `write(sym:value:)` with the code to write to your Realm file.

Add inside `write(sym:value:)`:

```
writeQueue.async {
   let realm = RealmProvider.sensors.realm
   guard let sensor = realm.object(ofType: Sensor.self,
      forPrimaryKey: sym) else { return }

   try! realm.write {
      sensor.addReadings([Reading(value)])
   }
}
```

The code is very similar to what you used in the previous section of the chapter, except that this time you use the dedicated `writeQueue` to schedule the tasks.

Let's run the project in the Simulator once again. Run the app, tap on **Background Queue** and check out the stats at the bottom of the screen (you will likely see different numbers).

```
Time elapsed: 00:10
Objects count: 5,107
Total writes: 5,106
File size: 31.46Mb
```

Above are the results when I run the code on my laptop. At first sight the numbers look great; there have been thousands of objects written to disk in 10 seconds.

However, when compared to the 7,389 written on the main queue, the 5,107 objects written on the dedicated background queue seem like a big let down!

And look at that file size: 31.46MB to store 5,000 objects! That is a significant difference, compared to the 0.21MB it took to write the same data on the main queue.

> **Note**: Depending on your computer these numbers can widely vary. The file size might start increasing at a higher rate after running longer than 10 seconds as well.

What gives?

You've already learned that Realm confines its objects to database snapshots created per thread. Working on the main GCD queue means you are always working on the main thread; regardless of whether you're working with async tasks or not, you're always working with the same snapshot of your Realm file.

Grand Central Dispatch provides an abstraction over threads called a **dispatch queue**. A dispatch queue will use a pool of threads to perform concurrent work. How big the pool or how often threads will be re-used is up to the implementation.

When you use a dispatch queue to offload intense Realm work, you're actually working *against* Realm instead of reducing its load. Run the project again, and tap **Background Queue**. After few seconds, pause the execution by tapping the pause icon above the Debug Console or going to **Debug ▶ Pause**, and have a look at the Debug Navigator Pane. You will see that the dedicated queue you use has spawned multiple threads. On my computer, there are around 70 active threads owned by the dedicated writer queue:

```
▶ ⬤ Thread 62  Queue: background (concurrent)
▶ ⬤ Thread 63  Queue: background (concurrent)
▶ ⬤ Thread 64  Queue: background (concurrent)
▶ ⬤ Thread 65  Queue: background (concurrent)
▶ ⬤ Thread 66  Queue: background (concurrent)
▶ ⬤ Thread 67  Queue: background (concurrent)
```

Try to imagine what's happening when the Sensors app tries to write this massive burst of incoming data to disk. You have 70 different threads constantly committing small write transactions to their own Realm snapshots, causing all other threads to auto-refresh their own snapshots.

Aside from the performance hit, all of these snapshots have the added pain of increasing the file size of your Realm!

The issue of a massive file size is actually pretty easy to solve. The problem only occurs when the Xcode debugger is attached to the running app. This seems to prevent Realm from properly compacting the file after committing write transactions. Run the app directly in your Simulator or on your device by tapping the icon directly, instead of runnning it from Xcode, and you'll notice the file size remains within a reasonable limit and stays relatively stable.

With the file size issue handled, the performance overhead of using so many concurrent threads still remains unsolved. To resolve this issue, you'll need to manage your own thread instead of offloading that task to GCD.

Writing on a dedicated thread

GCD is a great abstraction and a brilliant API for when you need to run some asynchronous work. Its many built-in optimizations are actually its downside in this specific use case of intensively writing into Realm. That's why in the third section of this chapter, you're going to manually manage a dedicated thread on which you'll perform all of your database's write transactions.

Open **Models/DataWriter/DataWriterDedicatedThread.swift**. You're going to, one final time, face an empty `DataWriterType` class. Regardless of its humble starting point, `DataWriterDedicatedThread` is going to go where no other writer class in this project has gone before.

Let's start by adding two new properties:

```
private var writeRealm: Realm!
private var thread: Thread!
```

`thread` is going to be the worker thread you'll use for writing to Realm. `writeRealm` is going to hold the `Realm` instance you'll use.

So far in this book, you've never held a reference to a Realm instance; you were always told to use a configuration to get a Realm for every context you had to read or write objects in. In the specific case of `DataWriterDedicatedThread`, you're always going to be writing to the same dedicated thread, so it's safe to keep a reference to the Realm itself.

Let's get to it, shall we? Add a new method called `threadWorker()` to configure and run the thread:

```
@objc private func threadWorker() {
  defer { Thread.exit() }
  writeRealm = RealmProvider.sensors.realm

  while thread != nil, !thread.isCancelled {
    RunLoop.current.run(
      mode: RunLoopMode.defaultRunLoopMode,
      before: Date.distantPast)
  }
}
```

You start by defining a `defer` block which will exit the thread when the execution completes. It's best practice to use `defer` for this since it *guarantees* the code will run after you exit the current scope.

Next, you fetch a Realm instance and store it to your previously defined `writeRealm` class property.

Finally, you run a `while` loop to keep the thread running until it's been cancelled by another process.

This is all the code you need to keep the dedicated thread alive and ready to write some data to your app's Realm. Of course, before using the thread, you also need to start it. You'll do that as soon as the class is initialized. Override the default `init` with a custom one:

```swift
override init() {
  super.init()

  thread = Thread(target: self,
    selector: #selector(threadWorker),
    object: nil)
  thread.start()
}
```

The code creates a new thread, defines `threadWorker()` as its entry point, and starts it.

One final point you shouldn't forget is to add a method to cancel the thread and clean the object state. Add `invalidate()`, which you'll call before destroying the writer object to cleanly wrap up its lifecycle:

```swift
func invalidate() {
  thread.cancel()
}
```

You'll call `invalidate()` whenever you want to cleanly destroy the writer class.

Since you manage the writer's lifecycle in the sensors view model, open **Scenes/ SensorsViewModel.swift** and insert into `deinit`:

```swift
(writer as? DataWriterDedicatedThread)?.invalidate()
```

This code, provided you are currently using a `DataWriterDedicatedThread` writer, will call `invalidate()` when the view model is deallocated.

Go back to **DataWriterDedicatedThread.swift** and add the code to store the sensor readings on disk.

Start by creating a helper `addReading(reading:)` method you'll use to write readings on your own thread:

```
@objc private func addReading(reading: [String: Double]) {
  guard let sym = reading.keys.first,
        let value = reading[sym] else { return }
}
```

You start by unwrapping the two values for the sensor symbol and the reading value out of the `reading` dictionary argument.

Similarly to the previous implementations, you'll fetch the corresponding sensor object and add the reading to its history. Append:

```
guard let sensor = writeRealm.object(ofType: Sensor.self,
  forPrimaryKey: sym) else { return }

try! writeRealm.write {
  sensor.addReadings([Reading(value)])
}
```

You write directly to your Realm file without using the `RealmProvider` proxy, since you already have a working instance stored in the class' `writeRealm` property. Both `workerThread` and `addReading(reading:)` are always executed on the dedicated thread so keeping the Realm reference around is a safe deal.

Now that we have our helper method, it's time to actually fill out your `write(sym:value:)` method to use it! First, add this line inside `write(sym:value:)` to make sure the thread, along with the writer, are properly initialized:

```
precondition(thread != nil, "Thread not initialized")
```

After you know your thread is available, invoke the `addReading(reading:)` method you created on your custom thread and pass the new reading as a parameter:

```
perform(#selector(addReading),
  on: thread,
  with: [sym: value],
  waitUntilDone: false,
  modes: [RunLoopMode.defaultRunLoopMode.rawValue])
```

This code calls `addReading(reading:)` and makes sure to execute the code on the given thread. A limitation of using `perform(_:on:with:waitUntilDone:modes:)` is that `addReading(reading:)` has to be defined as `@objc`, and the containing class (e.g. your `DataWriterDedicatedThread`), must be a `NSObject`. That limits its parameters to Objective-C compliant types which makes it impossible to pass the two parameters `sym` and `value` as a tuple or struct.

Luckily, for these two simple values its easy enough to bundle them up as a `Dictionary<String, Double>` like so `[sym: value]`. In your own apps, you might need a custom class to pass around more complex data structures.

Your new dedicated thread writer is now ready for a test drive. Run the project and tap on **Dedicated Thread**.

Running for `10` seconds in the Simulator on my computer produces the following results:

```
Time elapsed: 00:10
Objects count: 16,153
Total writes: 16,163
File size: 0.43Mb
```

Woah, that's a pretty significant difference!

From an average of around `7,500` objects written asynchronously on the main queue, to around `16,000` when using the dedicated thread, is an over `200%` increase in performance compared to your previous implementation. Neat!

Caching objects on the Dedicated Thread

Up until now, you didn't keep Realm objects around in-memory, since you couldn't guarantee you would always access them from the same thread, except in the case of view controller properties accessed only from main thread confined methods such as `viewDidLoad()` or `viewWillAppear(_)`.

Using your newfound knowledge, **you can guarantee** that the code in `addReading(reading:)` will always run on your shiny, new, dedicated thread. This allows you to prefetch some of the objects you'll always need and store them in your writer class instead of repeatedly fetching them every time you need to write data.

Let's fetch the three `Sensor` objects when you first create the thread and store them for future use. Add a new property to the `DataWriterDedicatedThread` class:

```
private var sensors: Sensor.SensorMap!
```

`SensorMap` is a type alias for `[String: Sensor]`, so it's basically a dictionary that allows you to get a sensor object by its symbol. In fact, the `Sensor` class already features a handy method to load all `Sensor` objects in a given Realm and return a `SensorMap` dictionary. This method is pre-bundled with the project as it doesn't do anything magical you haven't done before.

Scroll to `threadWorker()` and find the line `writeRealm = RealmProvider.sensors.realm`. This seems like a good place to fetch the sensor objects too. Below the said line, insert:

```
sensors = Sensor.sensorMap(in: writeRealm)
```

`sensorMap(in:)` grabs all `Sensor` objects and stores them in `sensors`. To make sure no object references remain, add at the bottom of the current method:

```
sensors = nil
```

This will make sure `sensors` is `nil` as soon as the thread is invalidated.

Time to go back to `addReading(reading:)` and make use of the new sensor map. First, remove all this code, which you won't need anymore:

```
guard let sensor = writeRealm.object(ofType: Sensor.self,
    forPrimaryKey: sym) else { return }
try! writeRealm.write {
    sensor.addReadings([Reading(value)])
}
```

In its place, insert:

```
sensors[sym]?.addReadings([Reading(value)])
```

You get rid of the database lookup and use your cached objects directly instead. This should further increase the performance. Give the app another try.

Interestingly, you'll discover there isn't really much of a performance difference, which points you to the fact that Realm *already* does this caching you just manually added, so there's no need to bother with it. This is an extra bonus when you're using Realm in a single thread.

Batched writes

You've improved the performance of your app significantly. But in the end, the biggest bottleneck comes from opening a Realm write transaction every single time a sensor reading comes through.

For every write transaction, Realm performs a number of tasks:

- Checks the transaction validity before committing.
- Double-checks the file consistency before confirming that the merge of the new transaction is successful.
- Sends change notifications to all observers about any relevant changes, if applicable.

- Refreshes the snapshots of all threads currently accessing the same file, unless configured differently with the `Realm.autorefresh` property.

This amount of overhead might seem negligible, but when you consider that there may be thousands of transactions per second, this has serious performance considerations.

In this final exercise, you're going to add some code that groups readings into batches of `1,000` and writes them in a single transaction. This approach should result in nearly a thousand-fold decrease in the number of write transactions.

> **Note**: Storing data in memory while you're waiting to write it could result in data loss if the contents of memory were to be lost. Take this into consideration if you plan to use write coalescing.

The solution is straightforward: you'll add an array that will hold readings as they come in. Once the count goes over `1,000`, you'll write these objects to the Realm.

Start by adding a few extra properties to `DataWriterDedicatedThread`:

```
private static let bufferMaxCount = 1000

private var buffer = [String: [Reading]]()
private var bufferCount = 0
```

Let's break these down:

- `bufferMaxCount`: Represents the maximum number of readings you want to keep in memory before persisting them to disk.

- `buffer` : A dictionary holding an array of readings for each of the sensor's symbols.

- `bufferCount`: A simple integer counter that keeps track of how many objects are currently buffered.

Add a helper method, `writeBuffer(_:)`, which you'll later use to write the batch of cached readings:

```
func writeBuffer(_ batch: [String: [Reading]]) {
  try! writeRealm.write {
    batch.forEach { sym, values in
      sensors[sym]?.addReadings(values)
    }
  }
}
```

This code loops over all the sensor symbols in the provided batch and adds the list of readings to each respective sensor object.

Time to build your buffer and use your new helper method. You'll need to modify `addReading(reading:)` once again to use your new buffer to hold the readings, instead of writing each of them separately. Remove the following line:

```
sensors[sym]?.addReadings([Reading(value)])
```

In its place, insert:

```
var bufferToProcess: [String: [Reading]] = [:]
```

You create a new local variable `bufferToProcess` to use in case there's a batch of objects to write to disk.

Next, if it's the first reading in the batch for the current sensor, you create the array to hold the sensor's readings:

```
if buffer[sym] == nil {
  buffer[sym] = []
}
```

Follow that by adding a `Reading` object to the buffer and increasing the buffer count:

```
buffer[sym]!.append(Reading(value))
bufferCount += 1
```

Finally, check if you've reached the buffer limit. If so, copy the buffered values and reset the buffer:

```
if bufferCount > DataWriterDedicatedThread.bufferMaxCount {
  bufferToProcess = buffer
  bufferCount = 0
  buffer = [:]
}
```

This code will store up to `1,000` `Reading` objects in `buffer`, copy them to `bufferToProcess`, reset the buffer, and start filling up the buffer again.

What's left is to write these buffered objects to the app's database when the buffer threshold is reached. First, check if there are any readings buffered. Add:

```
guard !bufferToProcess.isEmpty else { return }
writeBuffer(bufferToProcess)
```

Note: In the current example the buffered sensor data is modified from a single thread. Should you need to be able to modify the data set also from other threads

> you will need to use locks or other mechanism to guarantee atomic access to the buffer.

Try the app one more time and check the performance for the **Dedicated Thread** writing strategy:

```
Time elapsed: 00:10
Objects count: 30,000
Total writes: 253,949
File size: 2.10Mb
```

This time, the Simulator commits around `250,000` updates within `10` seconds. The number of persisted objects, though, is stuck at `30,000` and doesn't increase.

This is part of the app's logic: the sensor bars display the average of the last `10,000` readings, so `Sensor.addReadings(_)` removes any excess over `10,000` for each of the sensors.

Total Writes counts all readings added to the database, including those deleted readings considered to be over the `10,000` latest readings of each sensor.

Back to the main point of this section: batching multiple operations in one transaction can greatly improve the performance of your app. Realm is quite fast, but to persist your data it still needs to access the disk, so any optimizations you can make in that area will be a great help.

There is one final loose end to take care of: clearing the buffer when the writer is released from memory. If you didn't hit the `1,000` buffer limit before you released the class, there would still be some readings buffered which would be lost.

To take care of this edge case, scroll up to `threadWorker()` and find the line where you reset the `sensors` array: `sensors = nil`. Just before that line, insert:

```
writeBuffer(buffer)
```

This makes sure everything is wrapped up properly when the thread is invalidated. Therefore you won't lose any values when the writer is deinitialized.

With this last piece of code, the Sensors project is complete. Wonderful job!

Hopefully, the process of exploration you followed in this chapter gave you some ideas and insights on how to optimize your own code.

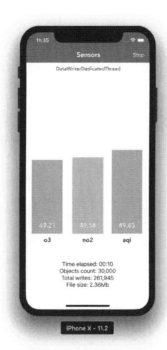

You won't often get into situations where you're writing to disk intensively and producing calculations over tens of thousands of values. But if you *do* ever work on apps with Realm underneath that need a solid threading strategy, you now have the knowledge to face that challenge.

Realm is a very performant database to begin with, but you can give it a helping hand by optimizing your data handling strategy when necessary.

Challenges

No challenges for this chapter!

This chapter introduced some more advanced and complicated aspects for using Realm to persist vast amounts of data. You definitely deserve a quick break for successfully finishing this one. Kudos to you!

Chapter 11: Beginning Realm Migrations

You've experimented with many ways to encapsulate your raw data as powerful and persistable Realm-backed objects. I would go as far as to say you've learned *most* of what there is to know about defining Realm schemas at this point.

But nothing in life (and code) remains static forever. So what happens, then, when the app you're working on becomes wildly successful and you need release a new version, and then another one, and another one?

As your app and its needs evolve, it's likely you'll need to deal with data you didn't necessarily plan for in your initial version, such as new objects or adding properties on existing models. You might even want to create new relationships or discard entities that you no longer need.

For memory-only objects in your code, you simply delete the code responsible for the class in question and — *poof!* It's gone!

However, in the case of Realm objects, or other data persisted on-disk, things are slightly more complicated. In this chapter you'll learn how you can migrate the schema of a Realm file as it evolves alongside your app.

Modifying an object schema

To define the object schema of a Realm file, you'd use the `Realm.Configuration` struct, or more specifically its `objectSchema` property which lists which objects are included in that particular Realm.

When your app starts, Realm introspects the classes you've defined in code, finds the ones that are subclassing `Object`, and creates a detailed map of those.

Later on, when you use a configuration to open a Realm from disk, Realm matches the schema of the objects defined in your code to the file-persisted schema:

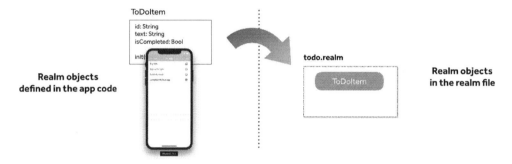

If the two schemas match, which would be the case if you didn't change anything in the interim, Realm can read and write objects from and to that file without any issue.

Quite the happy path, isn't it? But what happens if you add a new property to one of your Realm `Objects` that isn't part of your original schema? Imagine you had a `ToDoItem` object persisted to disk and you receive some new product requirements to add a `priority` value for each item:

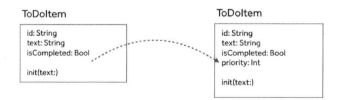

As soon as you try to open the file, Realm will detect there's a mismatch between the schema you have in your code and the file-persisted schema, at which point, `try Realm()` will throw an error.

```
0x108997900 <+0>: pushq  %rbp
0x108997901 <-
0x108997904 <-     Thread 1: Fatal error: 'try!' expression unexpectedly raised an error: Error Domain=io.realm Code=10  ⊗
0x108997905 <-     "Migration is required due to the following errors:
0x108997906 <-     - Property 'ToDoItem.priority' has been added." UserInfo={NSLocalizedDescription=Migration is
                   required due to the following errors:
                   - Property 'ToDoItem.priority' has been added., Error Code=10}
```

Realm not only detects the change but is also very explicit about what you've done to upset it: "Property 'ToDoItem.priority' has been added". The same will happen for any changes you make to your models. Here's the error description when you delete an existing property and remove the primary key in addition to the above changes:

```
"Migration is required due to the following errors:
- Property 'ToDoItem.priority' has been added.
- Primary Key for class 'ToDoItem' has been removed.
- Property 'ToDoItem.text' has been removed." UserInfo=
```

There's a shortcut to help you override these kinds of errors during development while your models are still constantly evolving. Realm.Configuration has a property called deleteRealmIfMigrationNeeded, which instructs Realm to simply delete the existing Realm before creating a new one if it doesn't match the current code schema:

```
let conf = Realm.Configuration(
    fileURL: fileUrl,
    deleteRealmIfMigrationNeeded: true)
```

When using this option, you'll never get a mismatch error during development. Just don't forget to disable this option before shipping to the App Store! Otherwise, you'll delete the user's data every time you ship a new app version with a newer schema, which is a fast route to one-star reviews.

Another use case for deleteRealmifMigrationNeeded would be if your app's data is ephemeral and you can recreate it at any time. In such case you can simply delete the whole database and recreate the data instead of performing a migration from one version to another.

What's a schema migration, anyway?

If you're already familiar with migrating database schemas, you can safely skip over this section. Otherwise, let me put things in perspective for you and explain what problem migrations aim to solve.

Imagine for a moment you're running a simple online store. Your code is located on your hosted web server along with a database server containing all product data, similar to this:

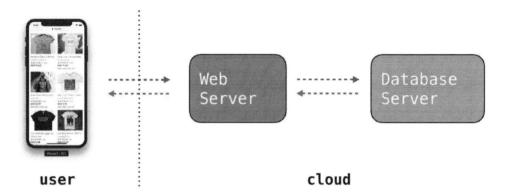

As the web site owner, you control everything to the right of the dotted line in the image above. You can adjust your code *and* the database in real-time. The user uses Safari as a stateless client to simply *view* content being served by the servers.

Whenever you make changes to the database, you can adjust your code to suit and **bam**! You're done. The next user that opens the web site will simply see the new information in their web browser.

In this scenario, you can see it's easy to control and synchronize the schema changes, since both the code and data are in your control and you can adjust them remotely without any user involvement.

Leaving the web application scenario aside, imagine you have a ToDo app installed on the user's iPhone. The app creates a Realm file in the **Documents** folder and uses it to persist objects. When the user upgrades the app to a newer version from the app store, the new app might use a newer object schema. Your code expects a "new" schema version, but the file located on the user's phone still has the "old" schema.

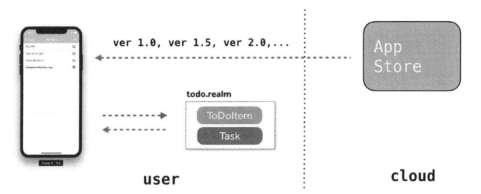

Simply deleting the old file often isn't a viable solution, as the user will lose their data. Using the old file schema with the new app schema is also not a viable proposition, since the new app depends on the new schema at that point.

Realm's approach is to let you specify a schema version in `Realm.Configuration`. Should Realm detect an older version on disk upon opening the file, it'll give you a chance to migrate the existing data to the new schema:

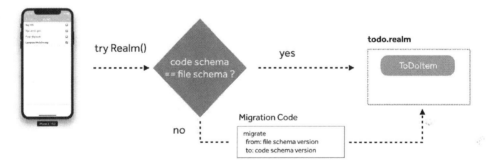

During a migration, which runs exactly once when you open the old file for the first time, you have access to both the old and new schemas. It's up to you to ensure that your old data fits the expectations of the new code and schema.

What tasks might you perform during a migration? This depends entirely on the changes you have made to the schema itself! To give you a general idea, here are a few example migration tasks:

- You've added a new object model to the schema, and the new code expects that there will always be at least one of these objects in the database. In your migration, you'll create that object and store it in the database before the new app version runs so that it matches your app's prerequisites.

- You've added a new text property named `title` to one of your objects with the default value of `"n/a"`. In your migration, you'll have to iterate over all of your existing objects and set their newly added `title` property to `"n/a"` to ensure your old objects are compatible with your new schema.

- You've renamed a property on one of the your existing models from `completed` to `isCompleted` to make it more "Swifty". In your migration, you'll call a special API that lets Realm know that the new property `isCompleted` should actually point to the old `completed` property and have the values copied over so they won't be lost.

Sounds complicated? Well, then … good news everyone!

Automatic migrations

You'll be *thrilled* to discover that Realm *automatically* handles most types of changes to your schema. Changes such as adding or deleting objects from the schema, adding or deleting properties on an object, adding indexes, and more are automatically performed during a migration.

What's left for you to do is limited to tasks that cannot be inferred by Realm, such as adding custom data and copying values from one object to another.

It's always best to keep in mind exactly which kinds of automatic schema changes Realm supports out-of-the-box:

- Incrementing the schema version number.

- Adding new Realm objects to the schema.

- Removing existing Realm objects from the schema.

- Adding properties to an existing Realm object.

- Removing a property from an existing Realm object.

- Adding a primary key.

- Removing a primary key.

- Adding an indexed property.

- Removing indexed property.

Realm will automatically apply all of these changes to the existing file structure during a migration. Once you successfully open the file, it will already have the new schema version number and be considered fully migrated.

Custom migrations

Whether or not your changes can be migrated automatically by Realm, you need to provide a migration block in your configuration object. The migration block contains code Realm will run once during the schema migration, and provides access to both the "old" and "new" schemas.

Let's take a look at a basic example:

```
let conf = Realm.Configuration(
  fileURL: fileUrl,
  schemaVersion: 2,
  migrationBlock: { migration, oldVersion in
    // do nothing
  }
)
```

This configuration tells the app it should use object schema version 2. If you update to this new version while you have an old version installed with schema version 1, Realm will call the provided `migrationBlock` to perform the migration from version 1 to 2.

`migrationBlock` provides two closure arguments:

1. `migration` is an instance of the `Migration` helper class, which gives you access to the "old" and "new" object schemas and provides you with methods to access the data in the "old" and "new" Realm files.

2. `oldVersion` is the schema version of the existing file, e.g. the one you're migrating *from*.

In the example above, the migration block is empty, which is a completely valid migration strategy; you're simply trusting Realm to apply any automatic changes that it can do by itself (e.g. anything from the list above).

Of course, the migration block could also be a free function, static method on one of your classes, or an inline closure as above. As your app evolves, your migration code can become quite complex, so you might want to offload that code into a separate file or class.

Realm Migration class

The migration object provided to your migration closure is the key to a successful migration. Before getting your hands on this chapter's playground, let's have a look at some typical tasks you'll perform by using the `Migration` class.

Schemas

First of all, `Migration` gives access to both the "old" schema (the one currently on the user's device) and the "new" object schema, which is Realm's introspection of your Realm objects. Those are accessible via two properties: `oldSchema` and `newSchema`.

Both properties are of type `Schema` and provide access to a list of all objects, the list of their properties, and the type and meta information for each.

A `Schema` instance contains the following detailed information:

You can iterate over the included objects and the list of their properties. Additionally, you can check which is the primary key, which properties are indexed, the type of each property, and if any are optional.

Data access

The old and new schemas provide you with information about the data structure, but do not give you access to the actual data itself. The `Migration` class has a set of methods that let you access the objects in both the old and new Realms.

Enumerating objects

You can access the existing data by enumerating over all objects of a certain type. The API is similar to `Realm.objects(_)`, with the key difference being that it provides you with the objects from both the old and new Realms *simultaneously*.

`Migration.enumerateObjects(ofType:_:)` iterates over the records of the required type and invokes your closure by providing you with a matching pair of old and new objects.

Here's an example of how you would use this API in a migration block:

```
migration.enumerateObjects(ofType: "Exam") { old, new in
    if old?["result"] == nil {
        new?["result"] = "n/a"
    }
}
```

The two closure arguments are of type `MigrationObject`. This is a catch-all type that acts much like a common dictionary. You can access properties by their name and get and set their values.

`MigrationObject` is the primary type you'll work with during a migration. Realm, naturally, can't provide you with the old and new version of a class. The app sees *only* the current version of the code so it has no way to create objects of a previous version of a given class.

As long as you know what you're doing, you'll get through your migrations relatively unscathed.

Adding and deleting objects

You'll sometimes need to either add new data or delete existing data. You can do this in a migration using the following APIs.

`Migration.create(_:value:)` creates a new `MigrationObject`. You provide a class name matching a local Realm object (as a `String`) and a dictionary to initialize the object with.

Once you open the Realm file and the migration has completed, you'll get back an object of the given type (instead of a `MigrationObject`) so you'll be able to work with it as you normally would.

Here's a simple example of using `create(_:value:)`:

```
migration.create("Exam", value: [
  "subject": "Computer Science",
  "result": "C++"
])
```

To delete an object during a migration, use `Migration.delete(_)`. You are most likely to call this method while enumerating objects from the Realm, like so:

```
migration.enumerateObjects(ofType: "Exam") { _, new in
  if let new = new, new["name"] == nil {
    migration.delete(new)
  }
}
```

The sample code above checks if any of the existing `Exam` records is "broken" — that is, has a `nil` name. If it finds any, it deletes them during the course of the migration.

Deleting all objects and metadata of a type

`Migration.deleteData(forType:)` lets you delete all existing objects of a certain type at once. As an added benefit, if the model was removed from the schema altogether, this API will take care of clearing all existing metadata related to the type.

Renaming a property

The last method you're going to cover is `Migration.renameProperty(onType:from:to:)`. When you rename a property in your code, Realm has no way to know that a property represents the same thing, given the fact it has a different name.

For example, when you rename `completed` to `isCompleted`, the only information Realm has is that `completed` was deleted and `isCompleted` was added. Therefore, it will delete all data stored in `completed` and add a new empty property called `isCompleted` to the class.

To preserve the existing data stored on disk, you'll need to help Realm by adding the following to your migration block:

```
migration.renameProperty(
    onType: "Exam",
    from: "completed",
    to: "isCompleted"
)
```

With that, your grand tour of the `Migration` class is over. It's time to actually play around with what you just learned and try some migration tricks in a playground.

Basic migrations

Open the starter folder for this chapter and, as you did previously, run `./bootstrap.sh` to install the playground's dependencies and build the project. Once the process has completed, you'll see the fresh playground in your Xcode.

The playground includes two simple Realm objects to start with: `Exam` and `Mark`. This time though, you're not interested in the objects themselves but only in their migrations.

App version 1.0

For each of this playground's examples, you'll simulate running a different version of an app and schema. You'll start with the first app version which uses object schema 1.

> **Note**: For this chapter, you'll build very simple additive migrations to get a grasp of how the API works. Usually, playgrounds won't work well for more complex real-life migrations.

Add to your playground's code:

```
// Initially install & run the 1.0 version app
Example.of("Run app ver. 1.0") {
}
```

For the purpose of this chapter, you'll consider the code inside the closure to be the code running in your app's version **1.0**. Start by adding inside the closure:

```
let conf = Realm.Configuration(
    schemaVersion: 1,
    deleteRealmIfMigrationNeeded: true,
    objectTypes: [Exam.self])
```

Your app version **1.0** uses a Realm schema version 1 and persists one kind of object in its database, of type **Exam**. You've written this kind of code many times throughout this book so hopefully nothing comes as a surprise here.

Next, add some code to create an **Exam** and persist it to your Realm file:

```
let realm = try! Realm(configuration: conf)
try! realm.write {
    realm.add(Exam())
}
```

To make sure everything went as expected, append to the closure:

```
print("Exams: \(Array(realm.objects(Exam.self)))")
```

Let the playground run and have a look at the Debug console:

```
 Run app ver. 1.0:

Exams: [Exam {name: ""}]
```

An exam has been successfully created and persisted to your Realm file. You *might* have more than one exam listed in there due to multiple runs of the playground— that's okay.

That concludes the code for your **1.0** app. Since this is the very first version of the app, there is no need to take care of any migration-related code at all. The goal was to create some data and migrate it in the next section.

App version 1.5

Next, you're going to simulate a run of the next version of the app, using a new schema, which is going to trigger a migration.

After the previous version's closure, add this:

```
// Simulate running the 1.5 version of the app,
// comment this one to simulate non-linear migration
Example.of("Run app ver. 1.5") {

}
```

You'll consider all code in the closure above to be the code base of your **1.5** app. A neat trick of this playground is that it'll play through all "versions" sequentially, so you can see how migrations happen from one version to the next.

Let's add some code to your **1.5** version (don't forget to insert this into the closure from above):

```
func migrationBlock(migration: Migration, oldVersion: UInt64) {

}

let conf = Realm.Configuration(
  schemaVersion: 2,
  migrationBlock: migrationBlock,
  objectTypes: [Exam.self, Mark.self])
let realm = try! Realm(configuration: conf)
```

This version uses a newer schema as compared to the previous app. This time, the code uses the version 2 schema, which has one change compared to schema 1 - a new class named `Mark` has been added to the Realm file:

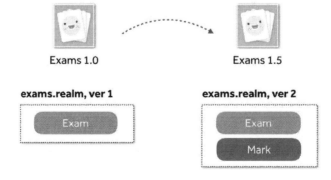

Since adding a new object is a change Realm handles automatically, you can leave the migration block empty. However, to make things more interesting, let's throw some custom migration logic in there.

Currently, the exams created by app 1.0 have an empty name value. You will address that while migrating your Realm to the next schema version and will set any empty exam names to "n/a".

Inside your migrationBlock(migration:oldVersion:) function, add:

```
if oldVersion < 2 {
  migrateFrom1To2(migration)
}
```

You confirm the oldVersion is 1, in which case you call a helper function named migrateFrom1to2(_). You might ask yourself: is there any need for that condition at all here? You'd be right by saying it's not very useful. But this kind of validation is part of a best practice pattern that will become obvious when you add additional schema versions later in this chapter.

You're still missing the migrateFrom1To2(_) helper function. Add it **outside** of the version 1.5 version code - you'll re-use this function later on, so you need it in the global scope of the playground. Append somewhere **at the top** of the playground:

```
func migrateFrom1To2(_ migration: Migration) {
  print("Migration from 1 to version 2")

}
```

As soon as the playground replays the code, you'll see that opening the Realm file with schema version 2 triggered the migration:

```
🛈 Run app ver. 1.0:
_____

Exams: [Exam {name: ""}]

🛈 Run app ver. 1.5:
_____

Migration from 1 to version 2
```

Finally, add the code to update broken Exam objects. Add to migrateFrom1To2(_):

```
migration.enumerateObjects(ofType:
  String(describing: Exam.self)) { from, to in
    guard let from = from,
          let to = to,
          let name = from[Exam.Property.name.rawValue] as?
```

```
    String,
            name.isEmpty else { return }

      to[Exam.Property.name.rawValue] = "n/a"
    }
```

You use `Migration.enumerateObjects(ofType:_:)` to iterate over all existing exams and find any in need of an update. Note how `from` and `to` are both optionals. Depending on the exact changes you performed on the schema, there might not be a corresponding object in either the old or new Realm.

For example, if you just added `Exam` in the latest scheme, `from` will always be `nil` since there won't be any exams in the existing file. Similarly, if you just removed `Exam`, the `to` parameter will always be `nil` since there won't be exams in the new file.

You use the code above to fetch the `name` property for each `Exam` object and check if it's empty via `name.isEmpty`. If the above `guard` statement was successful, you set the `name` of the target object to `"n/a"`.

To see the results of your new migration code, scroll to the code in the **1.5** closure — that's the closure you provide to `Example.of("Run app ver. 1.5")`, and append at the bottom of the closure just after `let realm = try! Realm(configuration: conf)`:

```
    print("Exams: \(Array(realm.objects(Exam.self)))")
    print("Marks: \(Array(realm.objects(Mark.self)))")
```

Once Realm opens the Realm file with the new schema version, this code will print the stored `Exam` and `Mark` objects:

```
  Run app ver. 1.0:
─────────────────────────────────────
Exams: [Exam {name: ""}]

  Run app ver. 1.5:
─────────────────────────────────────
migration from 1 to version 2
Exams: [Exam {name: "n/a"}]
Marks: []
```

You can see that the `Exam`, created in version `1.0` of the app with an empty name, has been successfully migrated and now has the default name of `"n/a"`. Exactly what you wanted all along. High five!

Add one last line to the closure, just after the two `prints`:

```
    try! realm.write {
      realm.add(Mark())
    }
```

The code adds a new empty `Mark` object to the Realm of version 1.5. This will give you something to migrate in the next version of your app.

App version 2.0

In this section of the chapter, you'll add one final version of your app to the playground.

This time though instead of adding or removing classes or properties the only change to the object schema will be to increase its number.

Why would you like to trigger another migration if there are no changes to the schema? The previous piece of code added to your 1.5 app creates some `Mark` objects with no values, which you'd like to fix in the new app version during the new migration.

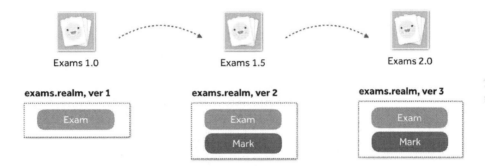

Look at the schema above for a moment. If your users always have the latest app version with each upgrade they will need to migrate from the previous version to the latest. However, some users might be a version or two behind - and you will also need to migrate their database schema correctly to the latest version.

That's why in your playground code you define your migration in sequential "steps", e.g. `migrateFrom1To2(_)` and `migrateFrom2To3(_)`. This way by checking what version the user has installed currently you can run sequentially all steps to migrate from the user's version to the current one.

The pattern in which you check for each version with series of `if oldVersion < X` conditions helps you run only the migration steps necessary for the current user. More about this you will learn in the next section of this chapter.

Start with adding the code for app version 2.0:

```
Example.of("Run app ver. 2.0") {
  func migrationBlock(migration: Migration, oldVersion: UInt64)
{
    if oldVersion < 2 {
      migrateFrom1To2(migration)
```

```
    }
  }

  let conf = Realm.Configuration(
    schemaVersion: 3,
    migrationBlock: migrationBlock,
    objectTypes: [Exam.self, Mark.self])
}
```

You simulate another run of the app and include all of the code you used in the previous version migration. The single change you might notice is the schemaVersion is set to 3 instead of 2.

All that's left is to add code to perform the migration from schema version 2 to version 3. Append **at the bottom** of the current migrationBlock(_):

```
if oldVersion < 3 {
  migrateFrom2to3(migration)
}
```

And next, just like before, you'll add the migration code in a free function in the global scope of the playground. Start by adding an empty stub somewhere towards the top of the playground:

```
func migrateFrom2to3(_ migration: Migration) {
  print("Migration from 2 to version 3")

}
```

What would the code for the migration from version 2 to version 3 look like? It'll actually be almost identical to the migration from version 1 to 2. Insert the following into your new migration function:

```
migration.enumerateObjects(ofType:
  String(describing: Mark.self)) { from, to in
    guard let from = from,
      let to = to,
      let mark = from[Mark.Property.mark.rawValue] as? String,
      mark.isEmpty else { return }

    to[Mark.Property.mark.rawValue] = "F"
}
```

This time around, you iterate over all Mark objects and set a default mark value for the broken records.

Go back to the closure of `Example.of("Run app ver. 2.0")` and append to the bottom of the code (just after defining the version 3 configuration):

```
let realm = try! Realm(configuration: conf)

print("Exams: \(Array(realm.objects(Exam.self)))")
print("Marks: \(Array(realm.objects(Mark.self)))")
```

This will re-open the existing database file, trigger a migration, and print the updated file contents. You should see the complete output in the console:

```
🛈 Run app ver. 1.0:
─────────────────────
Exams: [Exam {name: ""}]

🛈 Run app ver. 1.5:
─────────────────────
Migration from 1 to version 2
Exams: [Exam {name: "n/a"}]
Marks: []

🛈 Run app ver. 2.0:
─────────────────────
Migration from 2 to version 3
Exams: [Exam {name: "n/a"}]
Marks: [Mark {mark: "F"}]
```

The complete simulation of running the three app versions and the output after each successful migration demonstrates how you can apply your own custom logic to update the existing user schema and data when a new version of the app is out.

Linear vs. non-linear migrations

Now that your migration code is completed, let's take a moment to reflect on some of its design choices. In particular, the reasoning behind checking for the old version multiple times like so:

```
if oldVersion < 2 {
  migrateFrom1To2(migration)
}

if oldVersion < 3 {
  migrateFrom2to3(migration)
}
```

Checking for each version one after the other and performing each migration step **separately** lets you perform a combination of migration steps between non-consecutive versions of your app.

For example, if a user installs each version of the app (as the playground currently simulates), you always execute **just** the last step of the full migration sequence.

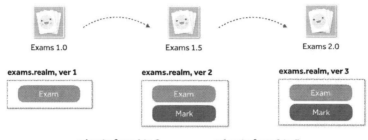

But what happens if the user had version `1.0`, didn't update for a while and got `2.0`? In that case she'll be skipping version `1.5`:

In the event the user has skipped a version, the migration will run through more of the steps to make up for the skipped migrations. In fact, you can simulate this in your playground as well!

Comment out the code that simulates the user running version `1.5` of the app and have a look at the console:

```
ℹ Run app ver. 1.0:

Exams: [Exam {name: ""}]

ℹ Run app ver. 2.0:
```

```
Migration from 1 to version 2
Migration from 2 to version 3
Exams: [Exam {name: "n/a"}]
Marks: []
```

When the user runs version `1.0`, the app creates the broken Exam object. Then the user runs version `2.0` which runs through both steps of the migration, first migrating to schema version 2, and then to schema version 3.

That concludes building your first schema migration! As said in the beginning of this chapter, building migrations is complicated, but you bravely pushed on. Well done!

In this chapter, you learned how to address schema changes as your app evolved. In the next chapter, you're going to work on a full project with three different app versions and delve further into the details of custom migrations, including building an interactive migration requiring optional user input.

Known issues

Last but not least, there are a few known limitations and issues with migrations in the current version of Realm which are worth noting:

- Lowering the schema version is not supported. If you try to specify a schema version lower than the one of the file on disk, you'll get an error thrown.

- Added properties don't have a default value applied. If you add a new property, e.g. `dynamic var title = "Default"`, all existing objects will get `title` added but its value will be an empty string instead of `"Default"`.

- Added primary keys aren't reflected in the new schema during migrations; the property is only marked as indexed. Once the migration has completed and Realm opens the file, the primary key is in place.

- Accessing a list of primitive types during a migration is not possible. Realm incorrectly casts lists to `List<DynamicObject>` which makes it impossible to access a list of non-Realm values primitives like `String`, `Int`, `Date`, etc.

Some of these are tracked as issues on Realm's GitHub repository and are likely to be addressed in future releases.

Challenges

Challenge 1: Adding another app version

In this quick challenge, add another app version to the playground: 2.5. Increase the object schema version to 4 and remove the Mark object from the schema. Use the proper Migration class method (mentioned earlier) to delete all meta information about Mark from the existing Realm file.

This should be a short and sweet challenge to warm you up for the next chapter where things will get more complicated as you navigate your migrations through some complex schema changes.

Chapter 12: Advanced Schema Migrations

In the previous chapter, "Chapter 11: Beginning Realm Migrations", you learned about migrations with Realm. Realm does a lot for you automatically but, you'll naturally want to implement some custom migration logic as well. After all, your app is a unique and special snowflake like no other so it's simply impossible for Realm to handle any possible migrations automatically.

You've previously worked on several migrations in a playground. You learned a lot about the `Migration` class and built a migration strategy for updating a Realm schema across several versions of your app. However, you can only do so much in a playground — so get ready for the real thing!

In this chapter, you're going to build a more complex migration in an Xcode project. The demo is designed in such a way that you can build three different versions of the same app. This will allow you to write code and simulate real-life app upgrades, all from the comfort of a single Xcode project.

Getting started

As this project is more complex than others in this book, it requires a little walkthrough before you get to write any code.

Open the starter project folder for this chapter and run `pod install` as usual to install the dependencies. Then open the project workspace in Xcode and peek around!

First of all, have a look at the Scheme selector towards the top of Xcode's window:

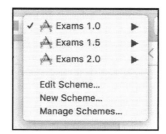

The three available schemes build the three different versions of the Exams app. The **Exams 1.0** scheme builds version `1.0` of of the app, **Exams 1.5** builds version `1.5`, and so on.

> **Note:** There's no magic behind the version selector. Each scheme defines a compile-time flag which enables or disables different pieces of code in your project. This way, the project can decide which pieces of code belong in each version of the app.

You can easily track which files change from version to version by looking in the **AppVersions** folder. It includes three subfolders where the changed files for each version reside:

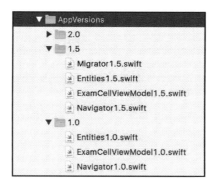

The files changed between versions are:

- **EntitiesX.X.swift**: Includes the Realm objects used in each app version.

- **MigratorX.X.swift**: Includes the migration code as it evolves across versions.

- **ExamCellViewModelX.X.swift**: Features the exam table cell view model which uses the Realm object to display information on screen.

- **NavigatorX.X.swift**: Features a central navigator class for the app.

Exams 1.0

To see what the app looks like, make sure that you've selected the Exams 1.0 scheme like so:

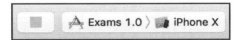

Then run the project:

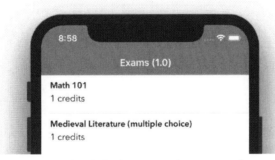

Version 1.0 creates two exams by default so users have some data to play with when they initially launch the app. The list displays the name of the exam and how many credits the exam good is for.

Open **AppVersions/1.0/Entities1.0.swift** to inspect the Realm schema for version 1.0 of the app.

Exams 1.0

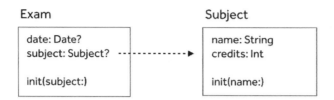

The object schema is fairly straightforward, especially to an expert such as yourself. In general, this project follows the structure of the rest of the projects in this book: you'll find the view controller and view model in **Scenes**, the Exams data model is in the **Models** folder, while RealmProvider and Path, that you know from before, are located in **Classes**.

Of course, since this is a chapter about migrations, version 1.0 of your app won't be that interesting for you, would it? The next version, 1.5, is where you can implement a schema migration, so I bet you've already eyeballed that scheme in the drop down menu.

Exams 1.5

Let's look at the next version of the app: 1.5. Your new version will feature two improvements:

- A user can mark an exam as passed.

- A user can separate multiple choice exams.

Start by selecting the correct Exams 1.5 scheme from the Scheme selector and trigger a build, as it might take a few moments to complete:

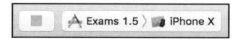

Updating the app code

Let's start by adding a couple of new properties to the Exam class to accommodate for the new features you're going to build. Open **AppVersions/1.5/Entities1.5.swift** and find the Exam class.

Add two new cases to the Exam.Property enumeration so it contains four cases in total, like so:

```
enum Property: String {
   case date, subject, result, isMultipleChoice
}
```

Then, add the two new properties to the class:

```
dynamic var result: String?
dynamic var isMultipleChoice = false
```

You add isMultipleChoice which is false by default, and an optional result where you can store the result of the exam as a free-form text.

Your object schema with the changes highlighted in green, is as follows:

Exams 1.5

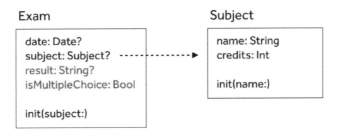

Scroll down and find the exams provider. It already features the updated version 2 schema and sets a migration block: Migrator.migrate.

Migrator is a new struct introduced in version 1.5 of the app. Open **AppVersions/1.5/ Migrator1.5.swift** to find its currently-empty implementation.

Before you get to building the migration logic, you need to update the app's UI with the new features. That'll give you a moment to better understand how the object schema changes will work in the new app version.

Open **AppVersions/1.5/ExamCellViewModel1.5.swift** to make some changes.

Add a new property to store the relevant exam:

```
let exam: Exam
```

Then, insert after the `guard` statement in `init(exam:)`:

```
self.exam = exam
```

And replace:

```
title = subject.name
```

With:

```
title = (exam.isMultipleChoice ? "⊠ ": "")
  .appending(subject.name)
  .appending(exam.result != nil ? "(\(exam.result!))": "")
```

Your view model now supports all of the new properties in the Exam class. Instead of adding `"multiple choice"` to the name of the subject (which was wrong to begin with), you now add a little icon in front of multiple choice exams. Additionally, if the user has already taken the exam, you display the result in brackets after the exam name.

Currently, Xcode complains about your `guard` statement missing an initialization of the exam property. To make it happy, add inside your `guard` (just before the `return`):

```
self.exam = exam
```

Finally, you'll make an additional change to the view model, and update the exam's status when the user taps the corresponding table row. The view controller calls `setExamSelected()` on the view model when the exam is tapped. Find `setExamsSelected` in your view model and replace its contents with:

```
guard exam.result == nil,
      let realm = exam.realm else { return false }

try! realm.write {
  exam.result = "I've passed the exam!"
}

return true
```

This will update the exam and set its `result` to `"I've passed the exam!"`.

With that, version `1.5` of your app is feature-complete, with only the schema migration left to code.

Adding the migration code

Open **AppVersions/1.5/Migrator1.5.swift** and add to the `migrate(migration:oldVersion:)` method:

```
if oldVersion < 2 {
  print("Migrate to Realm Schema 2")

  let multipleChoiceText = " (multiple choice)"
  enum Key: String { case isMultipleChoice, subject, name }
}
```

You start by adding the first step in what's going to be a cascaded multi-app migration code.

Additionally, inside the `if` body, you add some constants you'll need during the migration from schema 1 to schema 2.

The `Key` enumeration lists all object keys you're going to access or modify. You might be wondering what the point is to define `Key.isMultipleChoice` since you already have an `Exam.Property.isMultipleChoice` constant.

Well, think about it this way. You do have an `Exam.isMultipleChoice` property in this version of the app, but would you have it in the next version? Who knows?

You are welcome to use property names defined within their respective class, but its more convenient to declare the constants separately within the migration code to keep migration logic free from external dependencies.

Next, you'll add some code to iterate over all exams and migrate their data. Append inside the `if` statement:

```
var migratedExamCount = 0

migration.enumerateObjects(
  ofType: String(describing: Exam.self)) { _, newExam in

}

print("Schema 2: Migrated \(migratedExamCount) exams")
```

You'll count the exams being migrated and print that information to the console. In a real-life app, you'd add this to a log file or send it along with some anonymous stats as a useful insight into how successful your migration strategy was.

Now, for the real data update, insert into `enumerateObjects'` closure:

```
guard let newExam = newExam,
  let subject = newExam[Key.subject.rawValue] as?
MigrationObject,
    let subjectName = subject[Key.name.rawValue] as? String
  else { return }
```

This unwraps the new Exam object, traverses its `subject` relationship, and finally fetches the subject name as `subjectName`. You can now simply check if the name contains `"(multiple choice)"` and update the exam object if necessary. Add:

```
if subjectName.contains(multipleChoiceText) {
  newExam[Key.isMultipleChoice.rawValue] = true
  subject[Key.name.rawValue] = subjectName
    .replacingOccurrences(of: multipleChoiceText, with: "")
}

migratedExamCount += 1
```

You set the new `isMultipleChoice` property to `true` and remove the now unneeded text from the subject's name. Finally, you increase the enumerated objects counter for your stats.

The code above showcases how you can traverse object relationships during a migration, but to do that, you need to attempt to cast them to the type you expect them to be. The migration class, as explained in the previous chapter, isn't able to provide you with the previous versions of your classes, so you'll access all of your data as basic dictionaries.

Running the migration

It's time to try your new migration! Make sure you've selected version `1.5` of the app and run the project.

You should see the output of your `print` statements in the console like so:

```
Migrate to Realm Schema 2
Schema 2: Migrated 2 exams
```

Looking at the Simulator, your UI should reflect your schema changes:

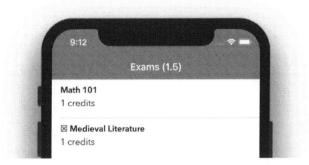

Tap the first row and notice the exam being updated with its new status:

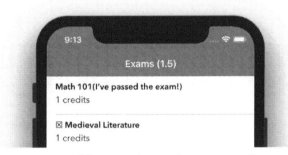

This looks like one very successful app update and migration. Congratulations!

Just as a friendly reminder, you can open the Realm in Realm Studio and confirm that the data looks as expected:

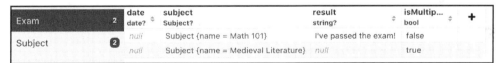

Exam	2	date date?	subject Subject?	result string?	isMultip... bool	+
Subject	2	*null*	Subject {name = Math 101}	I've passed the exam!	false	
		null	Subject {name = Medieval Literature}	*null*	true	

Exams 2.0

We saved the greatest challenge for last. It's time for Exams v2.0!

In the third version of the app, you'll replace the free-form, String `result` property of the Exam class and use a separate Realm model to store each exam's result. The idea is to have some pre-defined `Result` objects in the database such as `"fail"`, `"pass"`, and `"pending"` so you can better group and/or filter the exams in the database.

That's a pretty good design decision in general, but there's a little problem that you need to take care of before popping the champagne: you need to migrate the existing free-form property `result` to the new schema. This task is a bit tricky, as matching *any* free-form text to a group of pre-defined results can be a crapshoot.

In fact, this task is so non-trivial that you're going to need the help of the *user themself* to complete it. In the last section of this chapter, you're going to develop a simple **interactive migration**; you'll migrate as many objects as you can through the code, but should your migration not be able to figure out how to migrate some exams, you'll launch a custom migration UI and ask the user to complete the migration manually.

Realm does not offer a built-in way to create interactive migrations, so it's up to you to create any sort of custom UI and logic you'd need to get the required information to complete your migration.

> **Note**: The interactive migration you'll build in this section does **not** use Realm's standard migration. What you're about to build is a completely custom solution tailor-made for the context of your application. It might serve as inspiration in your own projects, as this approach could serve well in other migrations.

The plan is to complete all changes Realm can automatically take care of in a migration block, and drive the user into a separate workflow to conclude the remaining migration tasks:

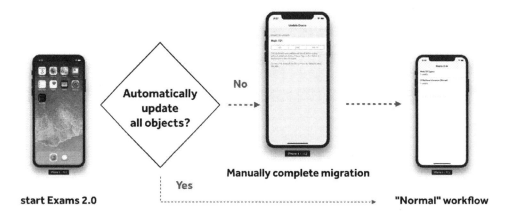

To get to a scenario where you *can't* update all exams automatically, you'll create a default `Result` of `"Not set"` and assign it to all `Exam` objects that don't have a free-form result assigned.

For all exams with some text-based result (whatever it may be), you'll ask the user to choose from the supported options list: `"fail"`, `"pass"`, or `"not set"`.

> **Note**: Keep in mind that an interactive migration like the one you're going to build should be your last resort. Having an interactive migration after all other migration steps are performed might make non-linear migrations in your app even more difficult to design and code.

Let's get started!

Updating the app code

Start by selecting the correct scheme from the Scheme selector:

> **Note**: Don't mind the build errors which would popup while you're adjusting the schema, you'll clear them all before running the app.

The changes you did to the entity classes in `1.5` are already included in the source code for version `2.0` to save you some typing. You're welcome!

You can start adding some code to cover the new features of version `2.0`. Open **AppVersions/2.0/Entities2.0.swift** and scroll to the Exam class. Replace:

```
dynamic var result: String?
```

With:

```
dynamic var passed: Result?
```

Once you make this change, rename `result` to `passed` in the `Exam.Property` enumeration as well, so it looks like this:

```
enum Property: String {
   case id, date, subject, passed, isMultipleChoice
}
```

The `Result` class will be pretty simple. Start by getting the basics in. Above your `RealmProvider` code, add:

```
@objcMembers final class Result: Object {
    enum Property: String { case result }
    enum Value: String { case notSet = "Not set", pass, fail }

    dynamic var result = ""

    override static func primaryKey() -> String? {
        return Result.Property.result.rawValue
    }
}
```

`Result` has a single text property called `result` which is also the primary key; nothing too crazy in my book. Continue by adding a helper method to create the three default `Result` objects.

Add to your `Result` class:

```
static func initialData() -> [[String: String]] {
    return [Value.notSet, Value.pass, Value.fail]
        .map { [Property.result.rawValue: $0.rawValue] }
}
```

`initialData()` creates three dictionaries needed to create the initial Realm objects. You might be confused by the fact that you're not specifying any Realm to be used here; this is because this code will be called from inside a Migration block, where a Realm instance isn't available.

In your new migration, you'll use the data from `Result.initialData()` to create the relevant migration objects and add them to the migration to be made available in the final migrated Realm file and during your custom interactive migration as well.

The code that's already in **AppVersions/2.0/Entities2.0.swift** includes yet another new class: `MigrationTask`.

This is a new Realm object to be added to version `2.0` of the app's object schema. You'll use it to persist uncompleted custom interactive migration tasks to your Realm file. Your automatic migration will go somewhat like this:

1. Automatically migrate all exams without a `result` value.

2. In case there are exams to migrate manually, create a `MigrationTask` with type of `askForExamResults`.

3. When the app starts, check for any pending migration tasks in the Realm file.

4. In case there are pending tasks, show the custom UI for the relevant task before moving on to the main app UI.

`MigrationTask` features several handy methods that wrap a lot of the logic in order to make your migration code a bit more readable:

- `create(task:in:)`: Creates a new object in a given migration instance.

- `first(in:)`: Returns a pending task in a given Realm, if exists.

- `complete()`: Removes the task object from its Realm when its completed.

The final `2.0` app object schema looks like this, with changes highlighted in green:

Exams 2.0

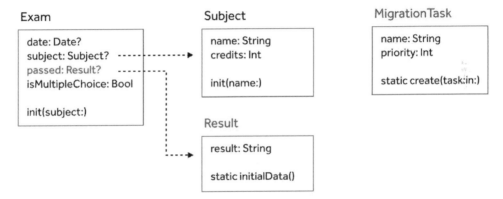

That wraps up the changes to `2.0`'s data entities, but there's still one more tiny issue to fix before moving on. You need to change one line of code in the exam table cell view model before the project will compile successfully.

Open **AppVersions/2.0/ExamCellViewModel2.0.swift** and find this line (it's easy — it's the one with a compile error):

```
.appending(exam.result != nil ? "(\(exam.result!))": "")
```

Replace the code with:

```
.appending(exam.passed != nil ? " (\(exam.passed!.result))": "")
```

Adding the migration code

Let's head to the `Migrator` class for version `2.0` and add start with the automatic migration code.

Open **AppVersion/2.0/Migrator2.0.swift**. The class includes the migration code from object schema 1 to 2. You'll add the code to migrate schema 2 to 3. At the bottom of `migrate(migration:oldVersion:)`, append:

```
if oldVersion < 3 {
  enum Key: String { case result, passed }
  var isInteractiveMigrationNeeded = false
}
```

You prepare for the migration by defining all keys you'll need to access, namely `result` and `passed`. This time around, you'll get to appreciate defining migration-specific key constants; `Exam.Property.result` doesn't exist anymore, as you removed it in this app version, but you still need this key's name to access its value from the "old" realm.

> **Note**: You'll face similar issues down the road if you remove `passed` in a later version of your schema. In general, removing properties or making other destructive changes makes migrations difficult. That's also the reason why it's important to be able to test all steps of your migrations in a similar fashion to how this project is structured.

Next, some code to create the pre-defined results. Append inside the new migration's `if`:

```
let results = Result.initialData().map {
  return migration.create(String(describing: Result.self),
value: $0)
}
let noResult = results.first!
```

You use the `Migration.create(_:value:)` method mentioned in the previous chapter to create a new record in the migration using a provided dictionary (or another data object). The created object will be merged into the finalized Realm as the migration completes.

You also grab a reference to the newly created default result.

Next, iterate over all Exam objects:

```
let examClassName = String(describing: Exam.self)

migration.enumerateObjects(
  ofType: examClassName) { oldExam, newExam in
  guard let oldExam = oldExam, let newExam = newExam else
{ return }

}
```

Inside the enumerateObjects(ofType:_:) closure, add code to either update an object or skip it:

```
if schema(migration.oldSchema,
    includesProperty: Key.result.rawValue, for: examClassName),
    oldExam[Key.result.rawValue] as? String != nil {
      isInteractiveMigrationNeeded = true
} else {
    newExam[Key.passed.rawValue] = noResult
}
```

You start by using the schema(_:includesProperty:for:) helper defined at the top of the file to check if the the old schema has a Results.result property at all. In case the user is migrating from 1.0 to 2.0 directly, they never had a chance to set any custom results, as object schema 1 does not have a Exam.result property.

In case there's an Exam.result property in the old schema and it's set to a String of some sort (oldExam[Key.result.rawValue] as? String isn't nil), you set the isInteractiveMigrationNeeded flag to true to let the user choose from the pre-defined list of results.

Finally, after enumerateObjects(ofType:_:)'s closure, check whether there's any need for manual migration. (It's important you add this code after the enumeration block.) If so, create a new migration task:

```
if isInteractiveMigrationNeeded {
    MigrationTask.create(task: .askForExamResults, in: migration)
}
```

This creates a new task object and adds it to the migration. Once Realm's migration is completed, you can check for pending tasks and show your custom migration UI and logic if needed.

Adding the interactive migration

The best place to implement the custom logic that displays your interactive migration UI is in the Navigator class. The role of this class in the Exams project is to only display the main app's UI — but you're about to change that.

Open **AppVersion/2.0/Navigator2.0.swift** and add a new class extension:

```
extension Navigator {
  func navigateToMigrationExamStatus(_ ctr:
UINavigationController) {
    let migrateExamsVC = MigrateExamStatusViewController
      .createWith { [weak self] in
        self?.navigateToMainScene()
```

```
        }
    ctr.setViewControllers([migrateExamsVC], animated: true)
  }
}
```

`navigateToMigrationExamStatus(_)` instantiates the
`MigrateExamStatusViewController` view controller and presents it on screen using
the provided navigation controller. `createWith(_)` takes a callback closure, which will
be invoked when the user taps **Done** on that screen. When that happens, you'll simply
want to pass back the control to the main navigation flow and prepare to present the
main scene.

Let's continue by adjusting `navigateToMainScene()` to look for pending migration
tasks. Insert into `navigateToMainScene()` right after the `guard` statement:

```
if let migrationTask = MigrationTask.first(in:
RealmProvider.exams.realm) {
  switch migrationTask.name {
  case MigrationTask.TaskType.askForExamResults.rawValue:
    navigateToMigrationExamStatus(controller)
    return
  default: break
  }
  return
}
```

This condition checks if there are any pending migration tasks, and if one is found, it
switches over its `name` property. In case a `askForExamResults` task was found, you call
`navigateToMigrationExamStatus(_)` to show the custom UI to migrate exam results.

This approach has some not-so-obvious features:

- If the user kills the app during a custom migration, the next time they start `Exams`,
  they'll still be presented with the migration UI.

- If there's more than a single pending migration task, their UI will be presented
  sequentially before the user reaches the main app UI.

- `MigrationTask.first(in:)` completely wraps the logic of fetching the next task so
  it can order tasks by priority, or perform any other decisions on how to proceed with
  the migration.

The custom migration UI is already included in the starter project. You can find its code
in **AppVersion/2.0/InteractiveMigrations**. There's a separate storyboard file, and a view
controller/view model pair to handle the UI.

Running the migration

Let's finally run the 2.0 app and see the migration in action.

Before running the app, make sure at least one of the exams has a custom result by tapping a table row while running version 1.5.

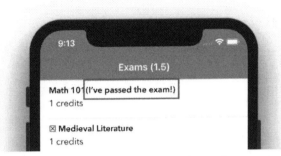

Since having a custom exam result is the trigger condition for your interactive migration, you can also double check in Realm Studio that you have a record like this one:

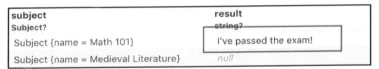

subject Subject?	result ~~string?~~
Subject {name = Math 101}	I've passed the exam!
Subject {name = Medieval Literature}	*null*

Now run version 2.0 and you should promptly see the custom migration view controller found in **Migrations.storyboard**:

At this point, the file contents will have results set for exams that had no result before:

subject Subject?	isMultip... bool ⇕	passed Result?
Subject {name = Math 101}	false	*null*
Subject {name = Medieval Literature}	true	Result {result = Not set}

One by one, you can complete the interactive migration by selecting one of the options ("Fail", "Pass" or "Not Set") for every exam. Once the list is empty, you'll see a **Done** button appear in the top-right of your navigation bar.

When you tap **Done**, the view model will complete the migration task and call its completion callback, presenting the main scene:

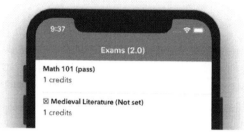

The next time you launch the app, the entire migration workflow won't happen at all, since Navigator won't find any migration tasks in the Realm file.

This concludes a deep-dive into Realm migrations over two entire chapters. By now, you know almost everything there is to know about migrating your data like a pro. Migrations can be difficult to design, since there's no common pattern to follow. The philosophy of migrations is reactive in nature, since you always end up designing a migration in response to the object schema changes you've made in the newer version of the app.

But let's be honest here — isn't your fully-migrated version of the app worth the effort? Of course it is!

Challenges

Challenge 1: Improve automatic result assignment

To complete the final migration for the Exams app, add code to check what free-form text result was assigned to each exam object, and whether it includes key words like "pass" or "fail", and if so, automatically assign one of the predefined results to avoid a manual interactive migration.

Section VI:Realm Cloud

Last but not least, you will learn how to enable automatic, real-time data-sync in your iOS application by leveraging the awesome powers of Realm Cloud.

Chapter 14: Real-Time Sync with Realm Cloud

In this last chapter, you will learn more about Realm Platform and take Realm Cloud for a test drive. You will develop a real, working chat app so you can chat with yourself (how sad!) or with your friends (yay!) using Realm Cloud as your backend.

Chapter 14: Real-Time Sync with Realm Cloud

In the very first chapter of this book, you learned about the two Realm products **Realm Database** and **Realm Platform**. While this book largely covers the Realm Database, we thought it would be a neat bonus to take a quick dip into Realm Platform as well.

Realm Platform is a server software which offers a multi-platform data syncing solution for applications using the Realm Database. If your app uses Realm Database, you can connect to a server with a few lines of code and get real-time data flowing across any connected devices that are running your app:

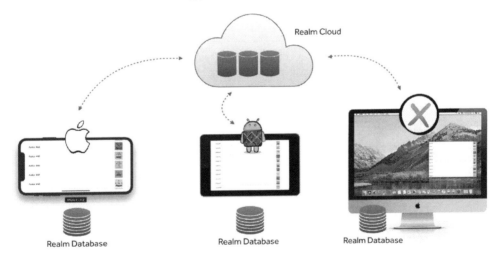

The Realm Platform has many benefits over similar solutions for manual synchronization:

- **Automatic data sync**: Realm takes care of keeping the server connection alive and synchronizes any data changes as needed.

- **Real-time two-way sync**: Realm does more than merely push up your local changes to its cloud; it also syncs down any changes *as they happen* in the cloud, across all devices and platforms.

- **No data conversions**: You don't have to fiddle with JSON, `Codable`, or other data transformations. You have the same database on your mobile device as you do in your cloud. When fetching from the Realm API, you'll get the synchronized data seamlessly from the server.

- **No conflicts**: Since you have Realm as your end-to-end data infrastructure, it can take extra care to avoid any synchronization conflicts.

- **Multi-platform real-time sync**: You can connect your iPhone, Android, tvOS, or macOS apps to the same server instance, and your users will instantly have their data on all of their devices across these platforms.

- **Self-hosted or PaaS**: You can either start lean by connecting to Realm Cloud which is already hosted, or you can self-host Realm Platform on your own infrastructure and have full access to your data, in-house.

The benefits of using Realm Platform are clearly numerous and the list above includes only covers a few of them. In fact, Realm Platform is so feature-rich that it could take an entire book to cover everything.

In this chapter, you'll get started with Realm Cloud and learn how to apply your existing Realm Database skills to develop an iOS chat application. This should put you on the right path with Realm Platform and leave you with the toolset needed to dive deeper at will.

Getting started with Realm Cloud

Realm Platform is Realm's realtime-sync server solution. You can purchase a software license and install the platform on your own in-house infrastructure, which usually works well for larger enterprises that have already developed server infrastructure and have the staff to run it.

In this chapter, you're going to look at the hosted Realm Platform solution called **Realm Cloud**. With Realm Cloud, you can get started in just a few minutes with a free account and pay for what you use when you go live in production.

As you might've guessed, your code will remain unchanged regardless if you're using the hosted version, or self-hosting on your own infrastructure which lets you scale up in the future if you ever need to do so.

Creating a Realm Cloud account

Note: Realm Cloud has just been launched at the time of this writing, so there might be minor differences between the screenshots and terminology included in the book .

You'll start by creating a free Realm Cloud account:

https://cloud.realm.io

You can sign up by providing either an email address or your GitHub account:

Once you create your account and log into Realm Cloud, you'll be presented with some welcome information. Skip that for now and click **Create New Instance**. This will create a new server instance and get you connected right away.

Realm Cloud offers a random name to speed up the process, much as you might be familiar with in Heroku. It might look funny at first, but its quite the time-saver for this chapter.

Create New Instance

Instance name

Rustic Wooden Towels

Confirm the creation of the server instance by clicking **Create New Instance** and give the service a few moments to spin up a new server. Once the activity indicator stops animating, you'll see the URL to your new Realm Platform server, like so:

Rustic Wooden Towels

Open in Studio   https://rustic-wooden-towels-bar.us1a.cloud.realm.io   Copy

You're done! You can now connect to your new server. Click on **Open in Studio**. Realm Studio, which has been your trusty companion throughout this book, will open on your computer and ask you to authorize it with Realm Cloud. You should then see your server's dashboard:

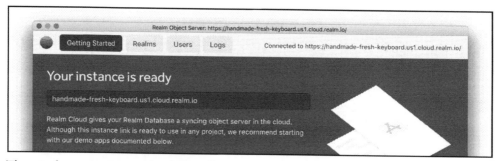

The window contains much of the information you need for your day-to-day work with your instance of Realm Platform:

- **Getting Started**: Contains your server address and links to tutorials to get started on different platforms.

- **Realms**: A list of all Realms stored on your server. This tab is where you can see all synced databases, open any database and inspect its contents, modify data on the server in real-time, and even add new objects or properties to the object schema.

- **Users**: Lets you create different users and passwords that are authorized to access your Realms. By default, you can connect anonymously to the server, but for production purposes you'd definitely want to set up some user accounts.

- **Logs**: Lets you inspect your server's logs directly from Realm Studio.

Click on **Logs** and check the activity on your brand new server so far:

```
❶ Autocreated admin token user: __admin
❶ Autocreated admin user: realm-admin
❶ Realm Object Server has started and is listening on http://0.0.0.0:9080
```

The server has been started and is listening for connections on port **9080**. Additionally, Realm Cloud created an admin user named **realm-admin**. You can use this user to manage the server, manage user access, and more.

For your app to connect to the server, you'll also need to create a non-admin user. Click **Users** and then **Create new user**. In the popup dialog, enter **chatuser** as the username and **chatuser** as the password.

Finally, click on **Create user** and you'll see your new user listed:

PROVIDER ID(S)	USER ID	ROLE
chatuser	85c4e20c4bbdc60d92518...	Regular user

While you're dealing with user access, open https://cloud.realm.io one more time and click on your server instance.

You'll be presented with several options, namely **Dashboard** and **Settings**. Tap on the **Settings** option where you'll see several authentication mechanism your Realm server can use:

Authentication	
Nickname	Enabled ∨
Anonymous	Enabled ∨
JWT	Disabled ∨
Username / Password	Enabled ∨

To secure your server instance, disable the **Nickname** and **Anonymous** authentication mechanisms. In this chapter, you'll only authenticate with a username/password pair so it's best to disable any unused authentication mechanisms.

Just one final point of interest on this drive-by tour of Realm Cloud: switch back to Realm Studio and click on the **Realms** tab. You should see a single Realm Database called **default** owned by *nobody*:

PATH	OWNER
/default	*nobody*

This database has been automatically created on your server so you can have a Realm to work with right off the bat. In fact, this default synced database is the server counterpart of the default local configuration — the one pointing to a **default.realm** file in your app's **Documents** folder.

You also just got a glimpse of one of Realm's powerful features: database access levels. Depending on the credentials you used to connect to the server, you are granted different privileges:

- **Admin users**: Can access and modify all files on the server.

- **Regular users**: Can create, access and modify files in their private user folder. Additionally, they can be invited by other users to collaborate on shared files. These users can also access files owned by the *nobody* user.

In this chapter, you'll use your **chatuser** user to connect to your instance and sync data from the **default** shared database.

With authentication behind us, let's talk about how you'd go about synchronizing your Realm server to your app's Realm data.

Accessing synced data

You have two different ways to open a synced Realm from your server:

- Sync the entire database from the server.

- Sync portions of a Realm database in real-time *only* when that data is needed by the app.

The first option simply "clones" a Realm from the server and keeps it synced with the client. This option is interesting, but not usually practical since syncing an entire database isn't the most efficient approach.

The second option, also known as **Partial Sync**, is what you're going to be using in this chapter. Partial sync is a very clever solution to real-time data synchronization.

It might be a difficult concept to grasp at first, but let's create a simple analogy to help you understand what it does and how it works.

Local notification subscription

You've used Realm notifications throughout the projects in this book. They work by providing you with an initial snapshot of a Realm collection and then provide consecutive updates as the collection changes.

Using this data, you can drive your app's UI like so:

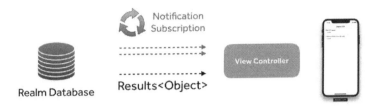

You use two distinct objects for this setup:

- **Results<Object>**, which gives you access to the result set you're interested in on-demand.

- **A notification subscription** via a NotificationToken, which pushes updates when the data in the collection changes in any way.

For example, you can fetch all User objects that have a name beginning with the letter J, access these objects in your result set and display them on screen:

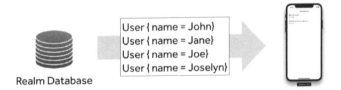

Remote sync subscription

That was pretty simple, wasn't it? The great news is that partial sync works in a very similar way.

You use two distinct classes here:

- **Results<Object>** to query your **local database** for some records of interest.

- **SyncSubscription<Object>**, which behaves very similarly to local notification subscriptions. While the subscription is active, any changes to the records will be synced up to *and* down from the server.

As soon as you invalidate the subscription, the locally cached data will be removed.

For example, if you create a `Results<User>` and **query** for all objects with a name starting with the letter J, your partially-synced database will initially return an empty result set.

When you **subscribe** to that same result set, Realm will immediately fetch any objects from the server that match your query and store them in your local Realm so you can work with them as you would with any local Realm records. Not only that, but if anyone added a new `User` either on the server or from a different client connected to the same Realm Cloud server, the changes will be reflected in your local database and you'll receive a change notification just as you'd expect for the newly inserted match.

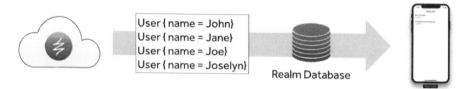

Partial sync requires a bit of a mind shift compared to working with a local Realm. You need to plan ahead to know which objects and queries you'll turn on or off, but the workflow itself remains largely the same.

The leap to building synced Realm apps isn't conceptual, but evolutionary; you'll find that this chapter's project is using many of the patterns you've gotten to know so well working through this book.

With this quick intro to partial sync, you're all set. Your server is set up and running, and you can get started with this chapter's project: **CloudChatterz**!

Getting started with CloudChatterz

CloudChatterz is another iteration of the chat app you worked on in Chapter 6, "Notifications and Reactive Apps". Instead of a mocked networking API like before, you'll simply connect your app to Realm Cloud and work with an actual live backend.

To get started, open the macOS Terminal app (or another similar app of your choice), navigate to the current chapter's starter project folder, run `pod install` and open the newly created Xcode workspace.

The project includes plenty of UI-related code and some Realm code that you don't need to work through for the thousandth time by now. You'll start by immediately connecting to Realm Cloud and getting real-time data sync running.

The project features three different scenes:

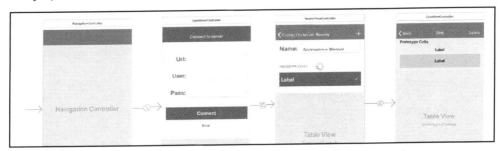

- **Login**: This is where you enter a server URL, username, and password to connect to your cloud. These are mostly pre-filled for the user.

- **Rooms**: This is where you set your chat nickname and choose a chat room to join to. Alternatively, you can start your own new chat room.

- **Chat**: This is where you, well... *chat*! You can see real-time messages from others in here and reply to them as well.

The object schema that's already part of your starter code includes three objects:

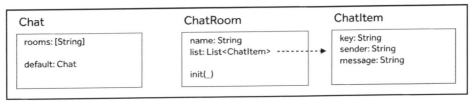

The odd part in this object schema is that `Chat` includes a list of all room names instead of linking directly to a collection of `ChatRoom` objects. This is not how you've created relationships so far in the book, so why was that design decision made?

When the app first starts you will synchronize the `Chat` object *only*. This will give you the list of available chat room names and whenever the user decides to join a room and chat to others, only then you will fetch that specific `Room` object and the messages it contains.

Synced realm provider

Just like previous chapters, you'll use a central struct called `RealmProvider` that provides you with access to your app's Realm. Open **Entities/RealmProvider.swift** and peek in.

For this project, the server URL, username and password will be included in your code. Find inside your `ServerConfig` struct the line `static let host = ""` and replace the empty string with the URL of your Realm Cloud instance as displayed in the Realm Studio Dashboard:

There is a single predefined provider named `chat`. Its configuration is pretty simple:

```
let chatConfig = SyncConfiguration.automatic()
```

`SyncConfiguration.automatic()` returns a pre-configured `Realm.Configuration` struct that points to the **default** database on the currently connected server. The default database will suffice for this chapter's project. Should you want a custom URL on the server or to use multiple synced files, look into `SyncConfiguration`'s docs.

There is one significant change compared to your usual provider struct in previous projects. Instead of a computed `realm` property, you have a `realm(callback:)` method.

`realm(callback:)` is currently empty though, so this will be your first step in building this project. Insert inside the `realm(callback:)` method:

```
Realm.asyncOpen(configuration: configuration, callback:
callback)
```

`Realm.asyncOpen(configuration:callback:)` lets you asynchronously open a remote Realm; you merely wrap Realm's own API to mimic the `realm` property you are used to from previous chapters.

Connecting and logging in

Run the project and you'll be presented with the login scene:

The text fields and the button are already connected to `LoginViewController`, so you'll only need to add the actual server authentication code.

Open **LoginViewController.swift** and add to `login(_)`:

```
let credentials = SyncCredentials.usernamePassword(
  username: user, password: pass)

SyncUser.logIn(with: credentials,
  server: server,
  timeout: 5.0) { [weak self] user, error in
    self?.serverDidRespond(user: user, error: error)
}
```

`SyncCredentials` provides factory methods to create connection credentials by using different authentication methods. For example `usernamePassword(username:password:)` creates a set of credentials by logging in with a username/password pair, `anonymous()` creates an anonymous connection credential, and so on.

Once you've created the credentials, you use `SyncUser.login(with:server:timeout:completion:)` to attempt to login to your Realm Cloud instance. Realm connects and returns either a validated user or error in the provided closure.

If you get back a user object, it means you've connected and you can start syncing data. In the code above, you simply call `serverDidRespond(user:error:)` which takes the user to the next scene — the chat room list — upon a successful login.

Believe it or not, that's all the code you need to connect to your cloud database server. Run the project another time, click on **Connect** and you'll see the next scene:

Adding a Partial Sync subscription

At this point, you don't know if there's any data stored on the server. You might as well be the very first user running the app, so the server database might not exist at all. Just like a local Realm, the server will create an empty Realm if you try to open one that doesn't exist.

The current project's database schema is designed so you can iteratively explore the data persisted on the server. The Chat Realm object contains a list of the available room names. When the user wants to join a given chat room, you'll start syncing that given ChatRoom object but *not* the other objects.

This way, your app will lazily sync the data the user needs at that point. The remote database could potentially store *thousands* of chat rooms with even more messages in each of these rooms, so it makes sense to sync just the room the user is interested chatting in.

In this section, you'll learn how to get the list of chat room names and display them to the user.

Open **RoomsViewController.swift** and add two new properties to the class:

```
private var chatSync: SyncSubscription<Chat>?
private var chatSubscription: NotificationToken?
```

chatSync is a SyncSubscription, which is the piece that creates the dynamic, real-time sync connection for a given data set to the server. chatSubscription is a NotificationToken that will aid you in receiving notifications about the state of the sync connection.

The code in viewWillAppear(_) already uses the Realm provider to asynchronously get a Realm instance. The default configuration you used for the chat provider gets the default logged-in user and handles all connection, authorization, and file URL details automatically. In the end, you simply call your own realm() method and you get a Realm instance returned in the closure:

```
RealmProvider.chat.realm { realm, error in

  ... use the realm object here ...

}
```

There's already some code inside the closure that takes care of storing the Realm instance in a view controller property and calls fetchRooms(in:), where you'll add your own code to fetch the actual room names.

Add to `fetchRooms(in:)`:

```
chatSync = realm.objects(Chat.self).subscribe()
chatSubscription = chatSync?.observe(\.state, options: .initial)
{ [weak self] state in
  guard let this = self, state == .complete else { return }
  this.spinner.stopAnimating()
}
```

With these few lines you start a live connection to the server:

- You query your local database for `Chat` objects and call `subscribe()` on the query to start syncing that local result set with the remote database.

- You then observe the `state` property on the sync subscription. When the state becomes `complete`, it means all matching objects (if any) from the server has been synced down to your local database.

Once the initial sync has completed, you can work with your local database as usual. If any other users add a new chat room on the server, you'll instantly get that change synced locally as well using the same subscription.

You can now add notification handling code just as you would with a local Realm in order to show the room names and to update the list whenever there are changes, regardless of whether those changes were made by yourself or by a remote entity such as the server, or a different user. The `RoomsViewController` class already includes the `roomNames` and `roomNamesSubscription` properties for you.

Add inside the `observe(...)` closure you just added:

```
this.roomNames = Chat.default(in: realm).rooms
this.roomNamesSubscription = this.roomNames?.observe { changes
in
  this.tableView.applyRealmChanges(changes)
}
```

`Chat.rooms` is a `List<String>` property listing available room names. You also subscribe for Realm notifications on that list and call `applyRealmChanges(_)` in case there are any updates, which updates your table view with the most up-to-date information.

As the last step, add to the view controller's `deinit`:

```
roomNamesSubscription?.invalidate()
```

Congrats! Your partial sync code is complete. It took two simple steps as outlined earlier:

- You used `subscribe()` on a result set to start syncing the matching data from the server.

- You fetched the objects from the local database and subscribed for change notifications, which would also be triggered upon remote changes thanks to the subscription above.

Run the project. You should see the **General** chat room appear in the list:

In fact, upon connecting, your app checks for available rooms in the database and creates the default **General** chat room if there aren't any. That change gets immediately synced up to the server as well.

Open the **default** Realm in Realm Studio where you can see the new data synced up:

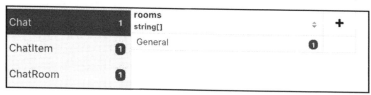

Your app created a single chat room named **General** and added it to the `rooms` list of the `Chat` object.

Creating more rooms

I'm sure the user would like to add new rooms to the chat. `RoomsViewController` already features a + navigation item which pops an alert asking the user to enter a new room name.

Once the alert completes, `createRoomAndEnter(withName:)` is called. This is where you'll add your code.

Append to `createRoomAndEnter(withName:)`:

```
guard !roomName.isEmpty,
   let realm = realm,
   let myName = name.text else { return }

let newRoom = ChatRoom(roomName).add(to: realm)
```

You use `ChatRoom(_)`'s convenience initializer to create a new room with the given name and use another helper included in the starter code called `add(to:)` to add the newly created object to your Realm.

As soon as that's done, Realm will queue that change and sync it to the server at its earliest convenience.

You can now proceed directly to the next scene. Append to the same method:

```
let chatVC = ChatViewController.createWith(
   roomName: newRoom.name, name: myName)
navigationController!.pushViewController(chatVC, animated: true)
```

Now you can create rooms and join them too! Before giving that a try, you'll add some more code to add a "joined" indicator to every room in the list. If the room with the given name is synced locally, you'll show a checkmark next to its name.

Scroll down to `tableView(_:cellForRowAt:)` and check out the code that configures the table cell for each room. You pass a Boolean to `cell.configure(with:isSynced:)` to let the cell know whether to show or hide the row checkmark.

Right now `isSynced` is hard-coded to `false`, so none of the rooms will have a checkmark. Replace `let isSynced = false` with:

```
let isSynced = realm?.object(ofType: ChatRoom.self,
   forPrimaryKey: roomName) != nil
```

You look up the persisted room object by its name and confirm it's not `nil`. Now `RoomCell.configure(with:isSynced:)` will correctly show or hide the checkmark.

You'd also like to refresh the room list when there are new rooms being synced down from the server. To achieve this, you'll subscribe to any `ChatRoom` changes and reload the list whenever there are any.

Scroll up to `fetchRooms(in:)` and append to the `observe(...)` closure parameter:

```
this.roomsSubscription = realm.objects(ChatRoom.self).observe
{ _ in
  this.tableView.reloadData()
}
```

This will simply reload the table whenever the local database changes.

To wrap up this code, add to `deinit`:

```
roomsSubscription?.invalidate()
```

Run the project and create some new chat rooms. You'll see them appear in the list as well as in Realm Studio as soon as the server syncs the changes to all clients (none have checkmarks since you haven't synced any rooms just yet):

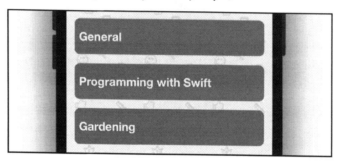

Dynamically managing sync subscriptions

The user can't currently add or see any messages in any of the chat rooms, which makes for a pretty boring chat app and a guaranteed fail on the App Store. Luckily, adding this to the app is pretty straightforward. In fact, it doesn't involve much more than what you've already learned about Partial Sync.

Let's start by adding sync subscriptions to each room the user joins. Open **ChatViewController.swift** and append in `fetchMessages(in:)`:

```
roomSync = realm.objects(ChatRoom.self)
  .filter(NSPredicate(format: "%K = %@",
    ChatRoom.Property.name.rawValue, roomName))
  .subscribe()
```

The structure of `ChatViewController` is pretty similar to what you already did in `RoomsViewController`. `viewWillAppear(_)` grabs an instance of the synced Realm and calls a separate method that starts the data sync.

In `fetchMessages(in:)`, you query the local database for the `ChatRoom` object with the selected room name and `subscribe()` to that result to keep it synchronized with the server.

This subscription will sync down the single room object that matches the room name predicate along with all messages in that room. Just like in `RoomsViewController`, you'll observe the state of the sync subscription and do some work when the initial sync completes.

Append to `fetchMessages(in:)`:

```
roomSubscription = roomSync?.observe(\.state) { [weak self]
state in
  guard let this = self, state == .complete else { return }

  this.room = realm.object(ofType: ChatRoom.self,
    forPrimaryKey: this.roomName)
  this.items = this.room?.items
}
```

Once the initial sync completes, you fetch the `ChatRoom` object from the database and also store the list of messages in the `items` property of the view controller. The view controller uses `items` to display a table view on screen with all chat messages in the room.

Like the rooms list, you'll want to subscribe for message changes as well, so your UI reflects the chat's latest state. Still inside the `observe(...)` closure of `roomSubscription`, append:

```
this.itemsSubscription = this.items?.observe { changes in
  guard let tableView = this.tableView else { return }
  tableView.applyRealmChanges(changes)

  guard !this.items!.isEmpty else { return }
  tableView.scrollToRow(at:
    IndexPath(row: this.items!.count-1, section: 0),
      at: .bottom, animated: true)
}
```

This subscription will apply any updates to the message list and try to scroll the table to latest added message.

Add one final line to the observe(...) closure to enable the **Leave** navigation item and allow the user to leave the room at their convenience:

```
this.leave.isEnabled = true
```

To cancel both notification subscriptions append to viewWillDisappear(_):

```
itemsSubscription?.invalidate()
roomSubscription?.invalidate()
```

Run the project and click on one of your newly created rooms. Once the data syncs down from the server, you'll see the default system message created for the selected room:

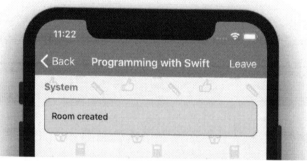

Woot! You're almost there!

Adding messages to the database is as easy as creating a ChatItem with the user's text and adding it to the Realm. The message will be automatically synced by Realm to the server and to any other connected clients.

Find the send(_) method in ChatViewController and add to it:

```
guard let text = message.text, !text.isEmpty,
   let room = room else { return }

ChatItem(sender: name, message: text).add(in: room)
message.text = nil
```

This code uses ChatItem(sender:message:)'s convenience initializer to create a new message from you, and calls add(in:) to add the message object to the current room.

Run the project, then select a different simulator in Xcode and run the project again. You should end with the CloudChatterz app available in both simulators. Open the app in both, and send some messages between them - just don't forget to pick different nicknames!

You can finally chat from two simulators and ask yourself some deep questions.

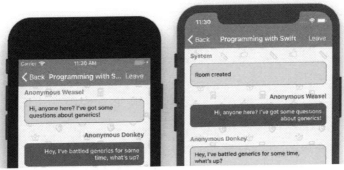

As mentioned in the beginning of this chapter, you can connect to the same Realm Cloud instance from iOS, tvOS, Android and other platforms supported by Realm. So if you have some free time and some Android skills, sit down and create a chat client featuring the same object schema and get it connected to the server.

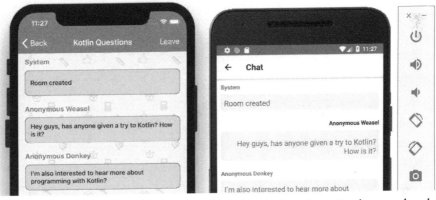

Of course, the chat app you've built in this short chapter is quite naïve, but you barely scratched the surface. Realm Platform has a lot to offer and should you want to learn more, head over to the platform docs located here:

• https://docs.realm.io/cloud

Challenges

Challenge 1: Leaving a chat room

You're not off the hook just yet! Your app's users can join rooms and get synchronized messages across their devices, but they seem to be stuck in these rooms forever.

In the `leave(_)` method of `ChatViewController`, unsubscribe from the room sync subscription before navigating back to the room list. This should be instantly reflected in the list and the room you just left should have no checkmark. Leaving **Gardening**, for example, should look like this:

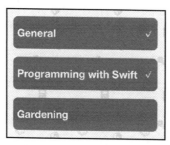

Once you're finished with this task, your CloudChatterz project is ready to play with. Put it on your phone and use it to chat with your friends!

I hope this quick tour of Realm Platform and Realm Cloud left you excited about the endless possible ideas you could use it for. Apps that utilize real-time data synchronization are pretty cool, and Realm Cloud makes building them a trivial task.

Conclusion

We hope you're excited about knowing how to make the most out of Realm and build powerful, solid iOS apps!

By leveraging Realm's fast, custom-made persistence engine, your own apps will be more responsive, safe, and fun to develop.

This book took you from a complete Realm beginner all the way to being a Realm pro. It's up to you now to apply what you learned in your own projects.

If you have any questions or comments about the projects in this book, please stop by our forums at https://forums.raywenderlich.com.

Thank you again for purchasing this book. Your continued support is what makes the books, tutorials, videos and other things we do at raywenderlich.com possible. We truly appreciate it!

– Marin, Shai and Chris

The *Realm: Building Modern Swift Apps with Realm Database* team

More Books You Might Enjoy

We hope you enjoyed this book! If you're looking for more, we have a whole library of books waiting for you at https://store.raywenderlich.com.

New to iOS or Swift?

Learn how to develop iOS apps in Swift with our classic, beginner editions.

iOS Apprentice

https://store.raywenderlich.com/products/ios-apprentice

The iOS Apprentice is a series of epic-length tutorials for beginners where you'll learn how to build 4 complete apps from scratch.

Each new app will be a little more advanced than the one before, and together they cover everything you need to know to make your own apps. By the end of the series you'll be experienced enough to turn your ideas into real apps that you can sell on the App Store.

These tutorials have easy to follow step-by-step instructions, and consist of more than 900 pages and 500 illustrations! You also get full source code, image files, and other resources you can re-use for your own projects.

Swift Apprentice

https://store.raywenderlich.com/products/swift-apprentice

This is a book for complete beginners to Apple's brand new programming language — Swift 4.

Everything can be done in a playground, so you can stay focused on the core Swift 4 language concepts like classes, protocols, and generics.

This is a sister book to the iOS Apprentice; the iOS Apprentice focuses on making apps, while Swift Apprentice focuses on the Swift 4 language itself.

Experienced iOS developer?

Level up your development skills with a deep dive into our many intermediate to advanced editions.

Data Structures and Algorithms in Swift

https://store.raywenderlich.com/products/data-structures-and-algorithms-in-swift

Understanding how data structures and algorithms work in code is crucial for creating efficient and scalable apps. Swift's Standard Library has a small set of general purpose collection types, yet they definitely don't cover every case!

In Data Structures and Algorithms in Swift, you'll learn how to implement the most popular and useful data structures, and when and why you should use one particular datastructure or algorithm over another. This set of basic data structures and algorithms will serve as an excellent foundation for building more complex and special-purpose constructs. As well, the high-level expressiveness of Swift makes it an ideal choice for learning these core concepts without sacrificing performance.

Realm: Building Modern Swift Apps with Realm Database

https://store.raywenderlich.com/products/realm-building-modern-swift-apps-with-realm-database

Realm Platform is a relatively new commercial product which allows developers to automatically synchronize data not only across Apple devices but also between any combination of Android, iPhone, Windows, or macOS apps. Realm Platform allows you to run the server software on your own infrastructure and keep your data in-house which more often suits large enterprises. Alternatively you can use Realm Cloud which runs a Platform for you and you start syncing data very quickly and only pay for what you use.

In this book, you'll take a deep dive into the Realm Database, learn how to set up your first Realm database, see how to persist and read data, find out how to perform migrations and more. In the last chapter of this book, you'll take a look at the synchronization features of Realm Cloud to perform real-time sync of your data across all devices.

Design Patterns by Tutorials

https://store.raywenderlich.com/products/design-patterns-by-tutorials

Design patterns are incredibly useful, no matter what language or platform you develop for. Using the right pattern for the right job can save you time, create less maintenance work for your team and ultimately let you create more great things with less effort. Every developer should absolutely know about design patterns, and how and when to apply them. That's what you're going to learn in this book!

Move from the basic building blocks of patterns such as MVC, Delegate and Strategy, into more advanced patterns such as the Factory, Prototype and Multicast Delegate pattern, and finish off with some less-common but still incredibly useful patterns including Flyweight, Command and Chain of Responsibility.

Server Side Swift with Vapor

https://store.raywenderlich.com/products/server-side-swift-with-vapor

If you're a beginner to web development, but have worked with Swift for some time, you'll find it's easy to create robust, fully-featured web apps and web APIs with Vapor 3.

Whether you're looking to create a backend for your iOS app, or want to create fully-featured web apps, Vapor is the perfect platform for you.

This book starts with the basics of web development and introduces the basics of Vapor; it then walks you through creating APIs and web backends; creating and configuring databases; deploying to Heroku, AWS, or Docker; testing your creations and more1

iOS 11 by Tutorials

https://store.raywenderlich.com/products/ios-11-by-tutorials

This book is for intermediate iOS developers who already know the basics of iOS and Swift development but want to learn the new APIs introduced in iOS 11.

Discover the new features for developers in iOS 11, such as ARKit, Core ML, Vision, drag & drop, document browsing, the new changes in Xcode 9 and Swift 4 — and much, much more.

Advanced Debugging and Reverse Engineering

https://store.raywenderlich.com/products/advanced-apple-debugging-and-reverse-engineering

In Advanced Apple Debugging and Reverse Engineering, you'll come to realize debugging is an enjoyable process to help you better understand software. Not only will you learn to find bugs faster, but you'll also learn how other developers have solved problems similar to yours.

You'll also learn how to create custom, powerful debugging scripts that will help you quickly find the secrets behind any bit of code that piques your interest.

After reading this book, you'll have the tools and knowledge to answer even the most obscure question about your code — or someone else's.

RxSwift: Reactive Programming with Swift

https://store.raywenderlich.com/products/rxswift

This book is for iOS developers who already feel comfortable with iOS and Swift, and want to dive deep into development with RxSwift.

Start with an introduction to the reactive programming paradigm; learn about observers and observables, filtering and transforming operators, and how to work with the UI, and finish off by building a fully-featured app in RxSwift.

Core Data by Tutorials

https://store.raywenderlich.com/products/core-data-by-tutorials

This book is for intermediate iOS developers who already know the basics of iOS and Swift 4 development but want to learn how to use Core Data to save data in their apps.

Start with with the basics like setting up your own Core Data Stack all the way to advanced topics like migration, performance, multithreading, and more!

iOS Animations by Tutorials

https://store.raywenderlich.com/products/ios-animations-by-tutorials

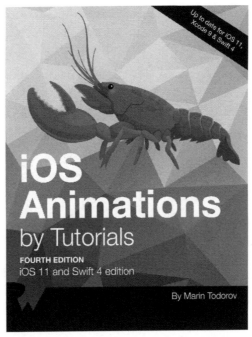

This book is for iOS developers who already know the basics of iOS and Swift 4, and want to dive deep into animations.

Start with basic view animations and move all the way to layer animations, animating constraints, view controller transitions, and more!

watchOS by Tutorials

https://store.raywenderlich.com/products/watchos-by-tutorials

This book is for intermediate iOS developers who already know the basics of iOS and Swift development but want to learn how to make Apple Watch apps for watchOS 4.

tvOS Apprentice

https://store.raywenderlich.com/products/tvos-apprentice

This book is for complete beginners to tvOS development. No prior iOS or web development knowledge is necessary, however the book does assume at least a rudimentary knowledge of Swift.

This book teaches you how to make tvOS apps in two different ways: via the traditional method using UIKit, and via the new Client-Server method using TVML.

Want to make games?

Learn how to make great-looking games that are deeply engaging and fun to play!

2D Apple Games by Tutorials

https://store.raywenderlich.com/products/2d-apple-games-by-tutorials

In this book, you will make 6 complete and polished mini-games, from an action game to a puzzle game to a classic platformer!

This book is for beginner to advanced iOS developers. Whether you are a complete beginner to making iOS games, or an advanced iOS developer looking to learn about SpriteKit, you will learn a lot from this book!

3D Apple Games by Tutorials

https://store.raywenderlich.com/products/3d-apple-games-by-tutorials

Through a series of mini-games and challenges, you will go from beginner to advanced and learn everything you need to make your own 3D game!

This book is for beginner to advanced iOS developers. Whether you are a complete beginner to making iOS games, or an advanced iOS developer looking to learn about SceneKit, you will learn a lot from this book!

Unity Games by Tutorials

https://store.raywenderlich.com/products/unity-games-by-tutorials

Through a series of mini-games and challenges, you will go from beginner to advanced and learn everything you need to make your own 3D game!

This book is for beginner to advanced iOS developers. Whether you are a complete beginner to making iOS games, or an advanced iOS developer looking to learn about SceneKit, you will learn a lot from this book!

Want to learn Android or Kotlin?

Get a head start on learning to develop great Android apps in Kotlin, the newest first-class language for building Android apps.

Android Apprentice

https://store.raywenderlich.com/products/android-apprentice

If you're completely new to Android or developing in Kotlin, this is the book for you!

The Android Apprentice takes you all the way from building your first app, to submitting your app for sale. By the end of this book, you'll be experienced enough to turn your vague ideas into real apps that you can release on the Google Play Store.

You'll build 4 complete apps from scratch — each app is a little more complicated than the previous one. Together, these apps will teach you how to work with the most common controls and APIs used by Android developers around the world.

Kotlin Apprentice

https://store.raywenderlich.com/products/kotlin-apprentice

This is a book for complete beginners to the new, modern Kotlin language.

Everything in the book takes place in a clean, modern development environment, which means you can focus on the core features of programming in the Kotlin language, without getting bogged down in the many details of building apps.

This is a sister book to the Android Apprentice the Android Apprentice focuses on making apps for Android, while the Kotlin Apprentice focuses on the Kotlin language fundamentals.